THE MAKING OF
"MAMMY PLEASANT"

WOMEN IN AMERICAN HISTORY

Series Editors

Anne Firor Scott
Nancy A. Hewitt
Stephanie Shaw

*A list of books in the series
appears at the end of this book.*

THE MAKING OF "MAMMY PLEASANT"

A Black Entrepreneur in Nineteenth-Century
San Francisco

LYNN M. HUDSON

✻

University of Illinois Press
Urbana and Chicago

First Illinois paperback, 2008
© 2003 by Lynn M. Hudson
Manufactured in the United States of America
1 2 3 4 5 C P 5 4 3 2 1

∞ This book is printed on acid-free paper.

The Library of Congress cataloged the cloth edition
as follows:
Hudson, Lynn M. (Lynn Maria), 1961–
The making of "Mammy Pleasant" : a Black entrepreneur
in nineteenth-century San Francisco / Lynn M. Hudson.
p.   cm. — (Women in American history)
Includes bibliographical references and index.
ISBN 0-252-02771-X (acid-free paper)
1. Pleasant, Mary Ellen, 1814–1904. 2. African American
women—Biography. 3. African Americans—Biography.
4. African American businesspeople—California—San Francisco—Biography. 5. Businesswomen—California—San Francisco—Biography. 6. San Francisco (Calif.)—Biography. 7. San
Francisco (Calif.)—History—19th century. 8. African Americans—California—San Francisco—History—19th century.
9. San Francisco (Calif.)—Race relations. I. Title. II. Series.
E185.97.P6H83   2003
979.4'6100496073'0092—dc21   2002003600

PAPERBACK ISBN 978-0-252-07527-8

For my father
Larry B. Hudson
(1931–95)

CONTENTS

ACKNOWLEDGMENTS

The history and memory of Mary Ellen Pleasant have been tirelessly kept alive for decades by librarians, volunteers, and historians of the San Francisco Bay area and the San Francisco African American Historical and Cultural Society in particular. My work would not be possible without their efforts.

I would like to thank the librarians and archivists at the following institutions: the San Francisco African American Historical and Cultural Society, the San Francisco Public Library, the Oakland Public Library, the California Historical Society, the Bancroft Library, the California State Archives, the Nantucket Historical Association, the California Society of Pioneers, and the Amistad Research Center at Tulane University. For two summers I benefited from the generosity of Adele Ames, who made it possible for me to start at the beginning of Pleasant's story. Special thanks to Ms. Ames for endowing the James Bradford Ames Fellowship for the study of African Americans on Nantucket and to Robert Johnson and the Africana Studies Department at the University of Massachusetts, Boston for administering the grant. New friends and colleagues on Nantucket welcomed me to the island and generously provided research help and guidance; thanks to Betsy Tyler, Helen Seager, Susan F. Beegal, and most of all Elizabeth Oldham, a diligent archivist, historian, and friend. Thanks to the Munson Institute of Mystic, Connecticut for the Paul Cuffe Maritime Studies Fellowship, which allowed me to finish my research on the East Coast. Financial support from my campus, California Polytechnic State University, San Luis Obispo, and encouragement from my colleagues in the history department have been invaluable. Former students and research assistants Alexandra Valdez and Shannon Smull tracked down obscure references and answered all queries. Pamela Ayo Yetunde assisted with legal research. Inspiration for this project was cheerfully provided by students in my courses at Cal Poly and the University of California at San Diego.

At Indiana University I was fortunate to study with Richard Blackett, who brought vast knowledge of African American history, sardonic wit, and tremendous patience to this project. Beverly Stoeltje helped me see the history and folklore of Pleasant in new ways, and my understanding of the West has increased tenfold under her tutelage. Wendy Gamber has generously added her insights in women's history and business history to many readings of my work and helped me participate in a broader scholarly conversation about my project. The Indiana University Research and Graduate School and the History Department of Indiana University, Bloomington offered much-needed support in the early stages. Tremendous thanks to the readers and editors at the University of Illinois Press for helping me to clarify my thoughts at the critical hour.

Many colleagues offered helpful comments on portions of the work in progress. Thanks to Susan Armitage, Quintard Taylor, George Lipsitz, Albert Broussard, Shirley Ann Wilson Moore, Barbara Loomis, Stephanie Shaw, Juliet E. K. Walker, Ellen Seiter, Mary Murphy, Stephanie Smallwood, Cynthia Chris, Gayle Fischer, Karen Rader, Cindy Hahamovitch, Scott Nelson, Elizabeth Oldham, Sharon Holland, Chana Kai Lee, Robyn Wiegman, and Angel Kwolek-Folland. I have also benefited from the wisdom and encouragement of Jacquelyn Dowd Hall, Trudier Harris, James Horton, Lois Horton, Julie Winch, and Elsa Barkley Brown, for which I am extremely grateful. In this study's formative years, I received scholarly advice and direction from Nell Irvin Painter, who taught me a great deal about writing African American history. A long time ago, in Santa Cruz, California, this book came to life with the help and inspiration of Bettina Aptheker, Pedro Castillo, and Marge Frantz; I thank them all for believing in my ability to tell this story.

Friends and family in California and Rhode Island offered their homes, their humor, and their support. My love and thanks to Toni Hudson, Patrick Gaganidze, Leslie Henriques, Ray Riegert, Mignon Henriques, Brenda Henriques, Mily Trabing, Susan Thomas, Choi Chatterjee, Omer Sayeed, Robert and Sandra Clark, and all members of the Ciunci clan. Amy Glass, Peter Geoffrion, and Julia Trimmer have been there for all the important moments. Kim Marlowe showed herself to be not only an exceptional sister but also a talented historian. I cannot thank her enough. In 1858 Mary Ellen Pleasant met abolitionist and feminist Mary Ann Shadd Cary in Chatham, Ontario. One hundred and thirty years later their biographers met in a coffee shop in Chapel Hill, North Carolina. I thank the Fates for bringing us all together and Jane Rhodes for making everything possible.

* * *

An earlier version of chapter 4 appeared as "'Strong Animal Passions' in the Gilded Age: Race, Sex, and a Senator on Trial," in the *Journal of the History of Sexuality* 9:1–2 (January/April 2000): 62–84. © 2000 by the University of Texas Press. All rights reserved.

THE MAKING OF
"MAMMY PLEASANT"

"Mary Ellen Pleasant?"

"Wasn't she a voodoo queen?"

"A madam?"

"A mammy?"

"Didn't she run a whorehouse for white businessmen in
  San Francisco?"

"Wasn't she Mammy Pleasant?"

"Didn't she work voodoo on that white woman and
  send her off her head?"

"Wasn't she Haitian?"

"Didn't she have a witchmark on her forehead?"

"A cast eye?"

"One blue eye and one brown eye?"

"Wasn't she ebony?"

"Yellow?"

"Wasn't she so pale you'd never know?"

"Didn't she come back as a zombie?"

"Didn't she have a penis?"

"Couldn't she work roots?"

"Didn't she make a senator's balls fall off?"

"Didn't she set fire to her own house?"

"Never heard of her."

—MICHELLE CLIFF, *Free Enterprise: A Novel* (1993)

INTRODUCTION

The Making of "Mammy Pleasant"

Every detail about Mary Ellen Pleasant's past is contested: her birthplace, her parents, her name, her occupation, and her wealth. She was called a mammy, madam, voodoo queen, and sorceress, and her history has been the subject of intense speculation by journalists, novelists, and folklorists. The life of Mary Ellen Pleasant (1814–1904) figures in U.S. popular culture, including film, fiction, stage, and television from the 1920s to the present. Although a participant in critical junctures in U.S. history—the Civil War, John Brown's raid on Harpers Ferry, the Gold Rush, and the urbanization of the West—she is largely absent from the annals of American historiography.

Historians have most often looked to churches, families, slave quarters, and female societies and clubs to trace nineteenth-century black women's history.[1] These are not the spaces and institutions where Pleasant is most visible. There are no traces of Pleasant as a clubwoman, heroic slave, self-sacrificing mother, devoted wife, or church deaconess. Perhaps this is what makes her history so unrecognizable to some and so disturbing to others. There *are* traces of her reputation as a boardinghouse-keeper and a financier and copious records of her work as a litigant fighting Jim Crow and challenging male authority. Yet Pleasant usually has not been welcomed into the canon of acceptable black heroines. Fragments of Pleasant's past are woven into accounts of blacks in the West and collections of notorious women in the West.[2] She appears fleetingly as a character in books that chronicle the wild days of the Barbary Coast and in studies of California history.[3] In *The Gift of Black Folk,* the patriarch of African American history, W. E. B. Du Bois, celebrates Pleasant as "quite a different kind of woman, strangely effective and influential."[4] However, her legacy continues to reside in places outside the academy and the historical profession.[5]

Pleasant's business activities in San Francisco ran the gamut from operating boardinghouses, traditionally women's work, to investing in mines and real estate, considered men's work. She financed enterprises that shaped the western economy in the second half of the nineteenth century. And she practiced the financial strategies of robber barons common to this era: stock speculation, inside trading, and monopoly. Pleasant also used tactics that fell outside the realm of traditional business—those most often practiced by entrepreneurs on the margins of the economy.[6] Parlaying the information revealed in her boardinghouses into capital became one of her most successful techniques. The secrets she knew—about real estate, stocks, miscegenation, and adultery—translated into social as well as economic power.

The cursory treatment of Pleasant's life in the historiography can be explained, in part, by the types of sources available to piece together the story of this remarkable woman. Like most nineteenth-century African Americans, Pleasant had limited access to the resources that produce lasting historical documents: leisure time, clerical assistance, and a wealthy publisher interested in printing her words. This does not mean that she did not leave records, however; Pleasant was literate and extremely savvy about history, the press, and self-representation. She wrote diaries and at least one autobiography and granted a series of interviews with the San Francisco press. Like Sojourner Truth, Pleasant "utilized the information systems of her time with phenomenal success."[7] Yet with few exceptions, historians have paid little attention to the sources that are available to tell Pleasant's story. This is probably because of the difficulty of fitting her into recognizable categories of the black subject or the heroine. Pleasant's entrepreneurial efforts were hardly selfless, and her relationships with other African Americans often were self-serving. Her record as an abolitionist warrants mention in the annals of freedom fighters, but reconciling this legacy with the less heroic aspects of her life has proved difficult. Pleasant's reputation as a mammy and a madam renders her a risky subject for those hoping to position her in the panoply of unsung black leaders. Finally, she contributed to the dilemma by guarding and shaping her past in ways that confound historians.

Pleasant sought control over her own history and the history of San Francisco's elite. At the turn of the twentieth century, writer and publisher Sam Davis claimed she knew "the history of [San Francisco's] people better than any other living person."[8] "In her breast are locked the secrets of hundreds of leading families," wrote Davis in his introduction to Pleasant's published autobiography, "and were she so disposed she might leave behind her memoirs which would shake the foundations of society."[9] Pleasant showed time and again that she was fully aware of the process of history; she witnessed her own past being packaged and tangled. Occasionally, she was a willing participant. "If a write-up about me put a blanket on somebody's bed or gave a household meat and bread," she said, "I would let them lay my character down in the middle of the road and let the whole world jump on it, and turn it over and let them go [at] it again."[10]

Feeling that her "silence might be misconstrued," Pleasant dictated her autobiography to Davis for his journal, *The Pandex of the Press*, and it was published in 1902. In it she refers directly to the already expansive legend she inspired: "I have frequently been asked to give the public a history of my life in order to vindicate myself and set at rest the many stories which have been published about me."[11] The second installment of the autobiography never appeared because of what the journal described as "an unfortunate misunderstanding between author and editor [Pleasant and Davis]." However, it is clear that printing the first installment of Pleasant's autobiography produced financial rewards for the publisher. "Persons who subscribed for *The Pandex* solely for the Memoirs" were instructed to contact their office for a refund.[12] Pleasant's story had been commodified long before her death.

In her autobiography, readers are first treated to the interpretations of a palm reader, H. Jerome Fosselli. "This is a very high type of hand, showing a keen and unusual order of intelligence," claimed Fosselli. Pleasant harbored a "marvelous ability to read motives" and a power to read the secret thoughts of others "that borders on the occult."[13] Whether these were Davis's, Fosselli's, or Pleasant's beliefs about her character—or all three— they certainly set the stage for the autobiography that followed. Pleasant described herself as a keen, quick-learning youngster and a forgiving friend. She let her readers know that she did "not harbor a vindictive thought" against people who had betrayed or maligned her.

Pleasant appeared conflicted about her role as autobiographer: "Now I have never cared a feather's weight for public opinion, for it is about the most ghostly thing I know of. No one but a rank coward fears it, for it don't know its own mind a minute or where it gets its ideas about anything. So I want it understood distinctly that I am not seeking any vindication which my own conscience does not call for."[14] Her disavowal of public opinion did not stop her from offering up pieces of her history to the public in this autobiography and in the press. Owning her past by providing her own version became very important to her at the end of her life. Unfortunately for scholars, much of Pleasant's other writing—most significantly, her diaries—have been lost or destroyed.[15] Thus, her history is based largely on accounts in newspapers, in other people's diaries, and in court cases. The latter source proves especially useful in tracking Pleasant's record as a civil rights litigant and property owner. Sifting through what others thought and said about Pleasant is a large part of the biographer's job, and with that comes the task of interpreting mythologies and folklore that surround Pleasant's life story.

Without a doubt her identity as "Mammy Pleasant" dominates popular and historical versions of her past. Although she made her dislike of the term quite plain, it became her name in the press, the history books, and the novels. At age eighty-seven, Pleasant told an interviewer from the San Francisco newspaper the *Call,* "Listen: I don't like to be called mammy by everybody. Put that down. I'm not mammy to everybody in California. I got a letter from a minister in Sacramento. It was addressed to Mammy Pleasant. I wrote back to him on his own paper that my name was Mrs. Mary E. Pleasant. I wouldn't waste any of my paper on him." Not one to be cowed by ministers, or men of any description, she continued, "If he didn't have better sense he should have had better manners."[16] As definitive as this remark appears, Pleasant had a vexed and changing relationship to the role of mammy.[17] Arriving in the city during the Gold Rush—a black woman who could keep your secrets and cook your food—Pleasant found mammy a handy disguise behind which she acquired wealth, power, and privilege. By the time the octogenarian agreed to the interview with the *Call,* she had represented herself in court as a servant to two prominent white families in the city: the Woodworths and the Bells. Yet in both situations Pleasant's relationship to the families was not simply one of domestic and employer; Mrs. Lisette Woodworth provided key testimony in Pleasant's 1868 lawsuit against Jim Crow streetcars, and the Bell family lived in the mansion Pleasant owned for nearly twenty years.

Pleasant became known as "Mammy Pleasant" partly because she was a black woman who performed domestic work; in nineteenth-century America, it is hardly surprising that she would be thus named. Her mysterious past as an African American who claimed to be freeborn, embraced abolition, and fought segregation discomfited many San Franciscans, who found her more appealing, no doubt, as "Mammy Pleasant." Coming to grips with the ways in which Pleasant manipulated the nation's much-loved icon of slavery and the ways in which mammy's association with docility, ignorance, and subservience worked for her and against her is part of the task of this book.

There is only one other book—now out of print—that claims to be a biography of Mary Ellen Pleasant: *Mammy Pleasant,* written by Helen Holdredge and published by G. P. Putnam's Sons in 1953.[18] Holdredge became the single most influential person to shape Pleasant's legacy. Hailed in the *New York Times* as a "fictionalized biography," the first edition of *Mammy Pleasant* sold out through orders before the book arrived in stores.[19]

After the initial success in the 1950s, it was reprinted in 1973 by Ballantine Books. Reviews of *Mammy Pleasant* praised the text for its "great and satisfying detail" and for "possessing a heaping measure of sinister and horrendous fascination."[20] Throughout the text Holdredge claimed that she had access to Pleasant's diary. This caused concern for at least one reviewer, who did not find the diary adequately cited: "It is too bad that Mrs. Holdredge does not quote from the diary of Mrs. Pleasant, which she often mentions. By the very lack of quotations, when the situation practically screams for them, this book becomes hard going at times."[21] Indeed, there are no footnotes to any of Holdredge's sources, adding to the suspicion that many of her accounts were invented.[22]

Following the success of *Mammy Pleasant*, Holdredge wrote *Mammy Pleasant's Partner* (1954) and *Mammy Pleasant's Cookbook* (1970).[23] Like the first book, *Mammy Pleasant's Partner* combined biographical detail—in this case about Scottish banker Thomas Bell—with unsubstantiated hyperbole. Pleasant appears throughout the sequel as Bell's manipulative, voodoo-practicing business partner. Holdredge culled the material for the cookbook from "Mammy's recipe books," which she claimed to have collected in her research. Undoubtedly, Holdredge hoped to capitalize on the belief that all mammies were excellent cooks, and the cover of the book claimed that Pleasant "cooked her way to fame, fortune and power." In addition to typical southern fare, one can find recipes for New England Abolitionist Beans, Voodoo Magic (a veal and pork loaf), and Earthquake Pudding, a variation of bread pudding. Although she had plans for other publications and hoped to see *Mammy Pleasant* made into a motion picture, none of this materialized, and the cookbook was the last of Holdredge's publications.[24]

While researching and writing these books, Holdredge developed an extraordinary collection of materials about Pleasant, ranging from recipes to account books to letters and newspaper clippings. During the 1930s and 1940s, she interviewed contemporaries of Pleasant. Black San Franciscans gave Holdredge much-needed information about Pleasant's abolitionist work and her relationship to her African American contemporaries. Another source that proved central to *Mammy Pleasant* were the diaries of Teresa Bell, Pleasant's protégé and business partner. Bell's diaries supply telling details about the relationship between the two women and give a daily account of the last twelve years of Pleasant's life. The diaries were a family heirloom given to Holdredge by her father, who had received them from Teresa Bell in 1909.[25]

Holdredge's interviews with Pleasant's contemporaries, much like those conducted with ex-slaves by the Works Progress Administration's Federal

Writers Project in the same period, are a rich historical source. At the same time, they reveal Holdredge's limited understanding of African American history and culture and her fondness for racist humor and stereotypes. In 1954 Holdredge wrote to her editor, Virginia Carrick, "Now I have honest-to-goodness bona fide goofer dust because it has been taken from the grave of a Voodoo Queen—and therefore I've got the proper kind of power."[26] Although this particular comment may have been tongue-in-cheek, Holdredge found many aspects—if not all—of black culture laughable. In the same letter Holdredge reported that she had finally located a man who had a photograph of Pleasant, and his name was Mr. Coon, "Yes, indeed, Mr. Coon had a picture of a coon," she wrote.[27]

Fascinated with what she perceived to be the exotic nature of black people, Holdredge, like many American authors, used black characters as a device to exploit American fears of blackness and miscegenation. As Toni Morrison has recently argued, much of what is characteristic of our national literature emanates from "responses to a dark, abiding, signing Africanist Presence."[28] In *Mammy Pleasant* we find not the comforting mammy we might expect from the title but an African American woman who embodies the dangers of blackness: miscegenation, voodoo, and power being used to control white people.[29]

In the heyday of her San Francisco career, Mary Ellen Pleasant had many real and imagined sources of power. But the most provocative source in popular culture, for many of her contemporaries as well as later admirers, was her supposed penchant for voodoo. In the press she was credited with supernatural powers usually described as voodoo, hoodoo, or conjuring. Her obituaries in the San Francisco press described her as a "Negro priestess" and "voodoo queen."[30] Voodoo derives from the religion of Dahomey in West Africa and has been merged with Christianity in the United States. Many claim that the practice of voodoo in the United States began in eighteenth-century Louisiana when the French brought Haitian slaves to the area.[31] In the nineteenth century voodoo was still practiced in New Orleans and maroon colonies across the New World.[32] The doctrines of voodoo require that its secrets be passed on orally and not written down; detailed records about the extent of its practice in nineteenth-century America are scant. Older black women often were the keepers of the religious doctrine and thus acquired certain social and political powers.[33]

It is not surprising that nineteenth- and twentieth-century popular culture portrays Mary Ellen Pleasant as a voodoo queen. Voodoo signaled secret knowledge, and secrets were precisely the kind of contraband Pleasant collected. Voodoo and conjuring, as Lawrence W. Levine has shown, were an essential part of slaves' effort to create a psychic and emotional space between themselves and their owners.[34] Furthermore, an association with voodoo emphasized African roots and, for some, implied Pleasant's connection to a slave past. As Pleasant's childhood unfolds in Holdredge's narrative, a ten-year-old Mary Ellen performs her first ritual: "Surely, if her mother and her mother's mother had both been Voodoo Queens, she should test her power and eventually, if she really believed that the spirit of the Great Serpent could speak through her, she might be given the voice to speak the Great One's words."[35] According to Holdredge, Pleasant became so obsessed with this "strange religion" that nothing would stop her from obtaining its powers.

The plot of *Mammy Pleasant* winds around Pleasant's uncontrollable savagery and evil impulses. Pleasant does not foam at the mouth, like her character in Charles Caldwell Dobie's 1926 novel *Less Than Kin,* but she does exhibit an unrestrained and biologically determined primitivism, as this description of her childhood indicates: "Already had begun a metamorphosis of which she was scarcely aware. In her veins beat a strange inspiration that drove her to fight for her own people, contending with a downbeat, savage and primitive, to which her sudden evil impulses would always yield."[36] Both Dobie and Holdredge depict Pleasant as a mammy who had unnatural control over others; her power was rooted in her African and Caribbean heritage.

The folklore about Pleasant's power, then, reveals quite a bit about her orbit if not about her actual deeds. Black San Franciscans interviewed by Holdredge offered similar narratives about Pleasant: She knew white men's secrets, she was accused of murder, she owned more property than anyone knew about, and she was a committed abolitionist. This seemingly incongruous set of characteristics provides an index of Pleasant's influence and its salience. Whether Pleasant actually murdered someone is impossible to prove, but the fact that many believed that she did is equally important.[37] Such rumors about Pleasant demonstrate how she was both feared and revered in San Francisco's black communities.

Mary Ellen Pleasant's friends and associates read like a roster of the nineteenth century's best-known African American abolitionists and leaders: William Howard Day, David W. Ruggles, Mary Ann Shadd Cary, and James Madison Bell. In California, she formed part of San Francisco's black elite—the "pioneer urbanites"—who organized California's black convention movement, the press, churches, and schools.[38] She followed in the footsteps of heroic men and women or, in some cases, they followed in hers. Frederick Douglass, for example, probably visited the segregated section of Nantucket known as New Guinea, the location of the African American Meeting House, where Pleasant had been one of the earliest attendees.[39] In her sojourn from the abolitionist centers of Nantucket, New Bedford, and Boston to the center of the California Gold Rush, Pleasant made a journey taken by thousands of Americans.

This study of a free black female entrepreneur in post–Gold Rush California challenges many historians' assumptions about the West. What little has been written about black men and women in the West often has romanticized their exploits as cowboys, miners, or explorers.[40] This book attempts to move away from that celebratory paradigm—which tends to essentialize the subject—and instead critically analyze the life of one African American woman and her milieu. Until recently, accounts of post–Gold Rush California, like western folklore, rarely discussed women as historical subjects; rather, they appeared on the sidelines as prostitutes or helpmates to men.[41] Pleasant does not fit this mold. As a helpmate, she seems to have been much more concerned about women; if she profited from sex in the West, it was as a madam, not a prostitute. Nor does she resemble the figures traditionally lionized as great black leaders of the nineteenth century: She denied a slave past, and even if she was born a slave, she became a literate abolitionist and entrepreneur.

By 1870, Mary Ellen Pleasant listed $30,000 in real estate and personal assets in the U.S. Census, the equivalent of at least a million dollars today. This wealth placed her in the upper echelons of black America. However, Pleasant did not fit the profile of a typical nineteenth-century black property owner. Most nineteenth-century African American property owners lived in the South, before and after the Civil War.[42] Men outnumbered women; in 1860 only one in five black property owners in the South was female.[43]

A handful of African American women did acquire substantial wealth and property in the postbellum era. The best known among these, Madam C. J. Walker (1867–1919), often is called America's first black female millionaire.[44] Her successful line of cosmetics and hair products expanded to include an international mail-order business, a training college in "The Walker System" of hair care, and a factory in Indianapolis. By the time of her death in 1919, more than 500 agents, mostly black women, taught "The Walker System," and Madam Walker had built herself a million-dollar mansion on the Hudson River. Mary Ellen Pleasant's entrepreneurial success predated Madam Walker's by several decades, yet their careers shared several attributes: Both built their empires on traditional female work, hair care, and domestic labor, both hired black employees and operated employment agencies of a sort (Pleasant in San Francisco and Walker on a national scale), and both were the subject of great speculation about their personal success and excesses. However, Walker's financial enterprise was global, whereas Pleasant's reached across California. And whereas Walker's wealth passed down to future generations, Pleasant lived to see hers whittled away by creditors, lawyers, and members of the Bell family.

Pleasant's work as a boardinghouse operator, laundress, and domestic placed her squarely in the tradition of black women's labor before and after the Civil War.[45] Ninety-five percent of southern black women who worked for wages on the eve of the war engaged in some form of domestic labor.[46] In the West, more than 92 percent of black women continued to work in domestic service as late as 1890.[47] However, Pleasant transformed her domestic labor into an enterprise. Whereas many men who had been "antebellum giants of black business" met their demise during the postwar era of restrictive black codes and antiblack violence, Pleasant's coffers grew, as did her list of properties.[48] For some, she became the symbolic representation of black capitalism. In an 1884 article in *The Cleveland Gazette* titled "The Colored Race: The Wonderful Progress Which It Has Made in Money Getting," Pleasant is heralded for her success in this regard: She "has an income from eight houses in San Francisco, a ranch near San Mateo, and $100,000 in government bonds."[49] Pleasant's moneymaking was national news.

The ways Pleasant managed her funds and invested her capital make it nearly impossible to track down property values and dollar amounts. Her business association with the family of Thomas Bell in San Francisco could not have been more convoluted; Pleasant hid money in accounts, controlled capital that was probably invested under someone else's name, and left little record of how she acquired her thousands if not millions of dollars. We know something about the extent of her enterprise from the press, her numerous court cases, probate records, and deeds, but these provide an incomplete picture.

Given the variety and type of sources available, writing a biography of Pleasant requires that the historian cast a wide net, one large enough to encompass fact, fiction, rumor, and myth. It is equally important to both follow Pleasant's actions over time and chart the fascination with her story. Mapping the terrain of those whose imaginations Pleasant captured also identifies her spheres of influence. It is in this way that I seek not merely to sort fact from fiction but to locate both of them in a variety of genres. It is the way they converge, the way one overlaps the other at particular moments in Pleasant's life, that forms the central thread of her story.

*   *   *

African American women's history is riddled with silences. Mary Ellen Pleasant's life is no exception. This study is part of a body of work that seeks to address the meaning of black women's lives in the face of gaps in historical knowledge. Indeed, one of the contributions of women's history, and African American women's history in particular, is its insistence that histories are worth knowing even if they are not what some would call complete.[50] There remain parts of Pleasant's life about which we cannot be certain. There is no available evidence that confirms the details of her parentage or her slave status. This book argues that the mystery concerning her past is a piece of evidence in itself. Pleasant left a contradictory and incomplete set of information about her history. This was partly intentional. She jealously guarded many details of her life as a means of controlling her representations.

Historians have recently come to see silence and absence as sources. What has not been said or left behind may tell us as much as the documents we have in hand.[51] Absences in Pleasant's story are abundant: If she was a madam or a voodoo practitioner, as alleged, she left no record of such activities. Like the silence that shrouded slave revolts, silence attaches itself to these activities by necessity. Prostitution was not yet illegal in San Francisco at the time Pleasant was said to have practiced it, but for business's sake—to protect clients—advertising this aspect of her enterprise would have been unwise. Voodoo requires a vow of silence of its practitioners. Pleasant therefore may have spoken volumes in her silence on certain issues.

Feminist scholars have been particularly concerned with the problem of silence in women's lives. The demands of social reproduction, paid and unpaid labor, and rigid codes of appropriate gender behavior silenced many women in the nineteenth century.[52] Slavery brought its own legally sanctioned silence in the form of literacy laws that forbade slaves from learning to read or write. Silences and distortions, secrets and rumors are woven throughout African American women's history.[53] In this book I have tried to pay attention to silence and absence whenever possible. When sources on Pleasant were silent on particular subjects, I have made note of it. I have listened to what others said or did not say about her. If I could substantiate oral traditions I have done so. But I have also analyzed the folklore about Pleasant as a source of her activities, her power, and her legend. What others *believed* she did is as important as what historians can verify that she actually did.

Few lives are recorded without missing pieces. Pleasant's story—silences included—reveals a life full of secrets, mysterious acts, and disguises. The texture of this study reveals, I hope, something of the texture of her life.

I

NANTUCKET

I was a girl full of smartness.

MARY ELLEN PLEASANT, *Memoirs* (1902)

"Some people have reported that I was born in slavery, but as a matter of fact, I was born in Philadelphia." So begins Mary Ellen Pleasant's brief autobiography, published in 1902, just two years before her death. Pleasant's wry sense of humor, sharp wit, and keen awareness of her own history permeate her autobiography. Her insistence that on August 19, 1814, she was born to free parents, like much of her past, remains a source of controversy. Many argue that Mary Ellen was born a slave. Some believe she was the daughter of a Virginia planter and a Caribbean voodoo priestess; others believe she was born into slavery in Georgia.[1] Though largely unsubstantiated, these beliefs merit attention; they point to the confusion about Pleasant's status and the presence of secrets about her past.[2] Many of the details of Pleasant's beginnings may never be known, but we can be certain about the tentative nature of black life in the first decades of the nineteenth century.[3]

If Pleasant's statement that she was freeborn was meant to hide a slave past, she would have had just cause. Slavery, and its requisite policing of black bodies, provided innumerable reasons for African Americans to hide, steal, and conceal themselves and their identities.[4] In the antebellum years, Pleasant could have found it too dangerous to reveal that she was born into slavery. Routinely captured and taken back into slavery, fugitive slaves necessarily denied their slave pasts. Yet by the end of her life—when Pleasant granted several interviews and published her autobiography—slavery had been officially abolished in the United States for a generation. However, Mary Ellen remained adamant about her history of freedom. Whether free or slave, she sought to be remembered as free.

At the dawn of the twentieth century, when Pleasant recorded memories of her childhood and parents, there were still many reasons to mask a slave past. Former slaves were thought by many to be savage and backward, with a questionable moral character. At best, a slave past was associated with illiteracy. In 1902, Pleasant may have hoped to distance herself from these assumptions. If she had been born into slavery, nothing convinced her that it was wise to say so. Even the success of Booker T. Washington's classic autobiography *Up from Slavery*, published a few months before Pleasant's own narrative, did not convince her of the benefits of claiming a slave past.[5]

She described her parents as a free but unusual couple: "My parents, as nearly as I know, must have been a strange mixture." "My father was a native Kanaka [Hawaiian] and my mother a full-blooded Louisiana negress," an elderly Pleasant recalled. She stressed their physical characteristics: "Both were of large frame, but I think I must have got my physical strength from my father, who was, like most of his race, a giant in frame."[6] This narrative has had a strong influence in defining the discussion about Pleasant's past. Her focus on race and physical characteristics and vagueness about her childhood have sparked tremendous speculation by biographers.

Pleasant did not reveal much else about her parents but did note that her father, Louis Alexander Williams, was an enterprising man "of great intelligence." "He was a commercial man and imported silks from India," she explained. About her mother, she said even less, "I was named after her, but I recall very little about her. I don't think she was as well-educated as my father, for I don't remember that she ever wrote me any letters."[7] It is quite possible that a Pacific Islander named Louis Alexander Williams and a free black woman from Louisiana became the parents of a baby girl in Philadelphia in 1814, as Pleasant claimed.[8] According to the U.S. Census there was an Alexander Williams living in Philadelphia in 1810 and 1820. He is listed as a white male, which is how Pacific Islanders were recorded in the census at that time; there is no listing for a Louis Williams. Pleasant's reluctance to paint a complete picture of her childhood may reflect the fact that she spent few years with them; she probably did not know her parents very well.

As a young girl, Pleasant was taken to the island of Nantucket, off the coast of Massachusetts.[9] It is from this place—a small island inhabited originally by Wampanoags and settled in 1659 by English colonists—that she dates her most vivid memories of childhood. Pleasant probably was raised and influenced by a host of adults, including the African American and European American inhabitants of Nantucket. It was not unusual for nineteenth-century African Americans to be reared by adults other than their biological parents. For example, Frederick Douglass wrote repeatedly about being separated from his mother to remind readers of the damaging effects of slavery.[10] Both Douglass and Pleasant grew up in families that did not include their biological mothers or fathers. Pleasant's supposed unfamiliarity or uneasiness with the institution of motherhood figured prominently in the legends woven about her in the twentieth century.

If masking a slave past, Pleasant chose an ideal city to locate her birth. Being freeborn to a merchant in black Philadelphia in the early nineteenth century would have placed her in the center of one of the most conspicuous and thriving black elite communities in the nation. As W. E. B. Du Bois, Gary Nash, Julie Winch, and other scholars have shown, Philadelphia was the location of the first independent black churches in the nation and also became a focal point for African American schools, commerce, and protest movements before and after the Civil War.[11] Perhaps that is precisely where she began her life or where she wanted to place herself by the end of her life.

Helen Holdredge, author of *Mammy Pleasant* and collector of Pleasant memorabilia, made much of slavery's effect on her subject. Pleasant, she claimed, was born a slave on a Georgia plantation near Augusta.[12] According to Holdredge's narrative, Pleasant's mother, a fearful voodoo queen, told a young Mary Ellen "that she had come from a succession of Voodoo Queens of Santo Domingo" and that she had been named after her father, a Virginia planter.[13] In this version, young Mary Ellen was bought by Americus Price, a Missourian, for $600 and sent to New Orleans. There she was educated by the nuns at Saint Ursuline's convent.[14] But it was too dangerous to keep a literate slave in slaveholding territory, so Price sent the eleven-year-old girl to Cincinnati to live with "dear friends," Mr. and Mrs. Louis Alexander Williams. She was moved to Nantucket as a bondservant when Price died a few years later. The Louis Alexander Williams who appears as Pleasant's father in her own narrative is a friend of Pleasant's owner in Holdredge's narrative.[15] Again, census records offer little clarification: The Ohio manuscript census for 1820 reveals an L. Williams in Cincinnati whose race is unknown. The 1830 census lists an L. Williams in the city who is head of a white household that includes a white female under age twenty. The absence of any comment by Pleasant about Cincinnati and Holdredge's dubious record as a scholar make it impossible to know whether Pleasant actually resided in that city.

Black San Franciscans who knew or remembered Pleasant provided rich detail about her early life. Many of these contemporaries—at least the ones interviewed by Holdredge—seem to confirm Pleasant's roots in slavery. It could be that they had information that is now lost to historians and chose not to believe Pleasant's self-representation as a freeborn woman. It is also possible that these narratives reveal more about Pleasant's significance in the early twentieth century (when the oral histories were collected) than about the facts of her life. But by basing her book, in part, on the testimony of African Americans, Holdredge—perhaps unwittingly—chronicles a set of ideas that black Californians held about Pleasant. That she was born a slave is one of the central tenets of these beliefs. It is clear that black San Franciscans took a certain pride in Pleasant's achievements, and perhaps describing her as a former slave helped draw attention to the distance she had traveled, literally and figuratively. This narrative of slave to aristocrat also works nicely as a Horatio Alger story and highlights the possibilities for African American success in San Francisco.

Oral histories informed much of Holdredge's work; one of her most important sources for *Mammy Pleasant* was Charlotte Dennis Downs, who grew up in the company of Pleasant.[16] Downs was the daughter of one of California's black pioneers, George Washington Dennis. Known for the successful livery business he opened in San Francisco in the 1850s, Dennis became a leader of the California Negro Convention movement. He proved to be one of Pleasant's closest allies. His son, George Dennis Jr., became Pleasant's personal liveryman in the 1870s.[17] Charlotte Dennis Downs helped Pleasant prepare one of her autobiographies.[18] According to Downs, "Mammy also said she was born in Cincinnati, Ohio. She was, however, a Hampden of Virginia. A daughter of John Hampden Pleasants. She was taken to Cincinnati by Price, a planter." Downs claimed that Pleasant recorded in her autobiography that she was born in Augusta, Georgia, and this undoubtedly is the source for the Georgia birthplace theory.[19] That particular diary—the one Downs referred to—subsequently disappeared.[20] Records from Georgia provide little help in the quest to find Pleasant's birthplace. If John Hampden Pleasants was her father, his residence is easily verified as Goochland County, Virginia, where he lived as a slaveowner.[21] He does not appear in Georgia state records, including the census.[22] One possibility is that Hampden Pleasants impregnated one of his slaves and sold her to a planter from Georgia. Another is that he visited Georgia or lived there temporarily and became the father of a slave girl.

Given the multiplicity of tales regarding Pleasant's birthplace and slave status, it seems safe to assume that Pleasant did not want the details revealed or did not know the details herself. When, at the end of her life, she revealed to publisher Sam Davis that she was born free in Philadelphia, she had already succeeded in camouflaging her past. To that end, Pleasant remained in control of her legacy.

Underneath the fascination with Pleasant's parentage lies another concern: How much "African blood" did she have? Was she of mixed race? Descriptions of Pleasant by her contemporaries ran the gamut from light-skinned to coal black. Given the significance assigned to color in nineteenth-century culture, it became increasingly important to determine her heritage—and thus pigmentation. For many nineteenth-century Americans, skin color served as an index for a range of attributes including level of education, sophistication, intelligence, and degree of self-control. Miscegenation received much attention in U.S. popular culture and, as we shall see, became the focus of the novels that took Pleasant as their subject.[23]

Most accounts of her appearance agree that she was a tall and formidable presence. Hallie Q. Brown, the lecturer and one-time president of the National Association of Colored Women, who met the eighty-year-old Pleasant in the 1890s, described her as follows: "She came forward and made herself known. . . . She was not a beauty as some have written. She was rather tall, slender, with sharp features, keen black eyes, very dark, almost black. She wore a purple silk dress, black velvet cape, purple bonnet and strings tied under her neck."[24] Hallie Q. Brown's description matches the photograph of Pleasant taken at roughly the same time. However, there is a great discrepancy in the written accounts of her appearance. For example, the color of her eyes has been much debated. Forty years after Brown described them as "very dark, almost black," Charles Dobie, a San Francisco writer who remembered seeing Pleasant when he was a young boy, claimed she had one blue and one brown eye.[25] Others have insisted that she looked coal black, not brown-skinned. Given the confusion over Pleasant's birthplace and parents, it is no surprise that a certain amount of obfuscation surrounds discussions about Pleasant's complexion. The disagreements about the color of her skin mirror those regarding her slave status and parentage.

Figuring out what Pleasant looked like is fraught with difficulty. A handful of drawings from the San Francisco press depict a wizened old woman in a bonnet during the last decade of her life. Photographic images of Mary Ellen Pleasant, and the question of their authenticity, stymie writers, publishers, and archivists. The best-known photo of Pleasant appeared in the journal that published her autobiography, *The Pandex of the Press;* it was taken when she was eighty-seven years old. Another photo of a regally attired younger woman in black dress and jewelry was the subject of a dispute between Helen Holdredge and a Hawaiian journalist, the California Historical Society, the Bishop Museum, and the State Archives of Hawaii. The Hawaiians claimed that the image was not of Pleasant but of Queen Emma of the Hawaiian Islands, wife of King Kamahameha IV. Holdredge, anxious to confirm the authenticity of the photograph, insisted that Pleasant was photographed at the Bradley & Rulofson studio on Montgomery Street in San Francisco in 1859.[26] This is the image that appears on the cover of Holdredge's bestselling book, *Mammy Pleasant.* Holdredge amassed extensive documentation, much of it quite convincing, to support her claim that the photo was authentic.[27] The archivist from the state of Hawaii at the time, Agnes Conrad, vehemently argued that this was not a depiction of Pleasant and pointed out that the jewelry on the woman looked exactly like that worn by Queen Emma, who was not in the habit of wearing "volume produced costume jewelry."[28]

Further complicating matters, Queen Emma traveled to San Francisco and posed for photographs at the same San Francisco studio in 1865 and 1866. Whether it is mere coincidence that the two women were photographed in the same studio or whether all photographs from Bradley & Rulofson studio are of Queen Emma remains difficult to know. The California Historical Society sided with the Hawaiian historians and exposed the controversy in the pages of the *California Historical Quarterly* in a 1976 article titled "Real Mary Ellen Pleasant Found." However, many continue to use the "Hawaiian" photo as a representation of Pleasant. The most recent book to have her face on the cover, Michelle Cliff's novel *Free Enterprise*, has the same contested image emblazoned on its dust jacket. The youthful face in the photo may be Pleasant's. Quite likely she deliberately modeled herself in style and dress after Queen Emma, whom Pleasant is rumored to have met at the Palace Hotel in 1880.[29]

Whereas much remains a mystery about Mary Ellen Pleasant's parents, her lineage, her likeness, and her complexion, it is easier to piece together the parameters of her life as a young girl. For example, it is likely that, whether slave or free, she was moved from home to home and town to town several times before her tenth birthday. The exigencies of slavery and freedom meant that nineteenth-century African Americans often lived unstable and uncertain lives. Just as slaves were customarily sold at least once in their lives, free black men and women often moved their homes to secure employment, escape slavecatchers, and attain a greater degree of freedom. Even those who believe that Pleasant was born a slave agree that she spent several years of her girlhood above the Mason-Dixon line. Whether in Cincinnati, as Holdredge claimed, or in Philadelphia, as Pleasant claimed, black life in the so-called free states remained risky in the first decades of the century.[30]

There are many reasons to believe that childhood for Mary Ellen consisted of restrictions, frustrations, and labor. If living in Cincinnati in the 1820s with Louis and Ellen Williams, Mary Ellen would have faced working conditions similar to those of other black domestic servants. Although Holdredge claimed Pleasant busied herself making lace, combing fur boas, and curling ostrich feathers for Mrs. Williams, it is likely that Pleasant worked for her caretakers (Williams or otherwise) and probably engaged in more arduous tasks than those mentioned. If young Mary Ellen "tried to bend [Mr. Williams] to her will with the power of voodoo," as Holdredge described, it probably did not work. As a young African American girl, she had little control over her working conditions. Cincinnati, in particular, regarded black workers as unwanted competition for Irish and German workers in this period and passed their own set of rigid black laws.[31]

Young Mary Ellen's caretakers—whether parents, guardians, or owners—made a decision in the 1820s that dramatically changed the course of her life. Pleasant was sent by boat to a place that, though only about thirty miles offshore, must have seemed a long way from the busy port cities through which she had traveled. A small, sandy island, Nantucket did not look like the places Mary Ellen had visited or lived. It did not bear lush forests like much of New England, nor did it sport a string of towns and cities. There was one town, Nantucket Town, which is where the ship carrying Mary Ellen docked. Predominantly heathland with ponds, much of the island did not yield arable land, leading the Frenchman J. Hector St. John de Crèvecoeur to describe late-eighteenth-century Nantucket as "a field which will not be fully cultivated in many ages."[32] What the island did have by 1820 was one of the busiest and most successful ports in North America, and this became Mary Ellen's new home. "When I was about six years of age, I was sent to Nantucket Mass., to live with a Quaker woman named Hussey," wrote Pleasant. "I never knew why I was sent there, and about all I know is that my first recollections of life dated from Nantucket."[33] That the island made an indelible impression on her is clear from her writings and interviews.

Work, business, and the creation of African American institutions all figured prominently in Pleasant's life on Nantucket. Her circumstances upon arrival were not uncommon for a young black girl in antebellum United States: working for a family for room and board and perhaps a slight allowance. Some have argued that Pleasant worked as an indentured servant for the Hussey family.[34] The main source for this theory appears to be an 1895 newspaper article, "The Life Story of Mammy Pleasance," that stated, "When she was nine years old she was bound out with Phoebe Hussey, a Quakeress."[35] Although the precise conditions of her labor were not yet known to her, Mary Ellen knew she would be a working girl. Nantucket proved a fortuitous stop on her journey to adulthood. It is here, in the midst of whalers, Quakers, and Yankee entrepreneurs, that she learned essential survival skills.

The island's name had become synonymous with whaling when Mary Ellen arrived in the 1820s. Indeed, by the time of the American Revolution, whalers from Nantucket dominated the fishery. The yearly bounty of whale oil—

so necessary for heat and light in the eighteenth century—skyrocketed from 3,000 to 30,000 barrels between 1730 and 1775.[36] As whaling expanded, so did the need for laborers. Nantucket merchants, most of them Quakers, shifted from crews of Indians to crews of white and black whalers.[37] The island's elite pursued the enterprise of whaling with something akin to religious zeal, making them some of the wealthiest families in early America.[38]

Landing in a society dominated by the Quakers must have raised many questions for young Mary Ellen. Their appearance alone—women in starched costumes and bonnets, men in similarly austere dress—certainly demanded her attention. Frederick Douglass, arriving in New England in the 1840s, took comfort in the Quaker presence, "The sight of the broad brim and the plain, Quaker dress, which met me at every turn, greatly increased my sense of freedom and security."[39] By the time of Douglass's arrival, the Quakers had long been associated with abolition, explaining Douglass's ease. Mary Ellen may have found a similar security, if not comfort, in the Hussey household. The residence certainly provided the curious young girl with an ideal vantage point from which to observe the island's activities because the Husseys' was a centrally located home near the bustling port.

Mary Ellen arrived in the care of Mary Hussey, or "Grandma Hussey," as the girl called her. Mary Hussey hailed from one of the island's first European families. By the end of the seventeenth century, a group of English settlers including the Husseys, Gardners, Macys, Folgers, Starbucks, and Coffins had successfully wrested the island from the control of Massasoit (King Philip) and various groups of Wampanoags (or Pokanokets). Indeed, these Quaker families dominated island economic and political life throughout Pleasant's stay. The Society of Friends had established itself on the island in the early 1700s, and from the earliest period, Nantucket's most prominent Quakers were also the island's most successful merchants and artisans.[40] Whereas the marriage of mercantilism and Quakerism remained a cornerstone of the island's culture, the relationship between the European American Quakers and antislavery was not always clear. Although Nantucket Friends publicly opposed slavery as early as 1716 and the state of Massachusetts abolished the institution in 1783, Mary Ellen did not enter a society devoid of racial animosity, the remnants of slavery, or segregation.[41] For Nantucket Quakers, the interests of the whaling industry and the establishment of an available class of free black sailors meshed nicely.[42]

At least as early as 1710, a few black people lived on the island. More black people arrived on the island in the eighteenth century as enslaved whalers and mariners such as Prince Boston, and like the black whaler, many freed themselves and their family members. By 1820, the free black population numbered 274 of a total population of 7,266.[43] Although Africans, African Americans, and South Sea Islanders may have applauded Quaker abolitionist principles, other reasons, namely economic, brought black men and women to the island. The labor demands of the maritime and whaling industry—as much as abolitionist principles—altered the demographics of Nantucket. The pre- and post-Revolutionary maritime boom, coupled with an epidemic of yellow fever in 1763–64 that decimated the Wampanoag Indian population, meant that captains needing large crews began recruiting black sailors.[44] As the profits from whaling increased in the nineteenth century, so did the island's black population.[45] By 1840, 578 black men and women lived on Nantucket, one of the largest free black populations in the state.[46]

Mary Ellen had come to a place where African Americans were free but segregated. Their houses were crowded in the southwestern corner of Nantucket Town in the area known as Guinea, New Guinea, or Newtown. Clusters of weather-beaten shingled houses adjacent to pastures and farmland hugged the edge of town. New Guinea naturally bordered the white part of town and was separated from it by a sheep gate at the end of Pleasant Street.[47] Contained within Orange, Atlantic, York, and Pleasant Streets, the neighborhood measured a mere two miles square, yet within its domain New Guinea hosted a thriving community of Africans, Cape Verdeans, and African Americans. The history and memory of slavery was also present in the community of black Nantucketers. Many ex-slaves lived in Guinea, and their presence caused anxiety among white Islanders who were anxious to maintain segregation.[48]

It is likely, however, that many spaces on Nantucket were integrated, given the cramped quarters of the tiny island. The narrow streets of Nantucket Town hardly accommodated the merchants and shoppers; black sailors, preachers, and entrepreneurs navigated the streets along with others. When Mary Ellen made her way up the cobblestoned streets from the dock to the Husseys', she noticed other brown and black faces, Quakers, bankers, whalers, and a whole host of busy characters. Her new caretaker, Mary Hussey, may have brought the young girl to the Friends women's meetings. It is also likely that Mary Ellen met some of the state's black Quakers, the most notable being Massachusetts sea captain Paul Cuffe. Most African Americans on Nantucket, however, worshipped at the African Baptist Church in the center of New Guinea, on the corner of York St. and Pleasant Street.[49]

Acquired by black leaders in 1824, the building at the busy intersection, called Five Corners, served as a staging ground for black Nantucket's most significant sites: its churches and schools. At the time Mary Ellen arrived, the African School held classes in the modest wooden building, and in 1829 nearly thirty children enrolled. Although Mary Ellen desperately hoped to be sent to school, she instead became one of the original members of the first church on the property, the York Street Baptist Church or African Baptist Church. Organized by sea captain Absalom Boston, nephew of Prince Boston, and three other trustees, this was the first black church on the island. In 1835 a second church, also on York Street, the Zion Methodist Episcopal Church opened to serve the needs of black residents. By the 1830s New Guinea supported shops, boardinghouses, grain mills, a cemetery, and two churches. For Mary Ellen, New Guinea provided a model of black entrepreneurship and institution building: public spaces and institutions that black people controlled. This surely impressed upon her the significance of black-owned businesses.[50]

The first church—the African Baptist Church—functioned as the community center and was reconsecrated in 1848 as the Pleasant Street Baptist Church by its new minister, James Crawford. Mary Ellen probably had left the island by then, but the records list the church's original members, and Mary E. Williams's name appears on that list.[51] It is further noted in the Church Book that in 1851, Mary E. Smith wrote a letter to the Pleasant Street Baptist Church. It is likely that by then Mary Ellen had begun using the name Smith, her first husband's last name. Membership in this institution signaled prestige and leadership to the island's black residents. For instance, the records reveal that not all black Nantucketers were welcomed into the church; some were denied membership and others were publicly castigated for inappropriate behavior. In her teen years, Mary Ellen could have taken spiritual and social refuge at the African Baptist Church, conversing with islanders, learning the politics of the community, and connecting with African Americans in a safe space away from the center of Nantucket Town. Black Baptist churches were critical institutions for black women's identity formation and political training.[52] A young woman who was developing an abolitionist politics and a sense for business could not have chosen a better location in which to flourish.

Most founders of the church were also entrepreneurs, like Absalom Boston. Boston, best known as the captain of the all-black whaler *Industry,* gave up the sea in 1823 and opened a store in New Guinea. As a third-generation islander, Absalom Boston had witnessed the transition from slavery to freedom first hand. His grandparents, Boston and Maria, had been manumitted by their owner, William Swain, in 1770, and the family settled in the part of New Guinea near the mill. In 1820, Absalom applied for a license from the county to open a public inn, and in 1830 he opened a store in New Guinea as well. Other black families maintained businesses in the neighborhood, and many were skilled artisans, mariners, and shop-keepers. Many of these families traced their ancestry not to Africa—as the community's name implies—but to Nantucket, where their ancestors had lived for generations.[53] Mary Ellen Pleasant also carried memories of Nantucket and of her friendships with her when she left the island. The business connections she made on the island in particular provided a bases for her future success in San Francisco.

Young Mary Ellen hoped that like many black youth in New Guinea, she would have the opportunity to attend school. "When my father sent me to live with the Husseys, he also gave them . . . plenty of money to have me educated, but they did not use it for that purpose," she explained, "and that's how I came to have no education."[54] Although there were several schools for girls on the island in the 1820s and 1830s, it is clear that they were not open to black girls. "I often wonder what I would have been with an education," she wrote in her autobiography. "I envy, as I always did, children who can write a good hand and spell correctly, and blame the Husseys for not giving me an education."[55] Pleasant's writings make it clear that she did not have a problem expressing herself. However, she was aware of the differences between the self-taught and the formally trained. Like many of the African American elite, Pleasant probably spent much of her life being denied access to the kinds of educational opportunities she craved. One of the best-known observers of Nantucket, J. Hector St. John de Crèvecoeur, remarked that the easiest way to understand a human society was to observe the ways they educated their children. In this regard, white islanders were no different from other northerners: They resisted educating the island's black children until forced to do so.[56]

Mary Ellen was soon put to work as a shop clerk, where she received an education of a different sort. Mary Hussey, like many Quaker women on the island, operated her own shop and hired female clerks. Pleasant described the shop's location as "under the hill on Union Street," which bordered the central business district and New Guinea. She remembered the work this way: "I was a girl full of smartness and quick at coming back at people when they tried to have a little fun talking with me. I was a good-looking girl, too, and people used to come in to hear what I had to say. I suppose I got into the habit of talking too much, for when young people find they can raise a laugh they are liable to talk too much. . . . All this brought custom to the shop, and I would call people in and get them to buy things of me. I was always on the watch, and few people ever got by that shop without buying something of me."[57] Keenly self-aware and near the end of a long life of deal-making, buying, and selling, Pleasant located her knack for capitalist enterprise in her youth. Pleasant viewed those early years as formative in her development and, more specifically, her development as a businessperson.

Pleasant described Mary Hussey's shop as a "huckster shop." Like many in Nantucket Town, it functioned as a dry goods store where islanders could get anything from candles to crockery to silks and buttons. In her autobiography, she made much of this Nantucket experience. She invested it with tremendous significance in terms of shaping her future in business: "Mrs. Hussey in her shop sold everything from fish hooks to a ton of coal. . . . Buying wholesale and selling retail was the way she did it and it paid. I was finally placed in the store as a clerk, and I could make change and talk to a dozen people all at once and never make a mistake, and I could remember all the accounts and at the end of the day she could put them down, and they would always be right as I remembered them."[58] From the window of Mary Hussey's shop, young Mary Ellen Williams watched as wagonloads of produce, whale oil, building materials, and the like jostled over the cobblestoned streets.[59] In the 1820s and 1830s, talk of whales, their oil, and their capture could be heard in all corners of the island. The Quakers controlled the whaling industry, which dominated island life in the first four decades of the nineteenth century. Not until the discovery of petroleum in 1859 did the prized sperm oil—and whaling—cease to be Nantucket's primary source of wealth.[60] Young shop clerk Mary Ellen sold spermaceti candles, entertained whalers' stories of "the one that got away," and watched shop profits ebb and flow with the industry.

Nantucket proved an ideal locale for an ambitious, headstrong girl to learn business. Indeed, Nantucket Town was overrun with woman-owned shops because of the abundance of so-called whaling wives who ran the town while the men were at sea. In the antebellum period, when whaling was at its peak, Centre Street had so many of these shops it came to be known as Petticoat Row. Nantucket women were notorious for their independence, bravado, and business acumen. Historian Lisa Norling finds ample evidence to suggest a semiautonomous female economy.[61] A female diarist of the nineteenth century noted that "all the dry goods and grocery stores were kept by women, who went to Boston semi-annually to renew their stock."[62] Abolitionist Lucretia Mott, arguably the island's best-known woman, remarked on the businesswomen of the era as well: "Look at the heads of those women, they can mingle with men; they are not triflers; they have intelligent subjects of conversation." This is precisely the kind of woman Mary Ellen Pleasant grew to be on that small island of businesswomen.[63] We cannot be sure whether these traits were encouraged in African American girls, however.

At the end of her life Pleasant looked back on her Nantucket years with a mixture of bitterness and nostalgia. Over the years she learned that the formal education denied her in Nantucket mattered far less than the lessons she had had in "human nature." Sharp-witted as she was, Pleasant also discovered that many learned citizens were, to her mind, quite dull. "I have run across a good many highly educated people who knew a whole lot about books," she said, "and nothing about the world or the people in it." She elaborated, "I have let books alone, and studied men and women a good deal. You can't learn all the book knowledge and all the human nature studies in a lifetime. You must slight one or the other. I have seen lots of people who talk all day and never talk sense a minute. If people talk sense and don't talk it with good grammar or use great words, they will be listened to. I have always noticed that when I have anything to say people listen. They never go to sleep on me."[64] When Mary Ellen Pleasant left the sheltered island of Nantucket as a young woman she took with her invaluable business skills, an informal yet substantial education, and political savvy that would last a lifetime.

2

SHE WAS A FRIEND OF JOHN BROWN

I'd rather be a corpse than a coward.

MARY ELLEN PLEASANT, *San Francisco Call* (1901)

She treasured a bitter hatred for slavery and a certain contempt
for white people.

W. E. B. DU BOIS, *The Gift of Black Folk* (1924)

After spending her formative years in Nantucket, Pleasant, then a woman in her twenties, left the island and probably settled in Boston.[1] For a young woman with abolitionist and business connections in New England, Boston was a logical stopping place. The maritime traffic between Nantucket and Boston had always been heavy, and Pleasant's associates on the island, black abolitionists and sailors, the Husseys and their descendants, all undoubtedly had ties to New England's largest city. Sources are sketchy on Pleasant's sojourn to and stay in Boston. Many believe Mary Ellen worked in a tailor's shop in Boston, where she met her first husband.[2] The site of a significant millinery and dressmaking industry, this place, like Nantucket, also supported a female economy where some women acquired economic independence from men.[3] Her years in New England gave Pleasant the skills, capital, and associates that made it possible for her to go West in the Gold Rush years.

What little has been written about Pleasant's time in Boston has focused exclusively on her quest for a husband. Helen Holdredge claims in *Mammy Pleasant* that Mary Ellen went to Boston for the sole purpose of finding a wealthy man to marry. While working at a tailor's shop on Merrimac Street, "she furtively watched his customers as they ordered their somber broadcloth suits."[4] "It was easy to learn who were the men of wealth among these conservative but affluent Bostonians, and there was one customer whom she watched particularly," wrote Holdredge. "He was James W. Smith, a big man with heavy features, an olive tinge to his skin, and the large black eyes of a Spaniard. Mary Ellen learned that his mother was a Cuban, that he was a Catholic and a widower with a daughter named Emma. He had considerable money invested in Cuban bonds and owned a tobacco plantation at Charles Town, West Virginia."[5]

Pleasant's first husband has many names and identities in the legends. Sometimes he is called Alexander Smith or James Henry Smith.[6] Additionally, there is a debate about his racial makeup, his status, and his wealth. That he was a wealthy plantation owner—some think Cuban—is also bandied about. Whether he was Cuban does not necessarily indicate whether he was of African descent, a concern that is fundamental to most who theorize about the first husband. Historian Lerone Bennett contributes to the mystery by citing a "six-page handwritten Autobiographical Fragment," unavailable to the public.[7] This document convinces him that Smith was a black man, the son of a black woman and the governor of a southern state.[8]

The unsubstantiated stories surrounding the first husband's identity bear a remarkable similarity to the folklore about Pleasant that claims she was the daughter of a black woman and a southern governor's son. The fact that this scenario is repeated about both Pleasant and her first—and even second—husbands may tell us more about how folklore and family narratives work and less about the identity of Pleasant and her husbands. The material realities of slavery in the United States produced generations of African Americans whose fathers were indeed white southern governors. Tracing one's genealogy to the governor's mansion signaled prestige, and that may also explain the popularity of the story line.

Many versions of the relationship between Smith, her first husband, and Pleasants (also spelled Plaissance and Pleasance), her second, exist; some are so convoluted they are barely decipherable.[9] William Willmore Jr., the son of one of Mary Ellen Pleasant's San Francisco employees, had this story to tell about how Pleasant met her husbands: "After years on Nantucket Island she went to Boston and worked in a tailor shop. Smith came there to have his suits made. Mammy sparked up to him and sure enough he took to noticing her. She got him to marry her, even joining his church to put herself on equality." In this version Smith took Mary Ellen Pleasant to his plantation and "it was there she met Pleasants [her second husband] because he was the overseer of Smith's plantation." Pleasant murdered Smith and got Pleasants to marry her "on a ship" as they fled the East Coast, according to Willmore.[10] J. Lloyd Conrich, Pleasant enthusiast and author of an unpublished and undocumented manuscript, "The Mammy Pleasant Legend," wrote, "The first thing that Mammy did after her husband's death was to take up with a Negro named Plaissance. By a strange coincidence, Plaissance happened to have been on one of her late husband's deep south plantations."[11] Strange coincidences become commonplace at this point in the legends of Mary Ellen Pleasant. Conrich also noted that much of the folklore "bandies the incest angle about" and some of it "indicate[s] that the younger Plaissance was her brother, inferring that they were both sex deviates."[12] Just as Pleasant's history has been the subject of American fiction, fiction about her has been the subject of American history. The relationship of Pleasant to her husbands is a prime example of the mingling of fiction and fact. In one of the most perplexing versions of the story, Pleasant's second husband, the enslaved John James Pleasants, was set free by John Hampden Pleasants, a cousin of Thomas Jefferson—and Mary Ellen Pleasant's father.[13] Virginia census records indicate that both John Pleasants, a free "colored" man, and the white slaveowner John Hampden Pleasant lived in Goochland County in 1840, adding some credence to the story.[14]

It seems likely that sometime in the late 1830s or early 1840s, Pleasant married a man called James Smith in Boston. Some believe Pleasant and Smith were married in St. Mary's Church in Boston. Pleasant claimed she sang in the choir of Saint Mary's.[15] A newspaper account describes her first husband as "a foreman, carpenter and contractor, who had a good business and possessed considerable means."[16] One characteristic of the first husband about which all the sources agree is his penchant for abolitionist work. Smith, whatever his background, committed himself to the fight against slavery. Many sources claim that when he died in the 1840s Smith was a wealthy man and that his will left a generous amount of money to his wife, Mary Ellen, for the purpose of continuing their abolitionist endeavors.[17] Locating traces of James Smith and his wealth in the records proves difficult; there is no James Henry or James W. living in Boston according to the 1840 census. Of the forty men named James Smith in that census, none fits the profile of Pleasant's first husband.[18] Finding Smith's will is equally puzzling; probate records from Suffolk County in the 1840s have no listing of a James Smith, with or without a middle name.[19]

The sum of money bequeathed to her by her first husband is also the subject of wild speculation. Many claim that it was as much as $30,000; one source claims it was $40,000.[20] W. E. B. Du Bois alleged that the amount was $50,000.[21] Pleasant told a reporter that she brought $15,000 in gold coin with her from the East when she traveled to California.[22] Even the lesser amount would have been a tremendous sum for anyone to invest in the 1850s, equaling nearly 200 times the annual earnings of a working-class white man in California, where the wages were already markedly inflated because of the Gold Rush.[23] Pleasant arrived in the West a wealthy woman.

Between the death of her first husband and her arrival in San Francisco during the Gold Rush, Mary Ellen met and married a man named John James Pleasants. Stories about his background are nearly as murky as those about the first husband. Whether she met him in the East, on a plantation, or whether he was an old acquaintance of hers is unclear. Pleasants reported to the federal census taker in 1870 that he was born in Virginia; census records also reveal that he was working as a waiter in New Bedford, Massachusetts in 1850.[24] It is possible that Mary Ellen and John met in New Bedford, a hotbed of abolitionist activity. New Bedford was the destination of many fugitive slaves on the Underground Railroad, including Frederick Douglass.[25] Scores of black men left New Bedford for the Gold Rush, and John Pleasants could have been among them.[26] Mary Ellen testified in court in the 1860s that she married John in 1847 in Nantucket. We have no reason to doubt this because the island had played such an important role in her youth and the Hussey family probably had become a surrogate family. Pleasant claimed that after her first husband died, she went back to Nantucket to live with the granddaughter of Mary Hussey, Phebe Gardner, and her husband, Captain Edward W. Gardner.[27] Phebe Gardner took a leading role in the island's Anti-Slavery Society, as did her niece Anna Gardner, who became a close associate of Frederick Douglass when he gave his inaugural address in the Nantucket Athenaeum.[28] It seems clear that Mary Ellen Pleasant had established herself in the tight-knit circle of abolitionists on the East Coast, from Boston to New Bedford to Nantucket, and like many black female abolitionists, she found friends, companions, and family within this circle. Mary Ellen and John probably married among friends and loved ones in the state of Massachusetts.

Mary Ellen set up household with John Pleasants—later the *s* was dropped—in California. The couple did not always live together during their marriage, and this has caused concern among some authors.[29] In fact, employment, rather than discord, meant that the two spent a significant amount of time apart. The demands of both jobs, Mary Ellen's as a domestic servant and John's as a ship cook, took them in two directions: land and sea. By 1865, John was listed in the San Francisco directory as a resident and cook on the steamer *Orizaba,* one of the many vessels ferrying goods and passengers to the San Francisco Bay. He continued to find lucrative maritime employment, working as a cook on the North Pacific Transport Company's SS *Pacific* by 1871.[30] The pay for African American seacooks equaled or exceeded that of sailors after 1850, and John Pleasant, unlike many men in San Francisco after the Gold Rush, acquired high-paying work that did not disappear with the gold.[31]

Mary Ellen Pleasant's marriages, like those of other black female reformers, were the subject of consternation and criticism during her lifetime. It was not uncommon for black women who had careers as abolitionists, reformers, or businesspeople to live apart from husbands and children. Sojourner Truth, Mary Ann Shadd Cary, and Frances E. W. Harper all left families behind to carry out their work as lecturers, editors, and writers.[32] Marriages of many African Americans living in the mid-nineteenth century did not necessarily involve continuous cohabitation, and women were judged harshly because of it. Female abolitionists often were accused of overstepping the bounds of appropriate behavior.[33] The actions of female reformers and abolitionists—public speaking, travel, political protest, and agitation—roused public opinion and placed their private as well as public lives under scrutiny.

John Pleasant's work as a seacook and Mary Ellen's work as a live-in domestic in the first decades of their residency in California meant that although they often claimed the same address, circumstances required that they live apart.[34] Whatever their precise arrangement, Mary Ellen and John Pleasant lived together intermittently for more than twenty years, worked together as abolitionists in Canada, and launched a legal battle against discrimination in California in the 1860s. Their partnership appears undeniable, although it has been clouded by the memory of Mary Ellen's later associations with white men, in particular. This erasure of Pleasant's black family and associates stigmatizes her in the minds of some who claim that she deviated from appropriate black female behavior.[35]

Mary Ellen and John Pleasants were also the parents of a little girl. Lizzie J. Smith was born in the East, probably in New England in the late 1840s, before the family left for California.[36] It is unclear whether John was with Mary Ellen at the time or whether he had already left for the West. It is likely that Mary Ellen left her daughter in the care of friends when she initially went West. Caring for a baby as she established herself in San Francisco may have been too difficult, and she might have thought it unwise to do so. This has led authors to make assessments about Mary Ellen's—never John's—parenting skills and moral makeup. Pleasant's daughter may have been left in the care of a Mrs. Martha Steele of Boston. According to one informant, Mrs. Steele brought Lizzie to San Francisco when she was a young girl.[37] We know from an announcement in the San Francisco black newspaper *The Elevator* that Lizzie married R. Berry Phillips in San Francisco in the spring of 1865, and Mary Ellen hosted a "splendid entertainment" in their honor.[38] Holdredge suggests, however, that Mary Ellen shirked her maternal duties: Pleasant "seemed to find an odd satisfaction in evading her obligations to her daughter," she wrote.[39]

The assertion that Mary Ellen Pleasant abandoned her daughter, and delighted in that fact, has been alluded to in several published accounts of Pleasant's life. One travel guide of San Francisciana devoted an entire page to Pleasant's "abandoned daughter," who "tracked her mother down" and became "a testy and unhappy" drunk. According to this unsubstantiated account, "Mary Ellen didn't display much grief upon her daughter's demise. In fact, according to one observer, she seemed uncommonly gay."[40] Elizabeth is reported to have died in her twenties, but there is no evidence to show that her mother found this to be a joyous occasion.[41] This characterization of Pleasant's relationship with her daughter affirms certain nineteenth- and twentieth-century fantasies about black women and motherhood. It was a common belief that although black mammies spoiled and cherished their white charges on the plantation, they were unfit to mother their own children.[42] Showing Pleasant to be an unfit mother confirmed the belief for some that she was unwomanly at best, perhaps sinister.

Pleasant probably traveled to California without kin, to be joined by both husband and daughter at a later date. All argonauts faced dilemmas about separating from loved ones; most left someone behind. Like the thousands headed to the gold fields, Pleasant probably struggled with questions about the risky journey, when to leave, how to travel, and under what conditions. She certainly pondered her future prospects as a lone black woman in a city known for its roughness. It seems plausible that Pleasant arranged to travel with abolitionist associates that she knew from New England. Upstart companies and networks of family and friends departed from the East daily after word spread of the discovery of gold in California in 1848. One of the most remarkable migrations was that from Nantucket, where more than 700 Argonauts left the island in 1849.[43] Passenger lists from that year alone indicate that no fewer than twenty-five members of the Gardner and Hussey families packed their belongings and set sail for California.[44] The islanders had ample reason to join the mass migration: Nantucket suffered a devastating fire in 1846, and the economic decline caused by New Bedford's dominance of the whaling industry left many seeking new opportunities. The intimate relationship that most Nantucketers had with the sea and the existence of a superior fleet of outfitted ships beckoned many to the Gold Rush. Whaling prepared Nantucket's men and women for long stretches of time at sea and long periods of waiting for those who left. From whatever port she set sail, Pleasant arrived in San Francisco to find many associates from her youth.

Pleasant dated her arrival in the West at 1849.[45] Like much of her past, the chronology of her sojourn is imprecise. The son of a black pioneer, John Allen Francis Jr., claimed that Pleasant traveled to San Francisco with his father on the steamer *Oregon,* which docked at San Francisco Bay on April 7, 1852. According to Francis, "Mammy Pleasant didn't come in 1849 as she said. She came in a sailing vessel from New Orleans, and my father John Allen Francis was aboard. They got here in April 1852."[46] Accounts of passenger arrivals reveal that when the *Oregon* docked in April of 1852, among its approximately 500 passengers were a J. Francis and an M. Smith.[47] The scenario Francis Jr. describes seems quite plausible. Pleasant retained the name of her first husband, Smith, for some years after his death, as was the custom. There could have been many reasons for Pleasant's reluctance to travel under the name of her current husband. Hiding her abolitionist past and that of her present husband or the desire to hide her tracks from those who were looking for her are two possibilities. It is also the case that traveling as a widow rather than an unaccompanied woman, married or single, brought certain benefits. John Francis Sr. became Pleasant's coachman in San Francisco, and if they sailed together, perhaps posing as husband and wife, it would have also allowed a less conspicuous crossing. Women rarely traveled to California alone, and although there were at least twenty women aboard the steamer, Pleasant would have attracted attention as one of very few African Americans. Also on board the *Oregon* was a T. Bell, perhaps the Scottish banker Thomas Bell who figures so prominently in Pleasant's life in the West. Bell and Pleasant could easily have become acquainted on their long journey to San Francisco Bay.

Vessels carrying passengers from the eastern seaboard to the Gold Rush usually waited for the end of the winter storms and struck out around Cape Horn at the tip of South America or made the trip via Panama across the Colombian Isthmus and then sailed north to California. Rounding the Horn could be treacherous; taking a steamer through the isthmus was the fastest route.[48] It took only fifteen and a half days for the *Oregon* to travel the 3,320 miles and reach San Francisco Bay once it left Panama. The entire journey from eastern seaports to San Francisco took most argonauts at least two months, sometimes as many as six. Captain Gardner, Pleasant's friend and one of the wealthiest men of Nantucket, made the trip in reverse, from San Francisco to New York, in eighty-three days and eighteen hours in 1853, a record-setting pace according to the Nantucket press.[49] Most of the migrants to the Golden Gate in 1849 made the trip around Cape Horn; only about one-third of those leaving the Northeast took steamers to Panama, and often they were the wealthier travelers.[50]

Although determining when she left the East is somewhat elusive, determining why she did is an easier task. With the discovery of gold in California in January 1848, the possibilities for westering African Americans seemed limitless. Frederick Douglass, in the pages of his newspaper *The North Star,* boasted of the opportunities awaiting black forty-niners, claiming that "the wealth of California is, as it should be, shared by colored as well as white men."[51] Drawn by stories of new-found wealth, Pleasant, like thousands of other migrants, may have felt tempted by the riches that could be had in the new territory of the United States. But gold dust alone did not explain the temptation for many African Americans to seek western climes. Black citizens had several compelling reasons to join the rush; the other regions of the United States offered little hope for economic and political viability at midcentury. Rights for black men and women diminished in the so-called free states, and slaveowners tightened their grip on centers of power from the local to the federal level. Perhaps the dangers of the Fugitive Slave Law of 1850 propelled Pleasant West. Part of a broader set of laws known as the Compromise of 1850 that also allowed for California to enter the Union as a free state, the Fugitive Slave Act gave slaveowners the federal support they needed to travel into states where slavery had been outlawed and reclaim their slaves. Reports of free blacks being harassed or enslaved in free states were common.[52]

Certainly the fact that California became a free state in 1850 made it more attractive to abolitionists such as Pleasant who were leaving the East. It was a Mexican province before 1848, when the Treaty of Guadalupe Hidalgo ceded the territory to the United States. Shaping white racial hegemony in this new free state was complicated given the large populations of Indians, Californios, and Mexicans.[53] The discovery of gold at Sutter's Mill, only days after the treaty was signed in 1848, guaranteed the creation of a multiethnic, multiracial West as gold seekers from Chile, Panama, Australia, and China joined others in the former Mexican province. Some historians have argued that African Americans were more welcome in California than they were in other regions of the United States. For example, Mexican authorities did not restrict entry into the province based on skin color, nor did they prevent interracial marriage. As one scholar claimed, "A darker skin color did not keep a Californian from attaining wealth or power" in the nineteenth century.[54] This assumption continues to hold sway in the literature of the black experience in the West.[55] High levels of employment, the lack of poverty, the presence of entrepreneurs such as Pleasant, and the visibility of a thriving black press are all cited as indicators that the West was a hospitable—perhaps even superior—place for black people to live.[56] Both contemporary accounts and historiographic ones have celebrated the West as liberatory for black people. Many of these accounts downplay the extent of white supremacy in the new state, and nearly all fail to take gender into consideration.

It is well known that women's presence in most of the mining camps in California was negligible, but even in the streets of San Francisco in late

1849, women were a rare sight; black women were even rarer. Pleasant's arrival, if in 1852, would have come at a time when the female presence was slightly more conspicuous. Nevertheless, only 464 African Americans made San Francisco their home in 1852; the ratio of men to women probably was around three to one.[57] California's population in 1850 was more than 92 percent male.[58]

Pleasant was very clear about her strategy once she arrived in California with capital: "I divided this money among Fred Langford, William West of the West & Harper. I knew these gentlemen at home. They put out my money at ten percent interest and I did an exchange business, sending down gold and having it exchanged for silver. Gold was then at a high premium. I had many bank books. I would deposit silver and draw out gold from friends in the banks where there was a good deal of silver. Most of this business was done through Wells Fargo through Mr. Confield and Mr. Zander."[59] Pleasant's inheritance from her first husband had made her wealthy, and she capitalized on her opportunities immediately. She invested wisely, channeling funds into the institutions that transformed the West such as Wells Fargo, which began operations in 1852, and later the Bank of California. And like most early Californians, Pleasant learned to operate in an economy obsessed with gold. The fact that she "did an exchange business" meant she also perceived the tentative nature of the metal markets and thus was better able to withstand the fluctuations that defined the Gold Rush economy.[60]

Her ability to triumph in the developing Western economy stemmed from her multifaceted relationship to the market: Pleasant operated simultaneously as an investor, a business owner, and a laborer. Like other successful capitalists, she diversified her investments in gold, silver, quicksilver, and property, and like most nineteenth-century black women, she worked. Pleasant's culinary talents allowed her to work for wages while she invested in real estate and other entrepreneurial activities. The highest wages in the early years of the Gold Rush went to female domestics, who received $13 a week and board; male laborers earned $11 a week.[61] By contrast, weekly wages to female domestics in the South in 1850 ranged from about $1 to $2.50.[62] Domestic servants in San Francisco earned ten times as much as those in New York City.[63] Not only did Pleasant bring capital to the state, but she also embodied what many wealthy men had been craving: someone to domesticate them.

The ratio of men to women in San Francisco in 1860 still hovered around 158 men for every 100 women.[64] This imbalance did not mean the same thing for all women. Some accounts of the Gold Rush have promoted the notion that an uneven gender balance meant special privileges for women.

This assumption is problematic on many accounts. First, it assumes that women earned more money and respect because men did not and could not provide domestic services for themselves; this is wrong on both counts. As historians of gender and sexuality have recently pointed out, a skewed sex ratio had multiple effects. Men necessarily performed so-called women's work in Gold Rush California, for example.[65] Second, this assumption often blurs the distinctions between western women; being a Chinese woman during the Gold Rush was vastly different from being a European American woman. Being one of just a few hundred black women in the city, Pleasant experienced the West in ways other women did not, although by working as a domestic she did the same work that most other women in California performed. Pleasant certainly profited by supplying domestic services, but she was not immune to unequal power relations simply because of this demand-heavy market.

Procuring jobs as a cook and housekeeper, Pleasant laid the groundwork for future enterprises. Rumors of her culinary skills abound.[66] Herbert Asbury, in the 1933 text *The Barbary Coast*, reports the scene at Pleasant's ship this way:

> Fewer than a score of cooks were in private service [in San Francisco], but they insisted, of course, upon being called "chefs." A notable exception to this foolery was Mammy Pleasant, a gigantic Negress from New Orleans, black as the inside of a coal-pit, but with no Negroid features whatever, whose culinary exploits were famous. She said flatly that she was a cook, and would be called nothing else. She arrived in the early part of 1850, preceded by her reputation, and was besieged by a crowd of men, all anxious to employ her, before she had so much as left the wharf at which her ship had docked. She finally sold her services at auction at five hundred dollars a month, with the stipulation that she should do no washing, not even dishwashing.[67]

Whether this is an accurate description of her landing we can only guess; Asbury provides no documentation. The image of a southern mammy fresh off the boat prevails in most descriptions of her arrival. And although these images are rife with stereotypic connotations, Pleasant did earn a sizable income in her capacity as cook and housekeeper, the very activities associated with mammydom. The Gold Rush provided an ideal market for women who could cook, clean, and keep house. Twenty years after gold was found at Sutter's Mill, most women who worked for wages in California did so as domestic servants; 7,735 women listed this as their occupation in the 1870 census. The second and third most common occupations for women in the state were those of laundress and seamstress.[68] Pleasant wasted no time capitalizing on her domestic skills and on the assumptions that as a black woman she excelled at these tasks. Her entrepreneurial success in the West—from its beginning—relied in part on the manipulation and exploitation of stereotypes about black women and mammies in particular.

Among her many offers, Pleasant chose to work as a housekeeper and cook for the men of Case and Heiser, who were commission merchants. In their establishment, Pleasant oversaw the upkeep of the house and supervised the other employees. Holdredge claims that Pleasant "selected a lover" from the guests at the boardinghouse.[69] More likely, Pleasant initiated financial relationships with the men at Case and Heiser. By the late 1850s, Pleasant had established herself as a cook for some of the most elite families and bachelors in San Francisco. This position proved valuable in myriad ways as investment tips and real estate deals came her way.[70]

While working as a cook, Pleasant supplemented her wages by purchasing laundries, perhaps as a result of her business connections made at Case and Heiser. James Allen Francis Jr. recalled that Pleasant opened a laundry as quickly as possible: "Mammy's first laundry was at the corner of Jessie and Ecker. People paid fantastic prices to get their laundry done, and Mammy decided that if she was to make money she should have several places. She opened another laundry on Clara Street and finally opened a laundry for the Pacific mail steamers out on Geneva and San Jose [Roads]. When she became wealthy and powerful no one ever remembered her laundries except those like my father who worked for her."[71] An employer of men such as Francis's father, Pleasant quickly expanded this part of her enterprise. And it is clear from accounts of Gold Rush San Francisco that she chose her business carefully. The cost of all services for the unwashed crowds were exorbitant. Laundry came to be so expensive that it became a public concern. In 1850, when the cost per dozen shirts fell from $20 to $5, the *Alta California* claimed, "The effect of the reduction is already manifest—tobacco-juice-bespattered bosoms are no longer the fashion."[72] Other sources indicate that after 1850, most laundries charged about twenty-five cents per item.[73] Despite a boom-and-bust economy, laundries turned a steady profit.

Laundering, like cooking, proved lucrative for Pleasant. Like other domestic jobs, it was also work that was most often done by women. So many women operated laundries in the city that one scholar estimates that 45 percent of women who were employed in San Francisco in 1860 worked as laundresses.[74] This female dominance of the trade shifted in the 1860s as laundries were increasingly operated by Chinese men. Targets of the Foreign Miners Tax of 1852, which deprived them of wealth accumulated in the gold fields, many gold seekers from China turned to the laundry business. By 1880, Chinese men accounted for 85 percent of the launderers in

San Francisco.[75] It is likely that Pleasant had closed her laundries by then because her boardinghouse business became so successful in the 1860s.

Pleasant's networks in California included abolitionist friends and colleagues she had known in the East. William West and Fred Langford, the "gentlemen from home" with whom she had entrusted her capital, continued to play a key role in her early days in San Francisco.[76] One source claimed that Pleasant "helped William West to establish a boardinghouse that was, in reality, a secret safe house for runaway slaves."[77] Abolitionist friends from Nantucket, New Bedford, and Boston probably formed a central part of her social and business life in the West. Pleasant participated in an abolitionist network that spanned the United States and abroad; she associated with abolitionists wherever she lived, be it Boston, San Francisco, or Chatham, Canada.[78]

That Pleasant simultaneously worked as a housekeeper and an abolitionist was common knowledge among African Americans. One of her contemporaries remembered, "Mammy, right from the beginning, when she was working for some men who owned a commission house, carried on her own affairs." "She got tied up because they were always entertaining," he explained, "so she got some men she'd worked along with in the Underground Railroad back in New Bedford. She'd send messages around to their offices and the action would be very fast."[79] Since Pleasant's youth in Nantucket, business and politics were never mutually exclusive; like most black abolitionists, she made a living while she worked for freedom.

San Francisco's black men and women quickly distinguished themselves as industrious settlers, although they were few in number. According to the census of 1850, there were only 962 "negroes and mulattoes" in the state, most of whom resided in the San Francisco and Sacramento areas.[80] The black population of these two cities increased at roughly the same pace in the 1850s; in 1852 San Francisco's black population was 464 and Sacramento's 338. By 1860, however, San Francisco's black population amounted to more than twice Sacramento's: 1,176 African Americans made San Francisco their home.[81] Many of the earliest black settlers in the city, like John Pleasant, were sailors and maritime workers. And although the Central Pacific Railroad also employed black men in the West, most had to work as cooks or porters. Both men and women found that the city offered the most opportunities for work in the service sector. One of the city's black newspapers, *The Elevator,* remarked on the abundance of domestic jobs for black women, claiming, "If there were one hundred capable house servants here, such as cooks, housemaids and laundresses, we would guarantee they could all find employment within a week or two."[82] Some men, and a few women, also advertised their businesses in the black press; these ads reveal the variety of the city's black enterprise: clothing stores, coal yards, restaurants, and music lessons could all be found in the small black community.

Although economic survival preoccupied most San Franciscans in the 1850s, black settlers devoted significant resources to forming social, cultural, and political institutions. In 1853, black leaders opened the San Francisco Athenaeum Institute, a saloon and meeting place for both elite and working-class African Americans. On the second floor the institute housed an impressive library, to which Pleasant contributed funds.[83] Charlotte Dennis Downs, whose father also contributed to the library, recalled, "Some people said she owned the Athenaeum Saloon but actually she had only helped James Ricker and Monroe Taylor with the money to open the business. It was on Washington above Stockton and it was kind of a club for Negro men."[84] The next year, the institute issued a report on the city's black community that served as an advertisement for the Athenaeum and as a useful index of productivity. In April 1854 the institute noted that the 1,500 black men and women in San Francisco, "notwithstanding their political disabilities," were in "a prospering condition."[85] There were 150 families with 75 children who were "not admitted to the common schools." Of the numerous accomplishments listed, San Francisco black citizens boasted three churches, two joint stock companies with a capital of $16,000, two restaurants, sixteen barber shops, four shoe stores, two furniture stores, one hundred mechanics, a brass band, a Masonic lodge, and a reading room with 800 volumes—obviously the institute's library.[86]

From the earliest years of statehood, black Californians pressed for the rights of citizenship. Their right to offer testimony in a court of law, prohibited in the state's constitution, was among their immediate concerns. Pleasant spearheaded campaigns to allow black testimony in courts, a struggle that lasted until 1863.[87] Many believe her to be a founding member of the Franchise League, organized by black San Franciscans in 1852.[88] Willmore remembered the organizing this way: "The Negroes were timid but not nearly as unthinking as many imagined. Sharp thinkers like Mammy and David W. Ruggles Senior formed an organization to protect them."[89] Franchise Leagues, like the vigilance committees that rescued fugitive slaves, organized across the country to combat slavery and secure the rights of black men and women. The precarious freedom of the state's African American citizens also prompted them to organize black conventions. In 1855, 1856, and 1857, African American men met to discuss California's antiblack legislation, and the antitestimony law in particular. These conventions served as springboards for future political activism: An Executive Committee of the Colored Convention planned forthcoming actions, and the city's first black newspaper, *Mirror of the Times,* grew out of these efforts.[90] Although black folklore and the historian Delilah Beasley make much of Pleasant's participation in the antitestimony law protest, the official records are silent on Pleasant's involvement in the black convention movement and the Executive Committee. However, her friend David W. Ruggles led the Executive Committee, and it seems likely that Pleasant participated in all the campaigns of the committee. We should not be surprised at the invisibility of black women in the records: Black conventions were notorious bastions of black manhood. Indeed, much of the rhetoric emerging from the nationwide movement centered on questions of masculinity and rights.[91]

The political activism of California's early black citizens flourished considering their numbers and the difficulties they faced in the free state.[92] Black Californians protested as the California Legislature tried throughout the 1850s to stop further migration of African Americans into the state. In 1851, 1855, 1857, and then again in 1858, anti-immigration bills were introduced in the legislature, although they never passed.[93] In 1852 California passed its own Fugitive Slave Law, compounding the dangers faced by fugitive slaves and free blacks alike. Slaveowners in California could capture their property without fear of legal repercussion. Indeed, until 1855, slaveowners were allowed to live in the state with their slaves, despite the fact that California entered the United States as a free state in 1850. Instances of slave sales were not uncommon in the first decade of statehood.[94]

Pleasant's efforts to rescue fugitive slaves in the West were well known to black San Franciscans. Charlotte Dennis Downs recounted numerous incidents when her father, George Dennis, and Pleasant worked together to free or hide slaves. One of the best-known fugitive slave cases was that of George Mitchell, a slave who had been brought to California in 1849.[95] "The owner was trying to hold George under the [1852] Fugitive Slave Act," Downs explained. "The judge pointed out that the act concerning the removal of a slave had expired. While the owner and his lawyer were swearing out affidavits, George was put under wraps by my father and Mammy, and they never did get a hold of him."[96] Historian Rudolph Lapp confirmed this outcome and noted that lawyers were able to stall the case until April 1855, when the California Fugitive Slave Law had indeed expired.[97]

The expiration of the law and the Mitchell case seemingly put an end to slavery in the free state, but in 1858 another case took black Californians by storm, and once again Pleasant played a significant role in the slave's defense. Archy Lee had been brought to Sacramento by his owner's son, Charles Stovall, in 1857. After hiring Lee out for his wages, Stovall got nervous and decided to move back to Mississippi, where there would be no doubt about the status of his slave. To avoid this fate, Lee hid in a Sacramento hotel operated by free black people, but Stovall had him arrested in January 1858, and thus began a series of legal maneuvers that lasted for months and involved the state's leading abolitionists and its highest court. After an initial victory in the lower courts, Stovall managed to rearrest Lee and was granted a hearing in the state supreme court. On February 11 the California Supreme Court ruled that although the state forbade slavery, Stovall was "in transit" and not aware of the laws and therefore was entitled to keep his slave.[98] This decision outraged black Californians and other abolitionists, who mobilized considerable resources for Lee's defense.

When Stovall attempted to secure Archy Lee's passage back to Mississippi on board the steamer *Orizaba* (where John Pleasant would soon be the cook), abolitionists readied their forces. According to Delilah Beasley, George Dennis and other members of the Executive Committee of the Colored Convention chartered a tugboat, met the *Orizaba* in the bay, and rearrested Lee for his protection. Pleasant, along with David Ruggles, orchestrated a fundraising campaign to cover the extensive costs of the battle, legal and otherwise.[99] Lee was again brought before district court; this time, Judge Freelon freed Lee in April of that year. Mary Ellen Pleasant hid Archy Lee in her home, concerned about the frenzied atmosphere after the case and the risks it might pose. It is likely that she helped Lee escape to Canada a few weeks later.

The combination of the Archy Lee case, the anti-immigration sentiment, and the antitestimony law signaled danger and injustice to many black Californians. Like African Americans in other parts of the country, many in the West questioned the viability of life in the United States. Mythologized in stories of the Underground Railroad and a place free from slavery, Canada had been one of the most popular havens for black emigrants from the United States, beginning in the 1840s.[100] Most black Californians who migrated to Canada went directly north to the city of Victoria, on Vancouver Island, British Columbia.[101] However, John and Mary Ellen Pleasant traveled to Chatham in 1858.[102] Chatham, located in what is now the province of Ontario, was a center of black abolitionist activity and the home of Canada's black newspaper, the *Provincial Freeman*. The Pleasants joined a small but active community of free blacks and fugitive slaves who made up a quarter of the town's population. Black Americans found Chatham fairly hospitable; men could own property, vote, and serve on juries, and their farms and businesses prospered.[103] Although we know very little about the Pleasants' more than 3,000-mile journey to what was called Canada West, we do know that their trip was exceptional because the other abolitionists they joined had lived on and around the eastern seaboard.[104]

In Chatham in 1858, thirty-four black and twelve white abolitionists gathered to offer their support to John Brown and his plan to end slavery. Brown, an Ohio abolitionist, had distinguished himself as a zealous evangelical in the fight against slavery. His efforts to battle proslavery forces in the Kansas-Nebraska Territory left him frustrated and fervently committed to ending slavery on a grander scale. His infamous raid on the federal arsenal at Harpers Ferry, Virginia was preceded by a series of clandestine meetings that, among other things, organized a provisional government of the United States. Brown convened what he called a "provisional constitutional convention" in May 1858 and secretly developed his plan to raid the arsenal and liberate southern slaves.[105] Chatham was an ideal location for Brown's activities; it was beyond the reach of U.S. law enforcement and, by the late 1850s, Chatham had approximately 800 black residents.[106] Located nearby, the fugitive slave settlements of Dawn, Elgin, and Buxton had established the area's reputation as a center of abolitionist activity.

In the fall of that year John and Mary Ellen Pleasant also participated in the rescue and defense of a free black man, Sylvanus Demerest. The Pleasants acted as part of the Chatham Vigilance Committee that rescued Demerest from a train as W. R. Merwin, a New Yorker, was attempting to kidnap him. Railroad officials arrested seven members of the Vigilance Committee. Like the Vigilance Committee that protected Archy Lee, the Chatham committee also took responsibility for the cost of their legal battles. As members of the Chatham Vigilance Committee, the Pleasants joined an illustrious society of some of black America's best-known leaders, including Martin Delany, Mary Ann Shadd Cary, William Howard Day, and Osborne Anderson (who was the sole black survivor of Brown's raid).[107] In October, Mary Ann Shadd, editor of the *Provincial Freeman,* requested funds to defray the expense of the trial. The Pleasants were both listed in 1858 as members of the fourteen-person Vigilance Committee.[108]

The spring and fall of 1858 were pivotal for black abolitionists in Canada. John Brown's convention and the Chatham Vigilance Committee brought together activists from across North America. The Pleasants must have felt committed to the task and to Chatham because they bought property in the town that same year. In September they purchased four lots in the township of Harwich in Chatham. Thomas Cary, Mary Ann Shadd's husband, and William Howard Day—both members of the Vigilance Committee— were the witnesses listed on the deed.[109] Another member of the committee figured prominently in the Pleasants' lives in both Canada and California.

James Madison Bell, secretary of the Chatham Vigilance Committee, housed John Brown during the convention and moved to San Francisco in 1860. Bell's decision to move west must have been influenced by his friends, the Pleasants; he followed a similar trajectory, raising funds and recruiting support for John Brown then moving to San Francisco, where he worked as a poet and joined the Pleasants' church.[110] Pleasant again found herself in the center of a vibrant, active abolitionist community. It is not coincidental that from Nantucket to San Francisco to Chatham she kept this company.

Among the legends that Mary Ellen Pleasant has inspired, none are more heroic than her role in John Brown's raid. Either as a jockey warning slaves of the raid or as the financier of John Brown's mission, she has appeared as a central figure in planning and executing the attack on the arsenal at Harpers Ferry in 1859.[111] Underneath these dramatic stories lies a web of complicated twice-told tales and, as Lerone Bennett points out, more mystery than evidence.[112] Her precise role in John Brown's raid remains elusive yet invested with tremendous significance for Pleasant and the history of abolition.

Her time in Chatham and her role in John Brown's raid is the part of her life she was most fond of retelling. Being remembered as an abolitionist was a priority for Pleasant as she approached old age. At the end of her life she granted several interviews with her friend, the editor Sam Davis. Davis, who in 1901 published Pleasant's autobiography in his short-lived journal *Pandex of the Press*, published an article two years later in *Comfort Magazine* under the heading "How a Colored Woman Aided John Brown." Based on an interview with Pleasant, this article documented Mary Ellen Pleasant's only testimony about her connection to John Brown.[113] "I have never made this statement in full to anyone," Pleasant told Davis in 1901, "but before I pass away I wish to clear the identity of the party who furnished John Brown with most of his money to start the fight at Harpers Ferry and who signed the letter found on him when he was arrested."[114] Thus begins the narrative that, for some, reshaped Pleasant's image and the history of John Brown's raid.

Pleasant's claim that she funded the raid inspired Sam Davis to test the validity of Pleasant's story. When he asked about supporting evidence she replied, "John Brown has some children still living in California and they would be likely to know about the money I advanced to John Brown."[115] The son, Jason Brown, was living in the Santa Cruz mountains south of San Francisco, and Davis questioned the eighty-year-old man about Pleasant and his father. "Yes, it is true, my father went to Chatham in '58 and met a colored woman who advanced him considerable money. I don't know her name." Susan Brown, the daughter, offered a similar response: She knew that her father "met a colored woman in Chatham and received considerable money from her," but he never disclosed the woman's name.[116]

The necessary secrecy surrounding the raid certainly encouraged Brown and his financial backers—the "Secret Six"—to remain close-mouthed about details.[117] Thus, it is not surprising that details about John Brown's mission and Pleasant's involvement have remained hidden. Neither literature about the Secret Six, Brown's papers, nor autobiographies of participants in the raid have confirmed Pleasant's involvement directly.[118] The details about a treasury draft that she had drawn up in the spring of 1858 seem to support Pleasant's contribution. Davis also checked on this and found proof that she indeed took a large sum of money to New York and had it converted to Canadian currency before she arrived in Chatham.[119]

Pleasant's role as a jockey, traveling around the South to warn slaves, is more difficult to substantiate. Her own version of the ride remains all that historians have to consider. Sometime between the fall of 1858 and the fall of 1859, when the raid took place, Pleasant claims she rode in advance of the raid to alert black southerners. "I then went back to the United States and secured a trusted man to go with me along the Roanoke River and incite an uprising of the slaves. I was dressed in the clothes of a jockey and he had horses along, and we posed as people connected with the turf."[120] Pleasant described the journey to plantations, hiding in slave cabins and talking Brown's plan over with the slaves. "They were very much taken with the idea of participating in the fight for their own freedom," she stated. "We arranged that when Brown made a stand at Harpers Ferry the negroes were to rise in every direction, but our plans were knocked all to pieces by Brown himself. He started the raid on Harpers Ferry before the time was ripe. I was astounded when I heard that he had started in and was beaten and captured and that the affair upon which I had staked my money and built so much hope, was a fiasco."[121] The raid was indeed a failure and fiasco. And by placing herself at the center of the action, Pleasant secured for herself a place in history.

When Brown was captured, she continued, "they found among his papers a letter from me. . . . It contained these words, 'The axe is laid at the root of the tree. When the first blow is struck there will be more money and help.' The [news]papers stated that such a letter was found and signed 'W.E.P.'"[122] Pleasant considered herself lucky to have escaped; she was well aware of Brown's hanging and the execution of many of his co-conspirators. "I went to New York as fast as I could," she told Davis; "I read in the papers that the detectives were on the track of W.E.P. who wrote the letter, and I had a quiet laugh when I saw that my poor handwriting had given them a false trail."[123]

Most historians hedge on the question of Pleasant's involvement in the raid. Lerone Bennett writes, "There is no documentary evidence to support her story, but she maintained with all her might until her dying day that it was true."[124] Holdredge downplays any sign of heroism:

> Her money did not go to John Brown but to the negroes, to aid them in get- ting out over the Underground not only to Canada but to such places as New Bedford and other New England stations and also to SF.
>
> She was investing money to stimulate the flow of Negroes to SF for every negroe [sic] there could be of some use to her . . . and if she helped them out of the South she would have a hold over them when they got there.
>
> There is no reason to believe that she contributed any large sum to John Brown's plan of rebellion.[125]

True to form, Holdredge waffles in her descriptions of Pleasant's abolition- ist activities. In the final draft of *Mammy Pleasant* she taints all Pleasant's work as devious and manipulative. But her notes to herself indicate that she was moved by the testimony of Charlotte Dennis Downs and David W. Ruggles, in particular, and inclined to believe their descriptions of Pleasant's efforts on behalf of African Americans.

Black San Franciscans found much more significance in Pleasant's trip east and her association with John Brown.[126] David W. Ruggles Jr. stated, "The money Mammy took East to John Brown was given to her by San Francisco negroes. . . . I heard my father say that she got the money to give John Brown from people here in San Francisco—very little of the money was her own and it wasn't anything like the amount that she said." But he insisted, "Mammy went East to meet John Brown; that I know is authentic."[127] William Willmore Jr. remembered, "Mammy made great preparations for her meeting with John Brown. She was very exultant, very uplifted, accord- ing to my father." Like Ruggles, Willmore repeated that Pleasant had served as a conduit, delivering donations from black San Franciscans to Brown's cause. "She turned the money she had collected from negroes into a bank draft before she set forth for Canada."[128]

Willmore went to great lengths to convince his interviewers, Helen Hol- dredge and a Mrs. Martha O'Donnell, that Pleasant contributed to John Brown's effort:

> You ask Charlotte Dennis Downs about it. She heard it from her brother who was Mrs. Mark Hopkins' steward. It must surely be true because you can't slow down that kind of learning. The wonderment is that the story even got repeat- ed at all—because you see Charles Crocker despised Mammy Pleasant. She had distributed money among strikers—people who were down on the railroad

builders. Charles Crocker was in Canada at the time Mammy met John Brown. With him was a man named William Stephens. Stephens knew a man who had seen—been the actual witness of Mammy giving the support money to Brown. The man who was the witness of this happening knew Mammy when she was married to her first husband because he was engaged in Abolitionist activities too. He was there and recognized her and that's a sure enough fact.[129]

Delilah L. Beasley, historian of black Californians, corroborated the story about the witness for her 1916 study. William Stephens of Oakland told Beasley that while employed on Crocker's private railroad car, he met a man whose father, a Canadian labor commissioner and abolitionist, had seen Pleasant give "a large sum of money" to John Brown.[130]

Mary Ellen Pleasant's request that the words "She was a friend of John Brown" be printed on her gravestone was honored in 1965 when the San Francisco Negro Historical and Cultural Society placed a marker bearing the phrase on her grave in Napa, California.[131]

3

JIM CROW SAN FRANCISCO

No more independent woman ever wore shoe leather.

San Francisco Examiner (1895)

Mary Ellen Pleasant returned to San Francisco on the eve of the Civil War. During the tumultuous years of the war and Reconstruction, she diversified her entrepreneurial activities, dramatically increased her income, and fought Jim Crow practices in the West's largest city. Pleasant began a series of court appearances in this period, challenging the state's treatment of African Americans and definitions of citizenship. By the end of the decade, she extended her reach to include many of the West's most influential political figures by establishing a lucrative boardinghouse business.

On her return from Canada, Mary Ellen Pleasant worked in the home of Selim and Lisette Woodworth in the tenth ward of the city.[1] Selim Woodworth, a former commander in the U.S. Navy, was one of San Francisco's wealthiest merchants.[2] Pleasant lived with fourteen other Woodworth family members and servants in what must have been an ample estate.[3] Her work as a domestic at this point in her career prompted San Francisco author Lloyd Conrich to ask, "Why is it that a woman who was able to give away thirty thousand dollars in 1858 and who was supposed to have been operating numerous prosperous businesses should, six years later, be working as a domestic?"[4] There are many possible explanations for the apparent contradiction between Pleasant's work as a domestic and her wealth. Nineteenth-century black workers had few employment choices; they were relegated to the most laborious and least profitable occupations.[5] The majority of black San Franciscans—of whom there were more than 1,000 in 1860—continued to work in service jobs, and most women who worked for wages did so as domestics.[6] Pleasant's options for other types of employment were few. Because Pleasant had already earned and invested money in San Francisco in the 1850s—when a large profit could be made from mining and real estate speculation—it is reasonable to assume that she left capital in the city. Her investments at the San Francisco accounting firm Case and Heiser probably increased substantially in her absence and were available when she returned from Canada. In that case, Pleasant may have worked as a domestic in the 1860s to maintain her disguise as San Francisco's most sought-after mammy. It is also possible that she had indeed donated her capital to John Brown's cause and found her resources depleted.

Working in the homes of wealthy merchants and investors put Pleasant within earshot of political and financial decision making. The proximity to San Francisco's elite families such as the Woodworths enhanced Pleasant's knowledge about the volatile economy, political climate, and the culture of the elite. This knowledge provided the basis for her own entrepreneurial success with the elegant boardinghouses she established later in the decade. The significance of her relationship with the Woodworths extended beyond the household to the state's Supreme Court, where Lisette Woodworth later was a key witness in Pleasant's discrimination lawsuit.

The Civil War years signaled a shift in Pleasant's civil rights activism in San Francisco. The state legislature abandoned its efforts to pass anti-immigration legislation in 1858, testimony rights were won for African Americans in 1863, and black leaders including Pleasant concentrated their efforts on combating segregation in education and public transportation and fighting for the right to vote.[7] Many authors, from Helen Holdredge to Lerone Bennett, characterize the 1860s as Pleasant's "civil rights phase" because in this decade her challenge to racism in the West's institutions was visible—and documented—in ways her previous work was not. However, this particular chronology is misleading because it erases the activism of Pleasant and other black San Franciscans in the antebellum years. Just as she did in the 1850s, Pleasant fought for racial equality in California during the Civil War and Reconstruction years; this time, however, she instigated her own lawsuit.

Black women's formal political participation was necessarily limited in this era, yet they participated in, and often were catalysts for, protests directed at the nation's segregated institutions. African American women regularly petitioned state legislatures, organized political clubs, and rallied local and state governments across the United States in the presuffrage and postemancipation decades.[8] In San Francisco, as in other cities, black women shaped political culture through their churches, literary societies, charity work, and entrepreneurial activities. The San Francisco black newspaper the *Pacific Appeal,* for example, regularly announced the meetings of the Daughters and Sons of Zion Benevolent Association (organized in 1860), which gathered at the African Methodist Episcopal (AME) Zion Church, and the Ladies Union Beneficial Society, which met at the African Methodist Episcopal Church. Pleasant attended the AME Zion church and probably participated in campaigns to help the needy, raise money for abolitionist and Union causes, and aid widows and orphans. Already known for her generosity, Pleasant orchestrated a benefit at the Mechanic's Institute Hall in December 1867; it was reported in the press that she was "assisted by a number of ladies," and the function was well attended.[9]

San Francisco's black businesses, churches, and philanthropic organizations thrived in the 1860s. By the end of the war they included three churches (Third Baptist, Bethel AME, and AME Zion Church), four Masonic lodges, several liveries (one owned by Charlotte Dennis Downs's father, George Dennis), ten laundries, two real estate agencies, and two newspapers (the *Pacific Appeal* and the *Elevator*).[10] Pleasant supported key institutions in the city's black communities, including the black press. *The Pacific Appeal* considered her an important patron. On July 25, 1863, the paper ran the following announcement: "Mrs. Mary Pleasants, of this city, has paid us $5 in advance, for two copies of the *Appeal,* up to January next. Such encouragement greatly relieves us, at times. The lady has our thanks."[11] In 1870, she was again praised in the pages of the press as "the ever-earnest lady and christian [*sic*]" for organizing a local benefit and celebration.[12]

In addition to creating their own press and business community, black San Franciscans occupied and transformed the city's public spaces. African Americans in San Francisco celebrated the signing of the Emancipation Proclamation on January 14, 1863, with a Grand Jubilee held in Platt's Hall. Reverend Jeremiah B. Sanderson, a well-known black pioneer, activist, and schoolteacher, read the proclamation to the crowd.[13] This was not a unique celebration; black San Franciscans regularly marked the occasion of West Indian emancipation with jubilees and parades, just as they did the anniversary of emancipation in the United States. The city's churches sponsored festivals, concerts, and fairs, as well as lectures and benefits of all sorts.[14]

In 1865 black San Franciscans participated in the fourth statewide Convention of the Colored Citizens, held in Sacramento in October of that year. These California meetings were dominated by the male elite of the state's black communities.[15] In attendance were Pleasant's minister, Reverend John J. Moore of AME Zion; a friend of the Pleasants from Chatham, Canada, the poet and activist James Madison Bell; and Pleasant's friend and associate David W. Ruggles. All-male conventions typically limited women's input, and this gathering was no exception. We have no record of women's response to this convention, but we can be sure that Pleasant and her female contemporaries must have known about it. The black convention movement shaped the social and political world in which Pleasant traveled.

Much of the proceedings of the fourth convention focused on the issues of suffrage and education, issues very dear to black women. Representatives also made it clear that black manhood was at stake. Reverend J. J. Moore, on the convention's State Executive Committee, stated "that the time had arrived for men to speak out boldly, and let the world know we think as men." "He is opposed to anything like cringing," the convention's minutes declared. Not surprisingly, these invocations of manhood, like others across black America, were meant to counter the abuses black men experienced as part of the legacy of slavery.[16] Admittedly, black Californians did not face the same attacks on their manhood in the form of lynching epidemics, Ku Klux Klan violence, and repeated cases of rape perpetuated against black women that their southern contemporaries experienced. However, this testimony from 1865 tells us that Pleasant's male friends and associates were not immune to the vagaries of racism and segregation, and they articulated their grievances in public meetings.

While California's black men convened in Sacramento, black women took the lead in the fight against segregation and discrimination on the city's streetcars in the 1860s. Mary Ellen Pleasant was in the forefront of this movement. Demanding her rights as a citizen was a recurring theme in Pleasant's life, as exemplified by her involvement in the struggle against segregated public facilities. Pleasant's public appearances in court held tremendous significance in her life. Paradoxically, it is the place where her power and status were most visible; it is also the place, as we shall see, where she was stripped of both.

Although it was celebrated by many leaders such as Frederick Douglass as a city rife with possibilities for African Americans, black citizens routinely experienced segregation and discrimination in San Francisco. Informed by the struggles of African Americans across the nation, black San Franciscans understood that they were part of a larger legal challenge. The black press in the San Francisco Bay area monitored battles against segregated streetcars in Philadelphia and other cities. For example, in 1862 the *Pacific Appeal* published the "Colored Citizens of Philadelphia's Petition to Ride in the Cars," documenting that city's efforts to desegregate their streetcars.[17] "A relic of barbarism still remains in Philadelphia," wrote Philip Bell, the San Francisco editor. He continued with ironic flair: "We know that the colored people were excluded from the city cars, some years ago, but we supposed Philadelphia had grown more civilized." While Bell chastised the citizens of Philadelphia, he was well aware that San Francisco in 1862 was far from "civilized."[18] This reference to "civilization" was meant to point to the uncivilized behavior of those ejecting African Americans from the cars.

Bell's comment also referenced the contemporary discourse of civilization, which, as Gail Bederman points out, was invoked repeatedly by white men to link male dominance to white supremacy.[19]

In the years during and after the Civil War, San Franciscans traveled by streetcars pulled along tracks by horses or mules. Cable cars did not become available until the late 1870s. By 1873 the city had eight horsecar systems or lines and more than eighty miles of track.[20] African Americans were prevented from taking these horse-drawn streetcars and the city's railway cars as a matter of course, and they were harassed on the cars if they succeeded in boarding. Underlining one of Reconstruction's primary concerns—the mixing of the races—segregation on public transportation kept black people in their place while preventing whites from mingling and therefore "mongrelizing" their race. Black bodies traveled across the country in these years, leaving plantations, moving from countryside to city, from black neighborhoods to city centers, all of which were dangerous transgressions in the minds of many Americans.

The study of segregated transportation and the efforts to dismantle it provides a window into a city's racial, class, and gender politics. Many historians have used these cases as barometers for measuring the level and type of resistance African Americans asserted against the restrictions of racial segregation. James McPherson referred to the Philadelphia struggle during Reconstruction as "a microcosm of the Negro's battle for equal rights and human dignity."[21] Evelyn Brooks Higginbotham points to black women's streetcar protests in the nineteenth century as a site of "the contestation over the conflated meaning of race and class."[22] And Robin D. G. Kelley reminds us that the study of black resistance in public space "offers some of the richest insights into how race, gender, class, space, time, and collective memory shape both domination and resistance."[23] As an indicator of black San Francisco's struggle against racism and segregation, the streetcar cases reveal the significance of black women's agency and the relevance of sex and gender to the language of citizenship. The resistance to harassment and segregation on public transportation in the West marks a site where women stake out claims to public space, articulate their class privileges, and also insist on treatment afforded to "ladies," a term reserved for elite white women. However, these efforts were not without their risks for African American women, including Pleasant.

Black women in San Francisco and other cities often took the lead in streetcar protests.[24] Many of the jobs working women performed required that they use public transportation. The majority of black San Franciscans worked in service jobs during the Reconstruction era, and most women who worked for wages did so as domestics.[25] Elite black women—unless they had their own carriages—took the streetcars and railways to shop or attend political and social events. But women spearheaded streetcar and railroad protests not only because they rode—or wanted to ride—the cars; it was a strategy calculated to confound and overturn racial and gender hierarchies. The gender of the rider presented a particular problem for conductors. As long as they had the proper fare, white women could expect to be welcomed onto the cars and treated as ladies on all forms of public transport. By the Civil War, railroad cars often were divided into "smokers" and ladies' cars to protect white women from the presumably male habits of smoking, cursing, and drinking. This practice fit nicely with many cities' postwar attempts to segregate public space. For example, Mary Ryan has shown that in Reconstruction New Orleans efforts to segregate streetcars were deemed necessary "as a means of providing for the comfort of ladies."[26] In fact, Ryan argues, "Gender . . . supplied the sexual prohibitions, codes of segregation, and rhetorical power with which to mortar the rising wall of segregation."[27] The problem for many cities, as Barbara Y. Welke explains came when "the person of color [was] in the shape of a lady."[28]

Two of the earliest reported incidents involving discrimination on San Francisco's streetcars occurred in March 1863, when, according to *The Pacific Appeal,* "two of our most respectable females were denied seats in one of the city railway cars." The unnamed women were told by the driver that they "should get out" after they boarded the car at Fourth and Folsom streets, even though none of the other passengers objected to their presence. The report of the incident in the *Appeal* drew attention to the class and gender of the riders to elicit sympathy from the paper's readers. Elite ladies should not be insulted by "coarse threats of ejectment," wrote the editor.[29] Harassment of black streetcar and railway riders continued that spring and summer. Other cities took notice. The *San Jose Mercury* admonished the white people of San Francisco: "The person who would object to riding in the same car with a respectable, well-dressed colored woman, would not object to having that woman as a servant in their families, to cook their food, or to fondle and take care of their children."[30] Keeping black women in their place as cooks and servants was, in part, what the streetcar incidents were all about. However, her status as a domestic did not prevent Pleasant from seeking redress; in fact, portraying herself as a maid became part of her strategy. Pleasant and two other black women, Charlotte Brown and Emma Jane Turner, took to the courts in the wake of the repeal on the testimony ban in 1863.

The first black woman in San Francisco to initiate a lawsuit against a railway company was Charlotte L. Brown. Brown was the daughter of James

Brown, a local black businessperson, associate of Pleasant's, and a well-known figure in elite circles of black San Francisco.[31] When a conductor ejected Brown from a car on June 26, 1863, she sued the Omnibus Railroad Company for $200. A month later, she was awarded $25 and costs.[32] The company's unsuccessful appeal affirmed the right of African Americans to ride the city's cars. The streetcar company's rationale for segregation was a common one: They were protecting white women from social contact with black people. Relying on this professed concern for the sanctity of white womanhood, Pleasant later shaped her case accordingly by ensuring that a white woman testified on her behalf.

Two white newspapers, *The Alta California* and *The Call*, were more sanguine; they were convinced that the Brown case had brought to an end the "war between the negroes and the Railroad Company." However, black citizens were not convinced that their problems were over. *The Pacific Appeal* responded with a description of the company's drivers, "who, if a colored person attempts to cross the street while their car is passing, are seized with a sudden fit of *negrophobia*" and speed away. The paper's comments drew attention to what many black readers already surmised: Discrimination and harassment on public transportation would continue on a variety of levels. One black citizen wrote in *The Appeal*, "Will the *Alta* and *Call* publish these lines, and let the public know that, so far as the people are concerned, the war, in a becoming manner, has just commenced."[33]

It probably came as a surprise to black San Franciscans when, a year after Brown's case, in 1864, a decision by Judge Orville C. Pratt of the Twelfth District Court abolished segregation on the city's streetcars. In his ruling, Pratt admitted that railroad companies had a right to manage their own affairs but had no right to manage the affairs of the general public. Preventing African Americans from riding the cars fell under the latter category.[34]

Pratt's ruling came as a response—albeit belated—to the Dred Scott decision, which Pratt found reprehensible: "It has been already quite too long tolerated by the dominant race to see with indifference the negro or mulatto treated as a brute, insulted, wronged, enslaved, made to wear a yoke, to tremble before white men, to serve him as a tool, to hold property and life at will, to surrender to him his intellect and conscience, and to seal his lips and belie his thought through dread of the white man's power."[35] Referring to discrimination on the cars as "a relic of barbarism," the judge dispensed with the practice. Or at least it appeared so. But Pleasant and other black citizens soon realized that Pratt's decision was not being observed by the streetcar companies. Many black riders were left to wait on street corners when drivers refused to pick them up.

After one such incident in 1866, Mary Ellen Pleasant decided to take action. That year she initiated lawsuits against two companies: The Omnibus Railroad Company and the North Beach and Mission Railroad. In the first case, Pleasant filed charges against the Omnibus Railroad Company for putting her off the car. On October 17, 1866, Pleasant withdrew her complaint against Omnibus. This warranted front-page coverage in the daily newspaper *Alta California:* "Mrs. Mary E. Pleasant, a woman of color, having complained of the driver of car No. 6 of the Omnibus Railroad Company's line, for putting her off the car, appeared yesterday in the Police Court and withdrew the charge, stating as a reason for doing so that she had been informed by the agents of the company that negroes would hereafter be allowed to ride on the car, let the effect on the company's business be what it might."[36] Why she withdrew her case is not entirely clear from this or other descriptions in the press. Was Pleasant searching, as savvy litigants often did, for a lawsuit that looked more favorable? By October 17—the day on which she dropped the charges—she was already in court testifying against a different streetcar company.[37] Perhaps she thought the case against Omnibus had been "won" in some way because she had exacted a promise from the authorities that black passengers would be treated fairly.

The action against the North Beach and Mission Railroad Company (NBMRR) proceeded quite differently, however. This time Pleasant pursued the case for two years. She hired the renowned George W. Tyler as her attorney in October 1866, and the suit continued until January 1868, when the California Supreme Court ruled on the case.[38]

Pleasant's original suit against the company was brought sometime in late 1866 or early 1867. In her testimony she explained that on September 27, 1866, she stood on Folsom Street waiting for the city's No. 21 streetcar to take her downtown to the city's plaza. Pleasant hailed the streetcar, but the driver refused to stop even though there was room on the car and she had her tickets. Her complaint detailed the company's policy of denying service to African Americans. She charged "that the agents and servants of defendant (NBMRR) acted under instructions received from said defendant requiring them to refuse to stop the cars of said defendant to allow 'colored people' or people of African Descent, to get on board."[39] Furthermore, argued Pleasant's attorney, she "suffered greatly in her mind" when she was denied service "and was compelled to and did proceed on foot to her destination, not being at the time in a physical condition so to do, causing thereby great suffering of body."[40]

This last claim—that Pleasant suffered in both mind and body—carried symbolic weight in light of contemporary racial discourse. Pleasant's lawsuit took place against a backdrop of heightened transgressions against the rights won by blacks in the years since the surrender at Appomattox.[41] The violence of the Ku Klux Klan and an epidemic of lynching became the most obvious expressions of white supremacy.[42] Just as black women shaped the discourse and strategies of Reconstruction in their campaigns against the lynching of black male bodies, in their streetcar cases they addressed the safety of black female bodies.[43]

When Pleasant, in her lawsuit, drew attention to her body, she conjured up well-known images of tortured slaves and injured black bodies. Antislavery rhetoric had long emphasized the "gruesome tribulations of the [slave] body."[44] By the time of the Civil War, pain and bodily suffering had become a pervasive social and cultural trope. The inability of slave women, in particular, to own their own bodies had become an important tenet of nineteenth-century abolitionist women's rhetoric.[45] As Elizabeth B. Clark argues, this rhetoric of sympathy for pained black bodies also signaled shifts in rights discourse and legal reasoning. When abolitionists commandeered an "identification with suffering others," they shaped not only the literature of the period but the legal arguments as well.[46] A practitioner of the abolitionist strategies associated with the Underground Railroad, Pleasant revised these in the Reconstruction era with great skill.

In addition to drawing attention to her bodily suffering, Pleasant accessed another strategy common to the abolitionist movement: She had a white witness from the upper class testify on her behalf. Just as Frederick Douglass was introduced to audiences by William Lloyd Garrison in the early days of his career and slave narratives often were prefaced by a white abolitionist to verify their authenticity, Pleasant enlisted a matron of San Francisco society to vouch for her veracity and respectability. This key witness was Lisette Woodworth, wife of Selim Woodworth and her former employer. Pleasant had lived with the Woodworth family and servants in the early 1860s.[47]

Asked to describe the circumstances of the NBMRR incident in court, Pleasant explained, "I went to Mrs. Selim E. Woodworth, on Folsom Street, and we were going out together, but I had an errand to do on Second Street. She told me to go and do my errand, and afterwards when it was done to meet her in the car on Folsom Street; to hail it when I came to Folsom Street."[48] Pleasant explained what happened next: "I hailed the driver of the car—his name is James Doyle—and he looked at me, and instead of stopping he passed on."[49] When she signaled the conductor (who stood at the back of the car), he said, "We don't take colored people in the cars."[50] Lisette Woodworth's testimony confirmed that Pleasant had been denied service because of her race and for no other reason: "I was in the car when she hailed it. I saw her hail it, and the conductor took no notice of her and walked into the car. Said I to the conductor, 'Stop this car; there is a woman who wants to get in.' He took no notice of what I said. . . . I said, 'I want her to get in.' His answer was, 'We don't take colored people in the cars.' I then said, 'You will have to let me out.'"[51] When Woodworth was questioned about the other passengers, she said there were only two other people on the car. Clearly Woodworth's testimony was meant to "prove" the legitimacy of Pleasant's suit. Black San Franciscans knew full well that the repeal of the testimony ban did not signal a willingness to *believe* what black people said in their own defense; it meant only that they had a right to speak in court. The positioning of Lisette Woodworth as her witness indicates Pleasant's understanding of the tenuous position of black San Franciscans in these critical years after the Civil War. It also reveals something of the interracial world in which black women—especially domestics—operated.[52]

A watershed in Pleasant's life, this case marked the beginning of a series of court appearances and the first time her image as mammy entered public discourse. When Tyler, Pleasant's attorney, asked Woodworth how long she had known the plaintiff, she replied that she had known Pleasant for ten years. She also told the court that she ordinarily called Pleasant "Mamma."[53] This term made it clear to the court that Pleasant and Woodworth knew each other as maid and employer, a relationship that was familiar to many in the 1860s. By the 1880s, headlines proclaiming the news about "Mammy Pleasant" were common in the local press, indicating the salience and popularity of the term.[54] The streetcar case established Pleasant as the city's mammy.[55] These representations of servant rather than entrepreneur or abolitionist had advantages for Pleasant in her early years in the West. In an era when representations of African Americans harked back to the "good old days" of slavery, Pleasant's strategy of self-presentation made sense. Many judges, juries, and attorneys found "Mammy Pleasant" a recognizable character and thus less threatening.

The combination of an elite white witness, the appearance of maid and employer, and Tyler's reputation and skill as an attorney may have influenced the court. The jury of the Twelfth District Court determined that Pleasant was "willfully and purposely deprived by the defendant of the exercise of a plain legal right, under circumstances showing an intent to insult the plaintiff, and the law presumes it to be malicious."[56] Pleasant was awarded $500 in punitive damages.

But the case was not yet over. On May 10, 1867, the NBMRR filed a motion for a new trial, claiming that the damages were excessive and appeared "to have been given under the influence of passion or prejudice," there was insufficient evidence to justify the verdict, and errors were committed at the trial involving the instructions given to the jury.[57] When that proved unsuccessful, the company appealed and the case went to the state supreme court.

The judgment was then reversed, with the California Supreme Court finding that the damages were excessive. "There was no proof of special damage," argued the court, "nor of any malice, or ill will, or wanton or violent conduct on the part of the defendant," so there was no cause for exemplary damages.[58] The court had issued a similar ruling in Emma Turner's case against the same company. Turner claimed she was pushed off of a car in 1866 because she was of African descent, and she was awarded $750. In both cases the Supreme Court found "no proof . . . to show willful injury."[59] The question of damages and intent—that is, the intent of the company to willfully insult black patrons and the damage they suffered as a result—became the focus. Because there was no proof of injury and no violent conduct, damages were not measurable, the judges reasoned. Therefore, Tyler's efforts to argue for damages based on injury to Pleasant's mind and body were unsuccessful.

The larger question of how to compensate African Americans for discrimination was a pressing one for Reconstruction era judges, juries, and politicians. The significance of Pleasant's case against NBMRR extends beyond the city's streetcar companies and their treatment of black citizens during Reconstruction. In terms of legal strategies open to black Americans, Pleasant's case indicated that courts often were unwilling to acknowledge—or, more accurately, to measure—the cost to black people of discrimination. It was not until 1893 that the California Legislature passed a statute that finally prohibited racial discrimination in places of public accommodation.[60]

This case set precedents in civil rights law, particularly in the determination of punitive damages.[61] When, nearly a century later, California revised its civil rights legislation, the question of the rights of the discriminator and the discriminated resurfaced.[62] A 1958 article on equal rights statutes in the *Stanford Law Review* cited *Pleasants v. NBMRR* to demonstrate that "an aggrieved party faces an almost insurmountable burden of proof in seeking to show that a refusal to admit him to, or a discrimination in the use of facilities of, a place of public accommodation, amusement, or entertainment resulted in *measurable* damages for which he is entitled to compensation."[63] Pleasant's insistence on equal treatment on public transportation in the 1860s clearly politicized public space. Struggles over racial segregation have provided some of the clearest examples of the ways in which women occupied and transformed public spaces in a period of the nineteenth century that was being ideologically carved into separate spheres. However loose and inappropriate the paradigm of separate spheres seemed in San Francisco, Pleasant nonetheless ventured into the male domain of the courts when she challenged the streetcar companies. Pleasant, along with African American women across the United States, claimed a fundamental right of citizenship during Reconstruction: the right to equal treatment under the law. In so doing, black women attempted to reconstitute institutions and politics in their cities.[64]

If the streetcar battles that Pleasant undertook signaled her challenge to the city's political and public culture, her career as a boardinghouse operator drew her into the semiprivate world of San Francisco's elite. As long as Pleasant kept the secrets of her guests under wrap, her financial empire appeared safe. When her business with the city's power brokers and robber barons (many of whom stayed in her establishments) spilled onto the streets, however, risks multiplied. The year Pleasant's streetcar case was heard by the state supreme court is the first year in which she was listed as a boardinghouse keeper in the city directory. In previous years she was listed as a domestic.[65] This indicates an important change in Pleasant's occupation but also in her self-representation. Pleasant had transformed herself from worker to entrepreneur—a shift very few black women of her day experienced. Controlling her own labor and the labor of others in her boardinghouses marked not only a financial change but an increase in status and political clout.

The significance of boardinghouses in the first decades of San Francisco's reign as the premier city of the West should not be underestimated. They provided food and shelter for an ever-increasing western population in the years after the Gold Rush.[66] As the editor of the *Overland Monthly* remarked in 1872, "Considered as a curious collection of boardinghouses, San Francisco is decidedly a success."[67] Indeed, by 1880 San Francisco had more boardinghouse operators relative to its total population than any other large American city.[68] Some establishments catered to miners; others, like Pleasant's, were expensive and exclusive. And boardinghouses, unlike hotels or bars, were owned by women.

Sometime after Pleasant left the Woodworths in the late 1860s, she began work as a domestic for Milton S. Latham of 638 Folsom Street. An ambitious politician, Latham was elected governor of California in 1859 but served only from January 9 to January 14, 1860, before resigning to take David C. Broderick's place in the U.S. Senate; Broderick had been killed in a duel with David S. Terry. Latham and Terry had been the leaders of the proslavery wing of the Democratic party in California.[69] Pleasant knew all of these men. In her shift from a domestic to an entrepreneur, Pleasant used these connections; associates of these men patronized her boardinghouses. Several writers have wondered how Pleasant acquired the capital to open her own boardinghouse the year after she was employed as a domestic. "Could it be that some Latham money financed her or was he just unusually generous with wages?" asks author Lloyd Conrich. Or, he wondered, did Pleasant blackmail Latham?[70] Perhaps Pleasant did blackmail Latham with secrets she learned in his home. It is just as likely, however, that Pleasant saved her earnings and chose to move into her own home. Her actual work as a boardinghouse operator probably was very similar to the chores she performed as a domestic at the Woodworths' and Lathams': she cooked, cleaned, shopped, and prepared elegant soirées. The difference was that she controlled her labor and the labor of others, and she derived a profit from her enterprise.

In 1869 Mary Ellen Pleasant moved to 920 Washington Street, where she established her most successful and most elaborate boardinghouse.[71] Its proximity to San Francisco's central plaza meant that Pleasant's business and she herself became public entities. The plaza, officially called Portsmouth Square, bordered Washington, Kearny, Clay, and Dupont streets; Pleasant's establishment was on the corner of Washington and Dupont.[72] Her property was strategically placed—near City Hall, the opera, and the largest gambling house—to attract the city's political and financial elite. A business's location on the plaza guaranteed publicity.[73] Pleasant's forays to the markets, banks, shops, and courts could be easily observed from the city center, as could the galas and meetings that took place at 920 Washington.

Operating boardinghouses was a common occupation for women who settled near gold and silver mines in the West. As many women realized, it was far more risky to pan for gold than to provide the much-needed services of boarding, cooking, and cleaning. The demand for shelter during the California Gold Rush proved steady and lucrative; as one woman newly arrived in San Francisco wrote to her daughter in 1849, "report says there are six thousand people here that have no shelter."[74] In fact, boardinghouses were the fulcra of the mining economy, helping to move wealth from the miners to the economy at large.[75]

In 1870, according to one study, boardinghouse and hotel keepers made up as much as 35 percent of all businesswomen in San Francisco, second only to laundresses, who were 42 percent of the total.[76] Pleasant's participation in both of these industries—laundries and boardinghouses—placed her among a growing subculture: female entrepreneurs in mining communities in the West. However, the cost of starting a boardinghouse in San Francisco could be prohibitive, and very few newcomers to the West had the capital to open the kind of establishment that Pleasant financed on Washington Street. Most boardinghouses and lodging houses in the city were located not on the central plaza, like Pleasant's, but in the area of the city south of Market Street (where Pleasant had waited to board the streetcar).[77] Pleasant's boardinghouses served the leaders of local and state commerce and politics: white men.[78] No doubt the skills she acquired as a shop clerk on Nantucket trained her well for her career in San Francisco.

The fact that women operated these spaces—and that an African American woman owned one of the most exclusive—points to a certain flexibility of racial and gender boundaries in San Francisco's economy. Women were an integral part of public life, not only as prostitutes or laundresses but as entrepreneurs and what would now be called networkers. Yet western women's worth often has been measured solely in terms of their sexual and domestic value, ignoring their agency in the region's politics.[79] In San Francisco, however, some women supervised—and profited from—the activities of prominent politicians and businessmen. Perhaps more than any other female innkeeper or boardinghouse owner, Pleasant maintained high visibility among the city's elite. Although she later opened other boardinghouses, her most famous business venture was at 920 Washington Street. According to one source, it was known "for its fine food and wines and its mysterious, lavishly furnished upstairs rooms which were set up as combined private dining and bedrooms."[80] Another source claims Pleasant served especially potent drinks in her establishment, including "cordials made from wild clover that grew in profusion on Twin Peaks," brandies made from elderberries and blackberries, and a concoction called Balm Tea, laced with "paralyzing gin."[81]

The costs of setting up an exclusive boardinghouse must have been substantial for Pleasant. Of the $15,000 she reported as real estate income in 1870, we can assume a significant portion of it reflected the worth of her boardinghouse on the plaza. The inflation of a mining economy, the scarcity of available land, and the risks of fires that plagued the city meant that San Francisco real estate costs were legendary. In addition to purchasing the lot, Pleasant outfitted the house with exquisite furnishings, drapery, and artwork, all presumably ordered from out of state. William Willmore, an employee of Pleasant, remembered that "luxury was expressed mostly in massive furniture like Mammy had in her upper Washington Street boardinghouse."[82] Another San Francisco boardinghouse operator, Mary Jane Megquier, complained of the costs she incurred setting up the business: "It takes a mint to begin, we have to pay $28 per dozen for the common wood chair and $60 for cane seats."[83] Pleasant incurred all types of costs related to serving guests extravagant fare, including not only food, but also linens, laundry service, and china. Like those of most consumable goods, food prices in San Francisco could be outlandish; Megquier reported in 1852 that she paid "five dollars for a poor miserable turnip" for her Thanksgiving supper.[84] The meals at Washington Street, like the decor, were lavish; Willmore remembered them as "sumptuous."[85] Pleasant's reputation as a gourmet chef probably helped to attract a wealthy clientele. And although we cannot know the precise number of guests Pleasant served, we know from the census that she listed nine boarders in 1870, and we can assume that she and her staff cooked for at least that many people on a regular basis.

By all accounts, Pleasant hired an extensive staff of black workers, including William Willmore, to serve her guests. Charlotte Downs, who also spent time in the house on Washington Street, claimed Willmore "was Mammy's confidant."[86] "He was a tall, dark Negro with white, even teeth and eyes of a flashing brilliancy."[87] The Willmores lived across the street from the boardinghouse, and Pleasant often hired Willmore's wife to "lend a hand with the cooking." His son, William Jr., remembered in a 1938 interview that Pleasant "liked me because she said I had good manners like my parents."[88] Willmore worked as Pleasant's steward, tending to her properties, carriage, and her horses, and according to his son, "he fared much better after he met her."[89] "My father kept the servants in line. Mammy used to say he was the one man she could get along with," recalled William Jr.[90] Like all other entrepreneurs, Pleasant concerned herself with maximizing profits at her boardinghouses. This entailed keeping a tight rein on employees and controlling the flow of information about herself, her business practices, and her guests.

The house at 920 Washington Street served as home for some of the state's leading politicians and thus attracted tremendous publicity. Charles Marshall, a clerk for the city tax collector, and Thomas Wright, a "master mariner" thought to be worth at least $40,000, were among the moneyed guests.[91] When Newton Booth, one of Pleasant's greatest admirers and also a boarder at 920 Washington Street, was elected the new Republican governor of California in 1871, Pleasant threw a gala and boasted proudly, "This is Governor Booth who has been elected from my house."[92] Pleasant was fond of repeating this story and proud of her relationship with the governor. According to a San Francisco detective, Pleasant "introduced Booth to Emily Putnam Smith and they had an illegitimate child."[93] This type of secret—about the state's governor—gave Pleasant obvious opportunities for blackmail. However, her friendship with Booth appears to have been genuine; when Pleasant attended his funeral she "shook so with sobs she had to leave."[94]

Washington Street also housed some of the best-known black residents and black institutions in the city. Pleasant's neighbors included the poet and emigrationist James Monroe Whitfield (1822–71). Whitfield ran a barber shop nearby on Kearny Street and lived next door to Pleasant at 918 Washington.[95] Most importantly, the San Francisco Athenaeum, the saloon and library that Pleasant helped to establish in the 1850s, was housed at 917 Washington. Drawing hundreds of African Americans to its halls and reading rooms, the Athenaeum ensured that this city block had become a place to meet and associate with the city's black residents.[96] And in the 1860s, all three of San Francisco's black churches resided in the neighborhood as well; Third Baptist, Bethel African Methodist Episcopal, and AME Zion, to which Pleasant belonged, were clustered in the section bordered by Washington, Larkin, and the San Francisco Bay.[97]

By 1870, Pleasant listed $15,000 worth of real estate in the U.S. Census and $15,000 as the value of her other assets. Her business success derived from the political habits and assumptions of mining moguls. While she invested in gold, silver, and quicksilver (mercury) mines, Pleasant also profited from the needs of the most successful investors of the day: the Bonanza Kings and their compatriots, who demanded elegant establishments in which to conduct their business. These men frequented her boardinghouses and revealed information—financial and social—that Pleasant used to increase her own wealth and status.[98] Pleasant's use of seemingly private space to further her enterprise may have played on the assumptions that white men had about African Americans and "help" in general: that domestics would not understand financial affairs.[99] The ways in which Pleasant exploited gendered and racialized codes of behavior constituted one of her most profitable strategies in court and at home.

Pleasant's association with boardinghouses made it easy to sully her reputation. These establishments were singled out as a social menace in this era because of their links to prostitution. One local observer complained that San Francisco's boardinghouses of the 1860s promoted "free and easy manners with the ladies."[100] Journalists of the day, her contemporaries, and the literature on Pleasant have all assumed that she operated bordellos as part of her enterprise. Charles Caldwell Dobie, author of several popular books on San Francisco, describes Pleasant's career as a boardinghouse keeper this way: "But one boardinghouse was not enough to feed Mammy's vitality. She opened others—of less pretensions and doubtless less respectability. Money flowed her way. Women were at a premium in San Francisco either as wives or mistresses, and Mammy was ready to import them to fill both needs. Her fortune grew."[101] Dobie is not alone in this assessment. William

Willmore Jr. refers to her businesses as houses "of ill fame." Given the racial subtext of Reconstruction and the stereotypes of oversexed black women, it makes sense that a successful and independent black businesswoman would be depicted in a way that emphasized sex and deemphasized business.[102] The characterization proved resilient. In nearly every decade since Pleasant opened her first boardinghouse, she has been called San Francisco's black madam. One article, published in the black press in the 1970s, describes her as "The Happy Black Hooker."[103]

Pleasant may have provided her boardinghouse guests with prostitutes or female companions. Prostitution was central to the mining economies of California, Nevada, and other western states, and some of Pleasant's patrons probably expected sexual services along with room and board.[104] However, the legend of Pleasant as black madam obscures the entrepreneurial aspect of her career: Her business activities, including those as a madam, meant that she absorbed profits from miners, politicians, and bankers and channeled them into her vast financial enterprise. Rather than either a madam or entrepreneur, she was probably both. Mixing business and pleasure, as all madams do, could reap tremendous rewards. Pleasant's reputation as a keeper of bordellos has served different functions in different eras: During her own lifetime it may have limited her access to certain circles of the black elite, and it may have sullied her reputation among the state's lawyers and judges. More recently, her reputation as a madam has obscured other salient aspects of her career and her abolitionist activities.

Pleasant entered into a new phase of her life in the 1870s: She continued her charitable activities and fundraising efforts but moved her home and headquarters to a hill above the city center.[105] At a time when many African Americans across the nation experienced a retreat from civil rights and the promises of citizenship, Pleasant reached her financial zenith. Pleasant's experience, like that of other black women, shifts the traditional periodization that interprets the end of Reconstruction as a period associated with African American defeat.[106] Pleasant's new house was on the corner of Octavia and Bush Streets, just west of the business district. It was a lavishly furnished multistory Victorian mansion with large grounds. Bennett claims the house was worth $100,000 at the time of construction, sometime in 1877.[107] This seems likely given the size of the house—thirty rooms—and the fact that the property encompassed two city blocks. In scale and opulence, the house on Octavia Street far surpassed any domicile Pleasant had previously inhabited, even 920 Washington Street. Servants at the mansion boasted of the "quaint and beautiful teakwood cabinets, inlaid bookcases, marbles, paintings, fine rugs and expensive hangings."[108]

Pleasant benefited directly from the huge profits made during the Nevada Comstock mining boom in the 1860s and 1870s. The San Francisco Stock Exchange opened in 1862 in response to Nevada's silver industry; profits from the Comstock transferred directly to San Francisco bankers and investors.[109] Pleasant's rise to prominence in financial and philanthropic circles can be attributed, in part, to this general economic trend; she was a keen manipulator of real estate and mining stock.[110] However, her fortune also became linked with the Scottish banker Thomas Bell. Bell, vice president of the Bank of California—the institution that reaped the most profits from the Comstock and the leading financial institution of the West—had met Pleasant earlier, and in the 1870s he became her financial partner and took quarters in her newly built home on Octavia Street.

Pleasant's mansion and her cohabitation with Thomas Bell made for intense speculation by her contemporaries. The press quickly coined the term "House of Mystery" and never ceased remarking on its secrets. After her death (1904) the house continued to fascinate San Franciscans. In 1933 Charles Dobie wrote, "Just to pass this house inspired me with an exquisite terror. Its mystery was not the mystery of ghosts but the mystery of flesh and blood enchantment. People were reputed to live beneath its frowning mansard roof but the only person I ever saw emerge was the black witch who held them all enthralled."[111] As recently as 1987, the *San Francisco Chronicle* claimed that Pleasant kept Bell as her prisoner in the mansion and fed him dog food.[112]

Speculation about a sexual liaison between Pleasant and Bell did not cease, but did subside, when he married a young protégé of Pleasant, Teresa Clingan. After 1878, the three of them, and eventually the Bell children, all lived in Pleasant's house on Octavia Street. Pleasant was assumed by many to be the mammy of the household, with Thomas and Teresa Bell serving as master and mistress. This masquerade proved to be advantageous for Pleasant, at least for a time. In actuality, Pleasant was living the life of a wealthy businessperson, tending to her property, directing her own servants, and spending exorbitant sums.

Pleasant's account books from this period show that large amounts were spent to purchase supplies for the house, including lumber, water, dairy products, and meat, as well as finery such as lace and jewelry.[113] San Franciscans watched Pleasant bargain and trade all over town. Charlotte Downs was told by her father that Pleasant "had a coachman, James Allen, dressed in a livery of a long black coat, white breeches, and a top hat. There was also a footman dressed the same."[114] Pleasant's carriage with liveryman and horses in tow was a familiar sight in the city center. Much like the mansions of the railroad magnates on Nob Hill, also built in the 1870s, the house on Octavia Street was a visual reminder of the owners' wealth. Unlike Nob Hill's estates, however, this palatial home was owned by a black woman. This fact was particularly disturbing to members of the press in Pleasant's next legal skirmish in the 1880s.

Pleasant's career flourished in the years between the Civil War and the end of Reconstruction. She had challenged the meaning of citizenship in the new state of the Union and testified about discrimination in the state's highest court. In addition, her status as an entrepreneur reached its zenith. Along with her exclusive boardinghouse and her Octavia Street house, Pleasant purchased other property in San Francisco and Oakland in the 1870s. In the next decade, the *Oakland Enquirer* noted that "Mammy Pleasance . . . is much the wealthiest colored person in this city; in fact, she is reputed to be worth two or three hundred thousand dollars."[115]

While Pleasant attempted to shift the boundaries of citizenship to include black people in her streetcar case, her efforts to maintain her financial enterprise were stymied by creditors, attorneys, and members of the court. Unquestionably, Pleasant's everyday acts as a businessperson exemplified certain kinds of freedoms not typically associated with black life in Reconstruction: the opportunity to engage in real estate speculation, practice vertical integration (buying laundries to serve one's own boardinghouses), and disguise one's assets. These acts were the very deeds that so rankled the status quo when Pleasant practiced them. So while black San Francisco temporarily profited from attacks on Jim Crow leveled by the likes of Pleasant, decades passed before they could practice everyday acts of freedom without dangerous repercussions to mind and body.

Powerful
And Sinister
Ruler
Mammy
Pleasant
1815·1904
HELEN
HOLDREDGE

Cover of Helen Holdredge's bestselling *Mammy Pleasant* (1953, paper-back). The photograph of Pleasant on the cover has been the subject of intense controversy. Holdredge insisted that it was taken in 1859 at the Bradley & Rulofson studio in San Francisco; Hawaiian archivists insist that the photograph is not Pleasant but Queen Emma of the Hawaiian Islands. (Author's personal collection)

Cover of Helen Holdredge's *Mammy Pleasant's Cookbook* (1970). Holdredge claimed to have in her possession "a number of Mammy's recipe books," which she used to compile this collection. (Author's personal collection)

MARY ELLEN ("MAMMY") PLEASANT AT 87 YEARS OF AGE
The first and only photograph taken since she was 13 years old

Mary Ellen Pleasant at eighty-seven years of age. This photograph accompanied her 1902 autobiography printed in the *Pandex of the Press*. (Courtesy of the Bancroft Library, University of California at Berkeley)

Mary Ellen Pleasant's mansion, dubbed the "House of Mystery," on the corner of Bush and Octavia streets in San Francisco, where she lived for more than twenty years with members of the Bell family. (Courtesy of the California Historical Society, George A. Berton Collection; FN-10810)

San Francisco in the 1880s, at the time of Pleasant's appearance in the Sharon trial, with the Palace Hotel in the background. (Courtesy of the Bancroft Library, University of California at Berkeley)

William Sharon. (Courtesy of the Bancroft
Library, University of California at Berkeley)

Sarah Althea Hill.
(Courtesy of the Ban-
croft Library, Univer-
sity of California at
Berkeley)

LITTLE BUTTERCUP IN JUDGE SULLIVAN'S COURT
"When I was young and charming, I practiced baby farming."

This cartoon, "Little Buttercup in Judge Sullivan's Court," appeared on the cover of San Francisco's magazine of political satire, *The Wasp* (August 9, 1884), during the Sharon trial. The caption reads, "When I was young and charming, I practiced baby farming," referring to accusations made during the trial and to the popular Gilbert and Sullivan play *H.M.S. Pinafore*. (Courtesy of the Bancroft Library, University of California at Berkeley)

"Re-engaged for a Short Season" pictures Pleasant on the right of Judge Sullivan, Sarah Althea Hill on his left; attorneys and other witnesses complete the orchestra. Pleasant's bare legs protrude from her gown. (Courtesy of the Bancroft Library, University of California at Berkeley)

Beltane Ranch, Pleasant's Sonoma County retreat, where she spent weekends and holidays in the last decade of her life.

Sketch by John Clawson that accompanied the 1899 article in *The Call*. Clawson's son, John Willard, also fascinated with Pleasant, wrote the 1922 melodrama *The Cat and the Canary*, based on Pleasant's cohabitation with the Bell family at the "House of Mystery." (Courtesy of the Bancroft Library, University of California at Berkeley)

Exposé in the May 7, 1899, edition of *The Call,* "Mammy Pleasant: Angel or Arch Fiend in the House of Mystery." This appeared during Pleasant's legal battles with the Bell family and shortly after Pleasant's eviction from her home on Octavia Street. (Courtesy of the Bancroft Library, University of California at Berkeley)

Still from John Willard's melodrama *The Cat and the Canary,* which opened on Broadway on February 7, 1922 and in London in October 31, 1922. Pleasant is played in blackface and maid's attire by Brenda Friderici in this production. The melodrama played repeatedly across the United States through the 1960s. (Author's personal collection)

Mary Ellen Pleasant city park. This plaque and several eucalyptus trees are all that is left of Pleasant's home on Octavia and Bush Streets in San Francisco. (Author's personal collection)

4

A MADAM ON TRIAL

You tell those newspaper people that they may be smart, but
I'm smarter. They deal with words. Some folks say that words
were meant to reveal thought. That ain't so. Words were meant
to conceal thought.

MARY ELLEN PLEASANT, *San Francisco Call* (1901)

Mary Ellen Pleasant had been a keen observer of the courts and a staunch
defender of civil rights from her earliest years in San Francisco. In every
decade since her arrival in the West, Pleasant figured in litigation as a plaintiff
or a witness.[1] Whereas Pleasant's streetcar cases of 1866–68 drew statewide
attention, her involvement in the divorce trials of Senator William Sharon
in the 1880s attracted the interest of columnists and politicians across the
country. Pleasant and an Irish American woman and purported prostitute,
Sarah Althea Hill, orchestrated Sharon's demise. This racialized and sexualized scandal tantalized San Franciscan and national audiences for years
as two lawsuits, *Sharon v. Sharon* (1884) and *Sharon v. Hill* (1885), captured the public imagination.[2] It is no wonder the pundits took such pleasure in the cases. The Sharon trials had all the ingredients of a Victorian
drama: voodoo spells, stolen underwear, voyeurism, sexually transmitted
disease, a secret marriage, a passionate or prurient widower, and unrequit-
ed love. The courtroom narratives that surfaced provide ample opportunities to view anxieties about race, sex, and, more specifically, Pleasant's power,
in Gilded Age San Francisco.[3]

Sarah Hill claimed she married William Sharon; Sharon insisted he paid
Hill for sex. Whether Hill acted as a wife or a prostitute preoccupied judges,
attorneys, and the press. Pleasant's high visibility as a key witness for Hill
and the presence of other African Americans in the courtroom ensured that
the trials—and the discourse inside and outside the courtroom—would also
hinge on issues of race. Furthermore, Pleasant's capital and her financial
support of Hill's case disrupted dominant assumptions about the place of
African Americans in post-Reconstruction America. San Francisco, like other
U.S. cities, rendered many of its black citizens powerless through de jure and

de facto segregation and discrimination. The enracing of Pleasant in this case is more complicated than assigning to her the role of mammy, voodoo queen, or madam, although all of these stereotypes were applied liberally. The knowledge about white men's secrets that Pleasant controlled, combined with her wealth, made her threatening in ways that mere blackness alone does not explain.[4] The legal contest between Sharon, Hill, and Pleasant, then, is also about Western wealth and capital; both Sharon and Pleasant had profited mightily from gold and silver mining and real estate speculation. Their wealth helps to explain why they could afford such a public and lengthy legal contest in the first place. But whereas Sharon's heirs eventually reaped the rewards of his millions, Pleasant and Hill paid dearly for trafficking in sexual secrets.

When William Sharon, lounging in his lavish personal suite at the Palace Hotel, was arrested on September 8, 1883, for adultery, most wondered how the wealthy widower—who had so successfully manipulated his financial affairs and those of others—could be taken to jail on those charges. In the months that followed, Sarah Hill's original charge of adultery was thrown out of district court on technical grounds, and her attorney, George W. Tyler, filed a new suit on November 1, 1883, in San Francisco's Superior Court. This suit, *Sharon v. Sharon*—which captured the limelight for years—was Sarah Althea Hill Sharon's request for divorce. Sarah claimed that the two had been secretly married in 1880 and charged William Sharon with desertion and adultery committed with nine women.[5] Seventeen years earlier, Pleasant had hired the same attorney, George W. Tyler, to handle her streetcar case.

Members of Sharon's defense team saw Pleasant as the evil mastermind behind Sarah's case.[6] One judge claimed, "Pleasant . . . was forced to admit after much evasion [that] she has advanced more than $5,000 [to Sarah's cause]."[7] The implication that Sarah worked as a prostitute and Pleasant as a madam informed much of the discourse in the courtroom. Proof that this was indeed the arrangement never materialized. Nevertheless, Pleasant's income—much of it obtained indirectly from secrets revealed in her establishments—caused quite a stir. Reporters consistently drew attention to Pleasant's assets, and her property in particular: "[She] derives a good income from eight homes, situated on Octavia, Clara, Stone, Scotland and Harrison streets, added to which is the revenues of a large ranch near San Mateo, besides that of $100,000 in bonds of the United States, while a ready sum awaits her call in our city banks."[8] Pleasant's capital and stature prompted suspicion. African American capitalists, often the target of brutal violence in the post-Reconstruction era, rarely appeared in court as key witnesses for white plaintiffs.

Sharon v. Sharon took place against a backdrop of 1880s abundance in California. It was an era of unprecedented wealth as well as scandal for investors and entrepreneurs.[9] Railroad and mining monopolies squeezed tremendous profits out of the West. And few profited more than city builder William Ralston's right-hand man, William Sharon.[10] Sharon served as a U.S. senator from Nevada between 1875 and 1881 but lived in San Francisco after 1872.[11] As the owner of the Palace Hotel, reputedly the largest hotel in the world when it was built in 1875, he was at the center of San Francisco's elite social circle. Sharon's background reflected a life of privilege and, to some extent, luck. Born in Smithfield, Ohio in 1820, Sharon studied law with Lincoln's future secretary of war, Edwin M. Stanton, in Steubenville, Ohio. Tempted by stories of the Gold Rush, Sharon took the overland route West in 1849. In San Francisco Sharon became partners with the men who controlled the Bank of California, the largest bank west of the Mississippi. Sharon's association with this circle of bank men—known as Ralston's Ring—led to his appointment as agent of the Nevada City branch of the bank in 1864. Together the San Francisco and Nevada offices controlled much of California finances and some of the most lucrative mining territory in the world: the Comstock Lode.

Not known for his charm or good looks, Sharon was described by one reporter as "a pale little man with a large head, ladylike hands and feet, and cold blue eyes."[12] With accusations of effeminacy such as this, journalists hoped, perhaps, to belittle Sharon's status. By the time he was elected to the Senate in 1875 he controlled the Comstock Lode, the richest silver mining region of the country, owning at least seven active silver mines.[13] Sharon also owned the Reno–Virginia City Railroad and in the year he was elected to the Senate he acquired Nevada's most influential paper, *The Territorial Enterprise*. His worth was estimated to be between $20 and $30 million in 1875.[14] Sharon's wife, Maria Ann Mulloy, died that same year, and Sharon later stated under oath that he began paying women monthly salaries to have sex with him in his apartment at the Palace Hotel.[15] Sarah Hill, he claimed, was one of those women.

Born in Cape Girardeau, Missouri, Sarah Althea Hill moved to San Francisco in 1871 after her parents' death.[16] Hill's exact age at the time of the trial is not known, but she was probably in her early twenties when she moved west. She lived for some time with her aunt and grandfather, then moved on her own from boardinghouse to hotel.[17] Sarah Althea Hill's background is rather sketchy. She was of Irish descent; her great grandparents probably migrated from County Antrim in the 1770s.[18] Her body, not her background, drew much more attention from the press: "[Her] face is shapely and oval, the features are regular, the mouth is well cut, the lips are rather full and are the most expressive feature. They look resolute, but betray also that their owner has a temper."[19] Her hair, described alternately as auburn or strawberry blonde, also elicited commentary. One reporter wrote blithely, "Her hair is auburn, and, if it is not false, is of luxuriant growth. That portion growing above the forehead is devoted to curls and ringlets, which fall in profusion over the dome of thought."[20] The press's earliest portraits of Sarah wavered on the brink of harlotry. Sarah countered this characterization with her own claims of blueblood stock. Before the trial, the *San Francisco Bulletin* printed a letter from a friend of Sarah's family, claiming that Sarah was a descendant of Revolutionary War heroes. Even Sharon's millions "would hardly compensate a handsome and accomplished young woman for his age and reputation and certainly no one can have a higher family connection than she has." Sarah and her family thought Sharon "of very low birth" and not equal to her social standing, according to the letter.[21]

On the morning of March 10, 1884, the divorce trial began in Department Two of the Superior Court in the San Francisco City Hall, with Judge J. F. Sullivan presiding. The public had already been treated to a few scandalous pretrial tidbits collected during the depositions, and, as a result, the courtroom was packed on opening day.[22] From the onset, the case raised the specter of Pleasant's "unnatural" relationship to Sarah and interracial alliances between women. Technically, the case hinged on the question of whether Sharon and Hill had been legally married in 1880. Many key witnesses for both the plaintiff and the defendant were African American women. On the first day of the trial it was clear that Sarah's interracial relationships and her alleged use of voodoo would be substantial issues for the defense in their attempt to discredit her. Sharon's lead attorney, William Barnes, made the following promise: "We will show how [Hill] visited the sanctums of fortune tellers, negroes, Germans, French and every race. We shall show how she obtained a pair of Sharon's dirty socks, had them charmed by a negro, and then wore them upon her limbs to charm him. How she wore one of his soiled undershirts and how she paid $25 for a pinch of pepper and salt a negro gave her to charm Mr. Sharon. She disclosed her secrets to a colored woman and did not confide in a relative. She had no one to confide in but a negro."[23] Questioning Pleasant's role as confidante formed a central part of the defensive attack. "Will anybody tell me," begged Barnes in his argument to the state Superior Court, "why it was that this unfortunate woman never confided the secret of her marriage to one respectable person of her own color, class, or rank in life?"[24] Pleasant occupied a conspicuous place in the courtroom from the first day. She sat behind Sarah in the first row of spectators. At seventy years of age, Pleasant appeared elderly yet stately in her seat at the City Hall. Her presence—and that of the other black witnesses—marked the courtroom as a site where racialized fantasies played themselves out publicly.

The courtroom scenario—of Sharon, the white patriarch, Sarah, the desirable young belle, and Pleasant, the desexualized elderly black woman—also resonated with American cultural icons rooted in the system of slavery. As long as these familiar roles were maintained by the principal actors in the case, and Pleasant played the role of the mammy, her danger to white San Franciscans, and especially white men, would be diminished.[25] At least that was what Sarah's attorneys were hoping; drawing on a familiar story line, that of the faithful mammy, the counsel planned to elicit sympathy for Sarah's case.[26] The other possibility raised by the specter of Sarah and Pleasant was that Pleasant was a madam—as many San Franciscans believed—and Sarah her employee. That, too, represented a familiar narrative, but one that Sarah's legal team hoped to avoid. Investing Pleasant with mammy-like characteristics and portraying Sarah as the helpless victim of Sharon's sexual desire became the chief legal strategy for Hill's attorneys.

For Sarah to elicit sympathy as a scorned wife, she must first show that Sharon had married her. To do this, Sarah explained to the judge that she hid her friend, Nellie Brackett, inside the wardrobe in William Sharon's room in the Palace Hotel so that Nellie might hear Sharon's promise of marriage. Miss Brackett—who testified that she heard more lovemaking than conversation—did vouch for the existence of a marriage. She testified that Sharon cooed, "Who is my own little wife and nobody knows about it?"[27] When Sarah was asked why she hid Nellie in the bureau, she responded, "Well, I wanted to prove to her that I was married to Mr. Sharon." The examiner asked, "You didn't want it for the purpose of proving it to anybody else?" Sarah answered, "I wanted her to tell Mammie Pleasant what she had heard and how he had talked to me."[28]

Sarah testified that Pleasant encouraged her to pursue the senator for the alimony payments he owed her. According to Hill, Sharon fell behind in his payments. In a heartless move, Sarah explained, Sharon had her evicted from the room he had secured for her at the Grand Hotel. Sharon's suite at the Palace Hotel and Hill's room at the Grand Hotel were connected by a footbridge that came to be known as "the bridge of sighs."[29] When Sharon had the carpet removed from Sarah's hotel room, she began writing a letter to Sharon about their arrangements, under the advice and counsel of Mary Ellen Pleasant, she told the judge.

Sharon's attorneys found Sarah's testimony implausible on several counts. Why did Sharon kick her out if they were actually husband and wife? And why did Sarah not mention the marriage or the marriage contract when she penned the letters to Sharon? In answer to the latter, Sarah replied, "I did not mention my contract, or the fact that I was his wife, because I did not want to anger him. . . . Mrs. Pleasance advised me to do so."[30] These remarks and others Hill made on the stand attested to Pleasant's central role in Sarah's life and in her case. Whereas Hill's attorney emphasized the natural affinity between a young woman and her mammy, the story that Sharon's attorney told was one of unnatural affinity: "Mrs. Pleasance occupies a very peculiar relation to the respondent in this case, one utterly inexplicable upon ordinary principle or upon any reasonable ground. Her intimacy with Miss Hill, as now related, was one that ought not to have existed. . . . They were together daily according to the present story."[31] Intimacy between Sharon and Hill was the explicit text of the trial, but intimacy between Pleasant and Hill was no less at issue.

Sarah's bad judgment could be measured, according to Sharon's attorney, by witnessing her descriptions of Mary Ellen Pleasant: "Miss Hill's descriptions of the woman to whom she attributes supernatural power must be given in her own language. She says: 'Mammie Pleasant was old and had the experience, and she had the experience of lots of girls and women; had the experience of the world, of being a servant, and being a wife, and being the head of families.'"[32] Sarah's portrayal of Pleasant reveals a conscious effort to cast Pleasant in acceptable roles for a black woman: as a wife, nurturer, and servant. But it was the mammy image that rang true to most observers of the trial. Many San Franciscans believed that Pleasant worked as a servant for Thomas and Teresa Bell on Octavia Street, and now some believed that she was mother and mammy to young girls such as Sarah.[33] Sarah's case hinged on representing her relationship with Pleasant in this way; were they to be seen as protégée and advisor—a more accurate description of their relationship—Sarah's argument would weaken.

Stolen underwear was the topic of extensive discussion in the second week of the trial.[34] The *San Francisco Chronicle*, which displayed sensational headlines since the trial began, printed the following one on March 19, 1884: "Sharon's Dirty Duds, Sarah Althea's 'Hoodoo': Socks and Shirts to Rekindle Love's Flame in Sharon's Bosom." Mr. Evans, one of Sharon's attorneys, "pulled out of the wrappers a sock so dirty and ill-smelling that Sarah Althea was compelled to hold her nose."[35] Sarah adamantly denied ever using the dirty underwear to put a spell on Sharon and asked Evans, "Are you through with your dirt?"[36]

There can be no doubt that the public—both in and out of the courtroom—was as titillated by the mention of voodoo as they were by the presence of Sharon's socks and undershirt. "At least thirty women" were in the audience the day the smelly socks were unveiled, a fact most reporters found remarkable. The *San Francisco Chronicle* described a room full of "fortune tellers, all witnesses in the case in connection with Sarah Althea's alleged devotion to Voudou."[37] Discussions of potions, charms, and voodoo appeared throughout the proceedings. Attorneys for both sides spent countless hours questioning black women who might have used, sold, or heard of charms, potions, or spells. On April 14, 1884, Frances Massey, an African American woman, testified that Sarah had come to her and requested aid and had brought her a pair of socks to charm. Mrs. Massey heard Sarah claim that she had also charmed Sharon's food. "Who told her to do that?" asked Barnes. "Oh, I would not like to tell; it is a lady I respect very much," answered Massey. Then the witness announced that the culprit was Pleasant.[38]

One of the more intriguing twists of the trial was the way in which both attorneys tried to use Sarah's involvement with voodoo as part of their argument. Barnes, who revealed a particular distaste for Sarah's black acquaintances, nevertheless called in a host of black witnesses who testified that Sarah had visited them for charms. He argued that by consulting voodoo practitioners Sarah was conducting herself as a single woman who "did not occupy the place of a loving, trustful wife."[39] Tyler seemed to vacillate between dismissing "hoodoo" as irrelevant to the case and hoping to prove that Sarah was manipulated by sorceresses such as Massey. Neither side disputed the validity or power of voodoo or spiritual practitioners. Many nineteenth-century Americans subscribed to various forms of spiritualism and the occult; voodoo was just one of the many. But voodoo signified blackness, and that fact was not lost on the participants, the observers, or the recorders of the case. Contact with voodoo, whether by Sarah or any other white person, signaled poor judgment and criminality.[40]

Trying to ferret out the "truth" about voodoo in a courtroom proved as farcical as hiding Nellie Brackett in a closet. Actual voodoo practitioners, those who drew on the traditions of the African diaspora, took a vow of silence as part of their beliefs. What these women described in the San Francisco courtroom sounded less like voodoo and more like love potions. But charms or potions touched by brown hands became voodoo in Victorian America. And the image of Pleasant running some kind of voodoo racket appealed to many because it underscored the blackness and the danger of Pleasant.[41]

Both sides of the divorce trial knew very well that Sarah's relationship to African Americans—and particularly to black women—was a key element of the trial. Barnes argued that Pleasant rounded up most of the black witnesses who appeared in court. According to Barnes and many others, Pleasant single-handedly launched Sarah's case and gathered her witnesses. In his argument before Judge Sullivan, Barnes exclaimed, "She is the best all-round witness Mr. Tyler ever had. She is a glorious old woman. I do not wonder that he loves her. I am not surprised that he canonized her. . . . She proved the existence of a contract in 1882. . . . She has produced a noble army of martyrs in the cause of Miss Hill. I do not wonder that Mr. Tyler expresses such sentiments of affection towards Mrs. Pleasance. Where would he have been without her?"[42] Mary Ellen Pleasant's testimony had nothing to do with potions or spells. She took the witness stand five times and offered significant testimony regarding the existence of a marriage contract. Because much of the case rested on the question of the contract, her testimony shaped the outcome of the trial. But her actual statements on the stand proved bland compared with those of other witnesses who confessed to selling potions, being in love with Sarah, or listening to Sarah and the senator have sex.[43] This blandness was an excellent strategy because it helped take the wind out the defense's sails; Pleasant appeared calm and subdued as Sarah's friend and helpmate.

When she first took the witness stand Pleasant testified that she found Miss Hill weeping at the Grand Hotel because Mr. Sharon had had her ousted from the premises. When Sharon kicked Sarah out of the Grand Hotel after their marriage had soured, explained Pleasant, Hill was desperate to find a room. "I have lived in San Francisco since 1849. I met the plaintiff in the Grand Hotel about two years ago. She wanted me to furnish a house for her. I asked to see the marriage contract to see if she had any guarantee for her money. The plaintiff showed the contract, and then I went to Mr. Sharon. I told him that I heard he had some kind of relation with Miss Hill and owed her money, and asked him if it would be all right if I furnished the house. Mr. Sharon said all right, go ahead and furnish it and he would pay the bills."[44] The encounter in the Grand Hotel in January 1882, Pleasant claimed, was the first time she and Sarah had met. This contradicted the defense's claim that the two had concocted the marriage contract two years earlier. Surprisingly, Pleasant was barely cross-examined by Sharon's attorneys.

Pleasant's claim that Sarah had told her about the marriage contract at this meeting became a pivotal issue in the case. Rather than focus on the contract itself, Sharon's attorneys argued that Pleasant was hardly a trustworthy confidante for such an important piece of news: "Mrs. Pleasance became the receptacle of the respondent's [Hill's] entire confidence. She was not only told of her marriage—informed her of her relations with Mr. Sharon generally—but when it came to the critical moment of expulsion from the hotel the respondent took the direction—think of it!—took the sound direction of this old negro diplomatist as to the character of the letters she should write to her husband!"[45] Pleasant's character as well as Sarah's was on trial, and Pleasant's first appearance in court whetted the appetites of a hungry press corps.

From the outset, courtroom discourse raised questions about the power of Mary Ellen Pleasant. Did she have an "unnatural" power over Sarah Hill? Did she operate a clandestine organization of women who made a career of tricking San Francisco men? As the trial progressed, other questions about Pleasant's presumably illicit activities surfaced. In particular, the framing of Pleasant shifted to include her alleged role as a baby seller.

Pleasant's name is first associated with procuring homes for babies in April 1884, the second month of the trial.[46] An astrologist, Mrs. Wanger, a "not unpleasant-looking woman of middle age," testified that in 1882 Hill planned to acquire a baby that she would use to blackmail Sharon. "How was she to get the baby?" Mrs. Wanger was asked. "Why, the same as other women; she said she would pull the wool over Sharon's eyes. The lady that gets the baby is here," announced Wanger. "Who was it?" Tyler asked. "Mrs. Pleasance; yes, she said that Mrs. Pleasance got the babies for Mrs. Bell, and Mrs. Bell pulled the wool over Tom Bell's eyes."[47] By then, Thomas Bell had been a business partner and resident in Pleasant's house for more than a decade. He played a strange but significant role in the trial. His testimony was needed to prove that Sarah Althea Hill was indeed at the mansion on Octavia Street on May 1, 1883. Another witness, a gravedigger named Gillard, had testified that he saw Sarah Hill using charms in a graveyard (presumably to put a spell on Sharon) on May 1, 1883. Bell testified that he had been in Mexico on a trip but arrived home at eleven o'clock on May 1 to have lunch, and Hill was in attendance.[48]

Bell and Pleasant both claimed that Sarah was at the house that day, although Pleasant herself was on an outing with the Bell children. In her testimony on July 22, 1884, Pleasant posed as a resident, not an owner, of the house: "I have lived at Mr. Bell's for nine years. On the first of May, 1883, I went to Patterson's ranch; I used Mr. Bell's team that day; I did not use my own; when I returned to Mr. Bell's the plaintiff was not there." In addition to Bell and Pleasant, four other witnesses testified that they knew Sarah had taken lunch at the Bell and Pleasant household. Pleasant probably secured these witnesses because it was in Sarah's interest to provide a solid alibi.

It was in the best interest of the defense, however, to draw attention to Pleasant's involvement in baby selling and bring the conversation back to that topic. Barnes attempted to do this by drilling one of the witnesses about the ages and names of the Bell children. One author describes the scene as follows: "Barnes and one of the witnesses were locked in a confused and heated exchange about the number and description of the Bell children as the time for adjournment arrived, and Judge Sullivan said pleasantly, if wearily, 'We'll give the babies a rest until tomorrow at ten o'clock.'"[49]

Indeed, when the trial resumed the next day, July 23, 1884, the press had a field day over missing babies. Whereas the previous days' headlines read, "An Alibi for Sarah: Where She Spent May Day of 1883," the *San Francisco Chronicle*'s headline of July 24 asked, "Where is Bertha's Baby?" A German American woman, Mrs. Weill, testified that Pleasant, at her request, had placed a certain Bertha Bonsell's baby in a "good home." Thus began a lengthy discussion in the press about baby selling, including a front-page cartoon of Pleasant in the political journal *The Wasp*. The caption of the cartoon, "When I was young and charming, I practiced baby farming," referred to a line in the popular Gilbert and Sullivan comic opera *H.M.S. Pinafore*, which opened a few years earlier.[50] The cartoon reinvigorated Pleasant's reputation as a baby seller. Good mammies nurtured babies; they did not sell them.

Tyler had brought Mrs. Weill into court to testify that she too had seen Sarah at the Bell household on May 1. But Barnes began his cross-examination in a different vein: "Do you know a girl named Bertha Bonsell?" asked Barnes. "Yes sir, she is in San Jose," answered Weill. "Do you remember when she was in the Lying-In Hospital and had a baby there?" pressed Barnes. Tyler objected immediately. And Barnes chimed, "We claim that this woman, Mrs. Pleasance, is at the bottom of what I shall claim is this mass of perjury that is being committed by these people. I want to show the relation between this woman on the stand and Mrs. Pleasance, and I want to ask her if she did not get this girl's baby from . . . the Lying-In Hospital and give it to Mrs. Pleasance to palm off on Thomas Bell."[51] Judge Sullivan allowed Barnes to further question Mrs. Weill, at which point Barnes asked her whether one of the Bell twins was Bertha Bonsell's baby. Mrs. Weill replied, "Not to my knowledge." But Mrs. Weill did explain that Pleasant helped her find a home for Bertha's baby and that the baby was "in a house on Bush Street." Although Barnes had not succeeded in proving that the Bell children were not Bell's, he had introduced solid evidence that Pleasant was in the business of finding homes for newborns.

The next day, Tyler called Pleasant back to the stand: "Did you ring in Bertha's baby on Mr. Bell?" he queried. "No sir," Pleasant responded. In a revealing yet nonchalant exchange, Pleasant chatted with Tyler about the babies: "Mrs. Weill asked me to get a home for Bertha's baby; I told her I would, and Mrs. Weill said she would get me a wet nurse for Mrs. Bell's twins; our babies were born ten or fifteen days before Bertha's; Bertha's baby was adopted by a lady on Bush Street," she explained. "Whose babies do you mean when you say 'our babies'?" queried Tyler. "I mean Mr. Bell's babies," Pleasant answered.[52] In this light Pleasant's work placing babies in homes looked more like charity or reform and less like black market baby selling or blackmailing. The image of Pleasant saving unwanted babies and placing them in good homes also conformed to the image of elderly black women—mammies—doting over white babies.

Pleasant's veracity continued to be dismissed with scorn by Sharon's legal team. In their final arguments Tyler and Barnes made much of Pleasant's role in the case. On August 12, 1884, Tyler "in a fury" let loose "his hot invective against Sharon." In his attempt to prove Sharon to be a perjurer, Tyler concentrated on Pleasant's testimony: "I claim that Mr. Sharon's statement to Mrs. Pleasance is a virtual admission that he signed the contract. He told her when she was talking about the case with him that he could prove that the plaintiff had been intimate with a dozen men since the contract was signed. If your Honor believes Mrs. Pleasance, this is an acknowledgment of the making of a contract."[53] Tyler placed before the judge a test of Pleasant's character and trustworthiness. Judge Sullivan was asked to weigh the faithfulness of this black servant: Was she a true mammy?

Tyler made his plea very directly: "Allow me to call attention to the character and testimony of Mrs. Pleasance. Mr. Barnes will no doubt try to malign her character; yet, while she was on the stand, he did not cross-examine her. Mr. Barnes adopted the most contemptible manner to discredit her and to shake her testimony in your Honor's mind. He said that Mrs. Pleasance had been ringing in other people's babies on Tom Bell; but what proof did he bring to prove any such outrageous statement?"[54] The baby-selling accusation clearly worried Tyler. A baby-selling mammy was not an image Tyler wanted before the judge. A defensive Tyler pleaded, "Mrs. Pleasance found a home for Bertha's baby. She has found homes for other unfortunate girls' babies. Is that anything against her?"[55]

Representations of Pleasant shifted greatly during the trial. In the early days of the trial Pleasant was described by the press as a "colored peddler of white laces."[56] She "first visited [Sarah] for the purpose of making a sale of some luxurious articles of female underwear which she habitually peddled to the class of white women with whom she associated," according to Sharon's attorneys.[57] But the image of underwear-selling mammy unraveled during the course of the case, and Barnes eventually described Pleasant as "the sole financier of the anti-Sharon syndicate."[58] The change in emphasis is noteworthy; initially the defense used the slavelike imagery of a lace-peddling mammy to describe Pleasant. But by 1885 this had been replaced by the image of a voodoo priestess deviously manipulating the unsuspecting Sarah with charms, potions, and financial wizardry.

Despite Barnes's best efforts—and a final argument that took six days in court—many observers sided with Sarah when all was said and done. However, the judge had given no indication of his opinion. Thus his verdict, delivered on December 24, 1884, came as a surprise to everyone. The opinion took two and a half hours to read, during which Sharon did not fare well: "The defendant was a man of unbounded wealth," the judge pronounced, "possessed of strong animal passions that, from excessive indulgence, had become unaccustomed to restraint."[59] It seems that Sharon's belief that he could indulge in excess with few, if any, repercussions disturbed at least one judge in town. The contract was deemed to be valid and Sarah was thus entitled to a divorce and alimony. Sullivan awarded Sarah $2,500 a month and $55,000 in attorneys' fees.[60] When Sharon heard the announcement of Sarah Althea Hill's award he told reporters that the judge placed a much higher value on Sarah than she did: "When she and I had to fix her value, she rated it at $500 a month."[61] This verdict privileged the madam's word over that of the client's, in this case Sharon's, at least in the eyes of many contemporary observers. One judge went so far as to describe Pleasant as a "magician and tamer of wild animals," crediting her with great power over the ex-senator's "strong animal passions."[62]

While awaiting her payments, however, Sarah appeared in the next courtroom drama: the federal case brought by Sharon that began in February 1885. *Sharon v. Hill* seemed like a repeat performance of the previous year's drama, only with a few new twists. Sarah was arrested and spent twenty-four hours in San Francisco's Broadway jail for refusing to deliver the necessary documents to Judge Sawyer of the U.S. District Court. Pleasant visited Sarah in jail, bringing her a basket of food. A crowd cheered when Sarah left the jail, and she took the opportunity to recite a poem she composed for Judge Sawyer.[63] This was not Sarah's only dramatic performance during the federal case: She also accepted the role of Portia in the San Francisco Grand Opera's production of *The Merchant of Venice* that year.[64] But Sarah's exuberance was short-lived.

Judge Sawyer was joined by Judge Matthew Deady of Oregon, and when they delivered their opinion on December 26, 1885, the rosy future that Pleasant and Hill had no doubt imagined shattered. The women had expected large sums of money from Sharon's estate, given the earlier verdict. This time, however, the contract was determined to be invalid. Deady, in particular, focused on the sexual improprieties committed, and although they had nothing to do with the validity of the contract, they were a blight on Sarah's character, not Sharon's. As he explained, "the sin of incontinence in a man is compatible with the virtue of veracity and does not usually imply the moral degradation and insensibility that it does in a woman."[65]

Deady also made his opinion of Pleasant quite clear. She was a "shrewd old negress of considerable means" with a "conspicuous and important" role in the case. Without Pleasant, he claimed, the case "never would have been brought before the public." "For my judgment," he wrote, "this case, and the forgeries and perjuries committed in its support, have their origin largely in the brain of this scheming, trafficking, crafty old woman."[66]

Although the federal case was not by any means the end of the legal skirmishes—appeals and ancillary cases waged on—it was in many ways the end of the partnership of Pleasant and Hill.[67] After Sharon's death in 1885, Sarah married one of her lawyers, David S. Terry.[68] Terry, well known in San Francisco as the former chief justice of the state supreme court, was murdered in 1889, and that precipitated a rapid decline in Sarah's mental health. By 1892, Pleasant was taking care of the widow, whom the papers described as "hopelessly insane."[69] Mrs. Sarah Terry told reporters that Pleasant's house at Octavia and Bush streets was her only sanctuary.

On March 9, 1892, however, Pleasant signed a petition for the health commissioners and had Sarah Althea Terry committed to the state institution for the insane. According to the *Chronicle*, "Mammy Pleasant appeared at once as complainant and friend, and of all the people present, male and female, was the only one who showed any sympathy for the demented creature."[70] Pleasant no doubt felt defeated. Her efforts to wrest Sharon of his fortune had failed, and she had not fared well in the courts. As Pleasant entered into another series of lawsuits with Teresa Bell over her own property in the 1890s, she felt the scars from this tiresome effort.

Pleasant's participation in the litigation was part of a complicated financial scheme that involved not just Sarah but many players among San Francisco's elite. Some authors believe that Pleasant's involvement in the case can be explained through a closer look at the Bank of California fiasco and the intertwined finances of Thomas Bell, William Sharon, and Mary Ellen Pleasant. When the Bank of California failed in 1872 and Ralston resigned as president, Thomas Bell and William Sharon were stockholders. Both Bell and Sharon desperately hoped to restore the bank to its glory days and save their own fortunes. Sharon maneuvered his way to the top of the bank's chain of command and bought up most of the shares. He also accepted responsibility for Ralston's debts and acquired Ralston's assets.[71]

Sharon's success cost Bell prestige and capital.[72] Pleasant's finances certainly were connected with those of the Bells, and it is likely that when Bell lost out to Sharon as president of the bank, both Bell and Pleasant also lost considerable capital and power as chief shareholders. Records do not reveal how much of Pleasant's money was tied up in Bell's shares or how much she stood to gain or lose when Bell's worth shifted. Nevertheless, the theory that Pleasant was out for "triple revenge," as one author calls it, may have some merit.[73]

The trials mark a site where power is made visible: Pleasant's, Hill's, and Sharon's.[74] For that reason it is a useful episode in which to examine how that power operated and how it was contested. Pleasant's power was contested by attorneys, reporters, and judges, who used stereotypes and a range of images, from the pilfering mammy to the money-grabbing madam, to discredit her status and power. But the courtroom narratives also reveal that power for women in the Victorian era was located in different places depending on age, race, and class. For Sarah, power emanated from her ability to portray Sharon as an adulterer unable to control his sexual impulses and herself as scorned wife. Pleasant's power emanated from her wealth, her secrets, and the comfort white America invested in the role of the mammy. Pleasant played her part well: On the stand she called herself Thomas Bell's servant, when in fact she was a business partner and co-mortgage holder.

For nearly a year, Pleasant rose every morning, dressed for court, took a team of horses downtown, walked into the courtroom, and sat next to Sarah Althea Hill. During the trials she never spoke publicly about the state of her finances or her contribution to Sarah's case. But her behavior indicates that she cared deeply about the outcome. After Sarah's brief victory was overturned in federal court, Pleasant took her under her wing again, and Sarah lived her last weeks before being institutionalized in Pleasant's mansion on Octavia Street. Because Sarah was broke and not entitled to alimony, Pleasant stood to gain nothing from these acts of kindness.

The trials made public the female friendships and homosocial networks in San Francisco. When Sarah was on the stand she testified that Pleasant "guided her through difficulties . . . but only as a great and true friend, you understand. Mammy expected nothing in return; absolutely nothing."[75] At least one titillated author wrote that there was something "outré" and "sapphic" in the relationship between Pleasant and Hill.[76] To read sexual intimacy into the relationship is to misunderstand their bond, forged, at least partially, on the basis of their perception of heterosexual relations in Victorian San Francisco. Pleasant and Hill shared a desire to make men—in this case Sharon—pay for sexual favors.

In his final argument, Barnes reveals the relationship to be more dangerous than one of mere confidantes: "Mrs. Pleasance occupies a very peculiar relation to the respondent in this case, one utterly inexplicable upon any ordinary principle or upon any reasonable ground. Her intimacy with Miss Hill . . . was one that ought not to have existed."[77] Their relationship proved threatening for a variety of reasons; that it was interracial probably was chief among the qualities that Barnes found so peculiar. And the intimacy between them became part of the discourse of the trials. Suggesting that it was a sensual or intimate relationship may not have single-handedly discredited Sarah, but the defense obviously thought that it might help to do so. As Martha Hodes makes abundantly clear, interracial intimacy and its policing defined Reconstruction politics.[78] This trial indicates that fear of this intimacy held fast through the Gilded Age.

The meanings that can be deduced from the trials are not only about personal relationships, however. The political implications of the relationships between Pleasant, Sharon, and Hill, and of the trials themselves, are vast. Sharon and Pleasant operated in San Francisco's world of high finance, stock speculation, and silver mining entrepreneurs. Their names were well known when the first trial began. But women—even famous ones such as Pleasant—encountered risks in public space that men did not. As Mary P. Ryan argues, nineteenth-century women entered a world of sexual objectification when they participated in a city's public life.[79] Furthermore, because African Americans were denied access to most public arenas and institutions—from restaurants to juries—the risk to Pleasant and the significance of her presence in court cannot be exaggerated.

Pleasant and Hill's experience also indicates that women infiltrated more traditional political arenas: places marked off as male domains. San Francisco's public sphere was more integrated—in terms of gender and race—than previous studies of the city have indicated.[80] Black women in San Francisco often were seen in public spaces. But they probably would have been seen performing service sector jobs.[81] The elite black women of the city attended church functions, literary societies, and the like, but a courtroom was public in a way that these spaces were not.[82]

This public arena made women easy prey for journalists. In the pages of the newspapers and magazines Pleasant was described and displayed. During the course of *Sharon v. Sharon*, she was depicted as a mammy and a baby seller. She became associated with the practice of voodoo, magic, and witchcraft. The risks to her career and reputation were far greater than those to Sharon because, as Judge Deady pronounced, male sexual misconduct could be expected and therefore tolerated. Pleasant was aware of the risks and careful to construct an unthreatening appearance and testimony. Yet the public scrutiny of the 1880s—the racialized and scandalous cartoons and headlines included—contributed to her financial decline and tainted her reputation with the very judges she faced in the 1890s.

5

THE HOUSE OF MYSTERY

Mammy Pleasant was accused of being a black leech who had
fastened herself on the Bell money sack until it was dry as a
sucked orange.

San Francisco Call (1899)

Mary Ellen Pleasant's days in the courtroom did not begin or end with the
Sharon cases. In the 1890s she spent increasing amounts of time in city hall
and state courts, at one point appearing in four cases concurrently.[1] The
decade also brought marked shifts in Pleasant's lifestyle: In 1891 she bought
a sprawling ranch in Sonoma County, north of San Francisco, where she
spent weekends and holidays. Then in her eighties, Pleasant experienced long
periods of illness, as evidenced by the frequent visits she paid to her physician, Dr. Peter A. Kearney, in those years.[2] Friends and well-wishers traveled to the ranch and to her San Francisco home for regular visits. But Pleasant's relationship with her boarders and sometime co–mortgage holders, the
Bells, deteriorated in these years, as did the carefully constructed appearance of Pleasant as the Bells' mammy.

After nearly two decades of living in the mansard-roofed mansion on
Octavia Street, the family and business enterprise of Teresa Bell, Thomas
Bell, the six Bell children, and Mary Ellen Pleasant collapsed. In the last
decade of her life, Pleasant lost most of her property and witnessed the demise of her enterprise. Judges, reporters, and editors got a better glimpse of
Pleasant than they had previously been privy to as Pleasant granted more
interviews, made more court appearances, and printed the first and only
installment of her autobiography in this decade. She also issued some of her
most fiery rhetoric in the last ten years of her life.

Pleasant spent the better part of the 1890s in litigation over the Bell estate and her own. The dramatic series of events began on October 15, 1892,
when Thomas Bell fell over the railing at the top of the stairs in the home
at 1661 Octavia street. He had retired to his bedroom at about 8:30 P.M.
According to police reports, Pleasant was also in the house that night, Teresa
was at Beltane, the Sonoma County ranch, and the three youngest children

were in bed.[3] At approximately 10:30 P.M. Pleasant reported that she heard Bell's voice, then the fall, and the servants' screams. He had fallen twenty feet to the basement floor, where one of the servants had discovered him lying unconscious. Doctors were called immediately and concurred that Bell had had a concussion. He never regained consciousness and was pronounced dead at 1:30 P.M. on October 16, 1892.[4] Thomas Bell was seventy-two years old when he died.

The newspapers reported the death as an accident, and a coroner's jury confirmed this fact.[5] On October 18 a formal inquest was held at the Bell and Pleasant household. This time Teresa Bell was in the house, but she remained silent. Pleasant, Fred Bell, the eldest child, the two doctors who had been called to the scene, Dr. Murphy and Dr. Kearney, and the servants all testified. The coroners concluded that Bell's death was caused "by falling over the balustrade of his residence" and "that his death was entirely accidental."[6] Demonstrating a certain intimacy she shared with Bell, Pleasant described his recent ill health: "Mr. Bell had been ailing for about two months now, and has been in bed since last Monday. He was badly run down, the doctor said, and besides he had a trouble of the skin that just kept him in torture."[7] Because Teresa Bell had been at Beltane Ranch when he died, she made no comments to the press about her husband's death.

Pleasant made it clear to the reporters that no one would ever know what really happened that night in what the reporters had dubbed "The House of Mystery": "Of course, we don't know just how the accident happened— nobody knows that—but we think Mr. Bell must have been dazed when he started down to the kitchen. I think he got to the bottom of the upper flight and then fell over the railing from the first step. There the railing is low, and it would be easy to fall from the stairs."[8] The examination of Bell's death provided the curious with another opportunity to scrutinize the relationships of the people living in the mansion. Partly because Bell had been a leading figure in one of the West's largest institutions, San Francisco's Bank of California, and partly because of Pleasant's reputation from the Sharon trials, the accident received much attention.

It is not clear what the immediate effect of Bell's death meant in terms of household dynamics. Pleasant was long suspected of being the director of the personal and financial affairs of the house. But just as mammies were suspected of running plantation households, there was an understood limit to this power; the master never acquiesced to the mammy in any matters of importance. With Thomas Bell gone, the charade of master and mammy was over. Pleasant's role in the house could no longer be cloaked behind the white patriarch. And she could be exposed for what she was: a self-possessed black woman in charge of a house full of wealthy people, including herself. As long as Thomas Bell lived, the house mirrored the white supremacist fantasy of a happy plantation household, a house in which white people controlled the affairs of black people. "Old Mammy Pleasant had lived with him for many years," explained one of Bell's obituaries.[9] "Old Mammy" without a master signaled trouble to many San Franciscans, who were anxious to read about Pleasant in the daily papers.

In the years after Bell's death, Teresa Bell and Pleasant were accused of mismanaging the Bell estate. The spoils were vast; in addition to real estate, Thomas Bell left behind millions of dollars' worth of stocks, mining claims, and cash.[10] The *Chronicle* claimed that the Bell estate yielded $40,000 a year at the time of Thomas Bell's death.[11] There was enough to provide all the children and Teresa Bell a tremendous inheritance.

Bell's will, dated February 3, 1892, stipulated that one-third of his estate be given to Teresa and that she be given a monthly allowance to support their six children: Thomas Frederick, Mary Teresa (Marie), Robina, Muriel, Reginald, and Eustace.[12] Teresa expressed dissatisfaction with her monthly allowance and petitioned for $5,000 a month. According to Teresa's attorney, the estate was amply able to provide this amount. However, the judge did not deem this necessary and awarded the family $2,000 a month.[13] Teresa was successful in another request, however, and Judge James V. Coffey agreed to set 1661 Octavia Street aside as a homestead for the widow and children. This appeared to eliminate any of Pleasant's claims to the property. Thus began Teresa Bell's and Pleasant's contest over the properties they inhabited, processes that continued for more than a decade.

Pleasant was willed nothing. She told at least one reporter that she requested that Bell leave her out of the will.[14] She held the deed for one of the San Francisco lots—the property encompassed two lots—and we can assume that she probably did not count on Bell's will for property or income.[15] One author believes, "If . . . Mammy was Bell's financial partner, her name would have been on their joint ventures. Mammy would have seen to that. . . . Bell's death and the terms of the will could never have had any material effect on what she personally owned."[16] It seems likely that Pleasant's financial relationship with Bell had been carefully orchestrated and did not depend on a settlement to be paid at his death.

The characterizations of Pleasant at the time of Bell's death rely on the image of the dutiful mammy. One newspaper describes the scene as follows: "She had nursed him all through his sickness and for days at a time he had not permitted any one else near his bedside. The negress looked upon him as more to her than a friend and employer, for she had been with and watched over his children from infancy and had been trusted by him in every way."[17] The trusting servant who is just like one of the family could not be better depicted. Yet in the same article the reporter admits that Pleasant built and designed the house that she shared with the Bell family—not a very mammy-like trait. "The building was constructed under the orders of Mammy Pleasant, that good-hearted old negress, who is known to almost everyone here through her strong and long-enduring friendship for Sarah Althea Terry."[18]

Seven years later, in 1899, Fred Bell accused Pleasant of Thomas Bell's murder. In Teresa Bell's diary of May 1899 she records that Fred Bell "believed that M. E. Pleasant threw Mr. Bell down the stairs." Fred Bell told his mother that Pleasant had given him instructions to change into his bedclothes and make it look as though he had been in the house but slept through his father's fall. Bell's murder was never substantiated, and no one was ever arrested for the crime. In the 1950s, Helen Holdredge provided lurid details about Pleasant's role in the "murder." *Mammy Pleasant* recreates the scene from the point of view of one of the servants, Maria Hall: "[Maria] saw Thomas Bell lying in a twisted heap on the floor at the bottom of the stairwell, and Mammy Pleasant kneeling beside him, facing her, but too absorbed in what she was doing to notice the arrival of the transfixed witness. Maria Hall, in that moment, saw something which was to haunt her for the rest of her life. Mammy, far from helping the broken and bleeding Thomas Bell, was using her long fingers to pull the protruding brains from a hole in the top of his head."[19] This grisly scene has become a favorite among folklorists and chroniclers of the Pleasant legend who use it to illustrate her savagery.[20]

The Bells and the divvying up of the spoils occupied much of Pleasant's time and energies throughout the 1890s. Five years after Bell's death, the family aired their dirty laundry in a very public way. In September 1897 Fred Bell petitioned to have the courts remove his mother as head of household and guardian of the younger children, claiming she was under the control of Pleasant. The petition stated that Mrs. Bell knew "absolutely nothing about her business affairs being controlled and directed by the said M. E. Pleasant, who is a negro woman of the age of eighty-three years or thereabouts, and neither a fit nor a proper person to guide, control, or direct any person other than herself."[21] Fred Bell's case began in Judge Coffey's court on September 8, 1897. After the first day's testimony, Pleasant received visitors and reporters at 1661 Octavia Street: "'Mammy' sat back in a big leather armchair and received her callers in a cold and dignified manner. . . . She talked for an hour before approaching the subject on which information was desired, and then very reluctantly made her statement."[22] That evening Pleasant explained that

Fred Bell had become an increasing drain on the family income. "This suit has been brought by Fred," she declared, "because some enemies of ours have urged him on, and his action is too shameful to speak about."[23]

Pleasant spoke all month in court, however, about the state of affairs at Octavia Street. Her power in the household was mentioned repeatedly by reporters and by Judge Coffey. And Fred Bell's attorneys claimed that Pleasant was behind Teresa Bell's every move. W. H. Schooler, Fred's lawyer, hoped to prove that Teresa Bell "had been the tool of 'Mammy' Pleasant in the squandering of a millionaire estate."[24] The issue of Pleasant's control of Teresa drove Fred's case from the beginning. Schooler exclaimed, Fred's "prime object in bringing this suit is not to strike at his mother at all, for he believes she is to some extent an innocent party. He wants to destroy the power of 'Mammy' Pleasant and show her up to people in her true colors."[25]

Pleasant's financial and personal activities came under tremendous scrutiny in this case. As in the Sharon trials, her name was splashed across newspaper headlines, and once again her relationship with a white woman was questioned—this time Teresa Bell. Although she was usually described as the employee of the Bell household, many accounts soon characterized her relationship to the members of the household as much more sinister. On September 16, 1897, the headline of the *Chronicle* indicated the nature of Fred's complaint: "Porterhouse for Mammy, Soup Meat for the Family." The article detailed Pleasant's role in the Bell house and the court testimony of one of the servants, the same Maria Hall whom Holdredge described as being at the "murder" scene. Hall described for the courtroom audience that "Mammy Pleasant and Mrs. Bell fared sumptuously on oysters, terrapin, chickens, quail, and porterhouse steaks," whereas "the bread the boys got was hard and stale." Pleasant's powers over other aspects of the household were also outlined: "The witness said she had never received any orders from Mrs. Bell and had never seen her give an order to anybody. She was entirely under the control of Mammy, who ran the whole house to suit herself."[26] There was probably more than a grain of truth in Hall's testimony: Pleasant did run her home on 1661 Octavia Street to "suit herself."

Pleasant's description of herself, in this particular case, was not altogether different from the one she gave during the Sharon trials: She described herself as a servant of the Bell household. When questioned in court about Teresa Bell's presence, she described Mrs. Bell as her "mistress" and "the noble woman." However, Pleasant's reputation as a simple servant came under attack. As this description of her appearance in court indicates, some observers were anxious to expose Pleasant as the autocrat of the estate: "Mammy Pleasant appeared in court in a costume that was oppressively stagy. She wore a rusty black dress, fastened at the neck, with a brass brooch, and her sharp-featured face was almost entirely hidden from view by an old straw poke bonnet, drawn tightly about her ears. Evidently with the intention of giving the idea that she was simply the kind of faithful colored nurse that the novels talk about, she had donned a white cotton apron, and over her shoulders she wore a green plaid shawl."[27] Pleasant's identity was the obvious subtext of Fred Bell's case against his mother, and exposing Pleasant as a masquerading "mammy" became part of the defense's strategy.

Fred Bell claimed—and the press reported—that Pleasant maintained complete control over every aspect of his mother's life. "Mammy seemed to exercise an unaccountable power over [Fred's] mother's mind," announced Fred's attorney. Mind control was the least of poor Fred's worries, however, according to his petition: "Thousands of dollars were being pilfered by Pleasant, a mammy-in-disguise," he claimed. In his petition to Judge Coffey, Fred Bell claimed that Pleasant disposed of valuable property including jewels worth more than $200,000. The entire estate was being squandered by Pleasant, and "her mistress" had no knowledge of this fact.[28] Meanwhile, Fred, his mother, and Pleasant continued to reside at the house on Octavia Street. "In the 'house of mystery,' in the home of my people peace would ever reign," claimed the young Fred Bell, "if that negress—'Mammy Pleasant'—was in some foreign clime. She is the cause of all our trouble and trouble will ever be until she departs. Just how she maintains the weird influence over Mrs. Bell I am unable to say."[29]

Fred Bell's petition of September 1897 provided yet another forum for public scrutiny and criticism of Mary Ellen Pleasant's personal and financial affairs. She was accused of starving the children, who ranged in age from eight to seventeen years old, and beating them. Numerous schemes involving laundered money and illegal mortgages were revealed by Fred Bell, his attorney, and George Eaton, a former bookkeeper for the Bell and Pleasant household. By the end of the month, many were calling Pleasant the defendant, pointing to her prominent role in the courtroom: "In this case the colored part of the population takes unusual interest for the reason that Mrs. M. E. Pleasant . . . is the real defendant in the litigation, though Mrs. Bell is named in the pleadings as the respondent."[30]

The complaints about Pleasant's control—this time over Teresa Bell and her children—echoed those aired during the Sharon trials: She had too much money and too much control over white people. The bond between Sarah Althea Hill and Pleasant seemed unnatural and distasteful to many observers of the 1880s trials. In the Bell case, however, the picture looked dangerously familiar: An older black woman was a maid for a wealthy, white family. Perhaps it was its familiarity—the plantation scenario—that so unnerved readers and observers. What could be worse than a mammy, a docile, obedient slave who is intimate with the secrets, the habits of a white family, who turns out to be working for the other side? The mainstream press played to these fears: "One after the other these mysteries of the family presided over by the tall old negress are being uncovered by the bitter litigation," claimed the *Chronicle*.[31]

Pleasant's business transactions play such a central role in Fred's case that we are offered a glimpse—otherwise unavailable—into her complicated financial affairs of the 1880s and 1890s. Among other things, Pleasant was accused of supporting young black women with proceeds from the Bell estate. In particular, a woman named Rebecca Boone seems to have held the deed to one of the lots on Octavia Street for a time. The same witness, Bayard Saville, who seemed so anxious to expose Pleasant's control of Teresa, testified that Pleasant altered the books to make it look as though four women lent the Bell estate $25,000. In a dramatic performance, Saville asked the judge, "Where did the $5,000 a month go that old Tom Bell used to pour into the lap of 'Mammy' as regularly as clockwork? What has been done with the money that the old woman swears she borrowed from these women of her own color?"[32]

Rebecca Boone, one of the four women, lived at 2016 Pine Street in San Francisco, property that Pleasant secured for her. Boone told the judge that she came to California from Cleveland, Ohio, as a girl with $500 that Pleasant had sent for the journey. Pleasant managed her money and bought her a house with the money from her parents: "She is sort of a guardian of my estate," explained Boone.[33] Fred's attorneys claimed that Pleasant signed over thousands of dollars to Boone and drained the Bell estate. "Only a couple of weeks ago," argued Fred's attorney, "Fred Bell overheard 'Mammy' talking to his mother about signing a note for $15,000 to Mrs. Rebecca Boone, in addition to the $10,000 already given to the woman." Pleasant had argued that Boone had lent money to the estate and she was only being paid back. "Now what do we find?" asked attorney Schooler. That "Mrs. Boone is also a colored lady, whose husband is a barber. And yet 'Mammy' Pleasant claims that this woman has advanced $25,000 to the Bell estate."[34]

Not everyone was sympathetic to the complaints of the millionaire's son and his attorney. There were those who accused him of being a spoiled brat and sided with Mrs. Bell and Pleasant. Some were convinced Pleasant was "a faithful old colored nurse and housekeeper" who was just doing her job. One news magazine, *The City Argus,* took up this sympathetic and paternalistic response to the controversy: "Mammy Pleasant has at all times had the confidence of Mrs. Bell and never has she wavered from the path of duty." Ever the devoted mammy, Pleasant was the image of a perfect house slave: "a vigilant housekeeper, who faithfully obeys every order of her mistress, a faithful, confidential servant, who can be entrusted with every matter, and honestly carry them out." It seems that to at least a segment of the population, attacking a faithful servant was unacceptable. The article concludes that Pleasant "is a real 'colored aunty' true as steel to friendship."[35]

At the onset this case looked like a rich teenager's ploy—Fred was seventeen when he initiated the suit—for the family fortune, but it was also a case about Pleasant's viability as a mammy: Was she faithful? Fred Bell's list of accusations—stealing jewels, giving money from the big house to other "colored" people, and tricking the mistress—reads like a master's list of complaints about his slave.[36] Probably that is precisely what Fred and his attorneys intended. If Pleasant could be exposed as a "mammy-in-disguise," he could gain the sympathy of the white elite. This was a valid strategy; members of the elite in Victorian America often complained about the class of servants available in an age when factory jobs lured European Americans away from household waged labor.[37] But perhaps Bell's legal team, and Bell himself, underestimated the pervasiveness and tenacity of the images of slavery. As the *City Argus* article makes plain, white America waxed nostalgic for the image—if not reality—of the perfect slave.

Relations between Teresa Bell and Pleasant deteriorated after Fred Bell's case, but the break also came after twenty years of sharing meals, living expenses, and the care of the Bell children. The two women kept close quarters: They had lived at the Octavia Street house since the 1870s, and in 1891, when Pleasant bought the Beltane Ranch in Sonoma County's Valley of the Moon, it served as their weekend home.[38] The valley was lush, harboring fruit trees, vineyards, and the homes of other refugees from the cities of San Francisco and Oakland. Jack London, the valley's most famous resident, built his country home "Beauty Ranch" in 1905 near Beltane. Pleasant bought her 985-acre ranch from the Savings Bank of Santa Rosa on June 8, 1891. The ranch sported a large mansion on a hill, southern style, with galleries on all its sides and outside staircases. Teresa, Mary Ellen, and the Bell children must have enjoyed the ranch tremendously. There was frequent train service between San Francisco and Glen Ellen (the depot nearest to Beltane), and Pleasant made the trip most weekends in the early 1890s. The younger Bell children rode horseback and made mischief at the ranch. Pleasant and Teresa both brought chickens, fruit, and other supplies up to Beltane for family meals.[39]

Running Beltane Ranch took a tremendous amount of work. A crew of men, employed by Pleasant, mended fences, stocked the house with supplies, cut wood, tended to the water supply and plumbing, and presumably kept the ranch in order when Pleasant stayed in San Francisco. The expense of keeping up the ranch became too much for Pleasant, however, and in 1892 she borrowed $1,000 on the mortgage. She also sold off some of the acreage in this period. On October 20, 1894, she signed the deed for the ranch over to Teresa Bell. Beltane was still 766 acres and worth at least $30,000 by the time Teresa acquired the deed.[40]

In 1892, while Pleasant still owned the ranch, Teresa Bell began writing a diary of events at Beltane. This is where Teresa recorded her frustrations with the workers, the children, and Pleasant. But in the early years, the diary reveals a much more mundane existence, a relaxing life of leisure in the country. Pleasant arrived on the weekends, and Teresa appeared to stay at Beltane most of the year. The journal lists visitors' comings and goings; on November 21, 1892, for example, Teresa wrote, "Mrs. P. came with turkeys and pies for Thanksgiving." At Christmas, Mary Ellen brought more turkeys to the ranch and presents for the children.

Both Pleasant and Bell spent a great deal of time with the children in these early years, bringing them back and forth from San Francisco to the ranch, riding horses in the hills, picking fruit, and visiting neighbors. By 1894, however, it is clear that both women were tiring of the children's antics. "The girls think of nothing but horses and riding," Teresa wrote on June 24, 1894, "and the boys expect meals to be left for them until they are ready to come. Mrs. P. is quite right about young America—they care for no one but themselves." In 1897, just before Fred filed his case, Pleasant told Reginald, then fourteen years old, that he had better go to Beltane or back to school because she would not have him living at Octavia Street "if he was allowed to make his own terms."[41] Pleasant, sick from a variety of ailments in this period, felt taxed by the boys' commotion in the house on Octavia Street.

The two women spent the majority of the summer of 1897 going back and forth to the courthouse, communicating through letters (ferried between the city and the ranch), and trying to foil Fred's case by presenting evidence of their household finances. On August 3, 1897, Teresa wrote, "M.P. is out looking for bills in the Fred Bell case. I am in a state of dread." Three days later Pleasant brought Teresa a lavish French hat, which she described as "quite an event as I have not had one in years." Pleasant also hid the coal at the house to make sure Fred could not use it.[42] Also that year, Pleasant and Bell made arrangements to mortgage the ranch, and they both signed a contract to that effect in February 1898. This was done to raise funds, apparently, because they both continued to spend time at the ranch, and Pleasant still had a financial and legal stake in the ranch, purchasing supplies and managing affairs. Teresa at least believed that she would "get possession of the place again in two years."[43] As it turned out, Pleasant was declared sole owner of the ranch in May 1899, when the two women were back in court fighting with creditors. This was a pivotal year in Pleasant's life. She was the subject of sensational exposés in the San Francisco press, her finances were whittled away in several courtrooms, and, perhaps most significantly, she was kicked out of her home of more than twenty years.

Teresa Bell, accusing Pleasant of squandering Thomas Bell's life savings, forced Pleasant to move out of Octavia Street and the house at the ranch, the places where Pleasant spent most of her time. This was a strange move considering the financial and emotional partnership the women had created in their two homes. However, it is clear that by spring of that year the relationship had gone awry. Teresa wrote on March 26, "Mary Pleasant and the 23 years of frauds she has worked off on me will last me for the rest of my life no matter how long it may be." And on April 8: "MP has had such success in working this whole family that she believes she is absolute owner of everyone and everything here, her constant gobble is how she owns everything here, it's all hers."[44] The confusing arrangement in which the property, children, and assets were shared between them had come apart at the seams. Pleasant witnessed the end of a business arrangement as well as a familial one. The change in her relationship with Teresa meant a shift in power relations: She would no longer function as head of household.

The row began on April 19, 1899, when a neighbor came to the ranch to see Pleasant about some money she owed him. Pleasant insisted that she would pay him the money and told Teresa she had "plenty of money." Teresa called her a blackmailer and told Pleasant that she had mailed a history of her evil deeds to the Bancroft Library, and the two began quarreling.[45] Pleasant accused Teresa of stealing an armchair from her house on 49 Clara Street, and the fight escalated. Teresa sent for a policeman to come out to the ranch, and a sergeant and two officers appeared but told her to call her attorney and file an ejectment suit. Pleasant was yelling instructions from upstairs and had one of the onlookers call police Chief Isaiah Lees in San Francisco, who was not in, but the clerk assured the caller that the chief would not go out to the ranch.[46]

The next day the two women fought in silence; Pleasant barricaded herself in her room and refused to leave. Teresa pushed in the door to the bathroom and threatened to have her removed. Pleasant finally gathered her things and left. "She passed out the door after her two trunks," wrote Teresa in her diary, "snarling like a mad dog." "I am glad, very glad to go," Pleasant told her. Teresa took great pleasure in this scene, describing it in great detail in her diary: "The wagon with the trunks stood before the door and the street and the steps opposite were lined with children and adults seeing the 'great Mary E. Pleasant' be turned out of this house, which she claimed could not be done."[47]

Teresa Bell firmly believed that the spectacle would result in Pleasant's defeat.[48] But as we know from subsequent court battles and the press coverage of the event, Pleasant's eviction from the house and the ranch did not mean her defeat. In fact, Pleasant had deeds to both these properties, albeit temporarily, after the eviction. The battle over Pleasant's mansion and the so-called eviction made front-page news on May 7, 1899, when *The Call* ran a full-page article titled "Angel or Arch Fiend in the House of Mystery." Again the relationship of Pleasant and Teresa Bell became public fare. "Perhaps Mrs. Bell and 'Mammy' have really quarreled. But more likely they have seemingly separated at Mammy's instigation and for a purpose," claimed *The Call*. On the other hand, the article noted, the ejection could be evidence that "Mrs. Bell has finally awakened to the fact that she has been as putty in Mammy's hands."[49]

Only weeks after the eviction, an insolvency suit initiated by Pleasant's creditors—which was pending at city hall—began. The creditors and the observers soon discovered that Pleasant's assets were so entangled with Teresa's that it would be difficult to extract much out of the old woman. According to some, the timing of Pleasant's eviction and the insolvency case may not have been accidental. Fred Bell accused Pleasant of instigating the move to avoid creditors. On May 11, *The Call* ran another story about the "House of Mystery" with the headline, "The Eviction of 'Mammy' Was a Ruse: Such Is the Theory of Young Bell." The reporter found Fred's description of the eviction convincing and claimed that it was general knowledge that Pleasant was dodging her creditors. "That the eviction of 'Mammy' was simply a little strategy to mislead this army of creditors is generally accepted," the article argued, "and each succeeding day of the proceedings to declare 'Mammy' insolvent results in the unfolding of a fact or action lending strength to the theory."[50] The tone of this article reveals the hostility many San Franciscans felt toward both Pleasant and Bell in light of their partnership. "Mrs. Bell, who would have the world believe her to be 'Mammy's' enemy, sits beside the deposed queen of 'the house of mystery,' during the proceedings," it is reported. "As of old," the story continued, "'Mammy' and Mrs. Bell exchange their views in whispers, and on their faces no trace of enmity is manifested." The image of the two scheming women outwitting their creditors was potent, one "that is not unplausible," claimed *The Call*.[51]

Pleasant and Bell's ownership of the ranch was at issue before the court on May 10. "'Mammy' was placed upon the stand," wrote the reporter on the case, "and in half an hour was between two fires of extremely unpleasant heat." Pleasant either had to swear that she owned the ranch (then valued at $100,000) and risk losing it to the creditors and being charged with perjury because she had claimed to be insolvent, or she would have to agree with Teresa's statement that she had deeded it to Teresa in 1898. Pleasant admitted to the judge that day in court that she owned claims amounting to $50,000. "This made the creditors jubilant and 'Mammy' likewise morose."[52] Pleasant and Bell may have manipulated the deeds to dodge creditors, as many implied, but their partnership was not as solid as Fred Bell believed. Teresa recorded her angst about the insolvency case in her diary, and it is clear—from her perspective—that she felt herself to be in a battle with Pleasant over the properties. When the judge proclaimed on May 17, 1899, that the ranch belonged to Pleasant and Pleasant was insolvent, Teresa wrote in her diary that she had "never met with quite such a disappointment."[53] It is possible that the two were trying to hold onto the ranch together and Teresa was merely disappointed that they lost it. But it is also clear that she had lost faith in Pleasant as a financial partner.

The next day, May 18, Teresa recorded her most telling description of Pleasant: "Mary E. Pleasant has been my evil genius since the first day I saw her. She has simply had me for a pocket book to help her have a standing which otherwise she never could have reached. A demon from first to last."[54] Comments such as these have caused speculation about the precise nature of Teresa and Mary Ellen's relationship. Teresa alternated between casting herself as Pleasant's victim and as Pleasant's prop or savior. The two probably functioned in different ways at different times for each other; it was a mutually constituted relationship that both women appeared to manipulate for their own ends. Whether framed as a mother-daughter relationship or as an intimate friendship, the relationship was central to their lives in every conceivable way: emotionally, financially, and socially. Furthermore, as Teresa indicated by the preceding comment, the relationship may have allowed Pleasant entrance to certain circles from which she was otherwise barred. On the other hand, Pleasant's business acumen and financial connections certainly kept Teresa living in the opulent style to which she had become accustomed.

Confusion about Pleasant's property had been pending in another case that began in Superior Court in 1898, *Pleasant v. Solomons*. In this case George Eaton was appointed as an assignee of Pleasant or receiver of her estate because she was determined to be an insolvent debtor. Pleasant brought the suit so that she could recover real estate on Sutter Street—the lot adjacent to the Octavia Street lot—from Lucius Solomons, who had been Pleasant's attorney in 1897. But in 1898 Pleasant charged that Solomons had committed an act of fraud and tried to cheat her out of the lot on Sutter Street. The three-cornered suit, as it was called, also involved Teresa Bell, who said the Sutter Street property belonged to her, and thus she became an intervenor in the suit. Arguments of the case were heard in Judge John Hunt's courtroom in September 1899.

Pleasant thought she was being framed—made to be an easy target for creditors—and protested the handling of the case from the onset. Angered by the court-appointed assignee, George Eaton, she reminded the judge that she had cases pending against Eaton and Teresa Bell. Pleasant drew attention to the fact that although she brought the suit, she disapproved of its trajectory and was opposed to giving testimony. She objected vehemently when called to the stand, stating, "This is simply a fishing expedition by my opponents. They want to find out what I have so they can keep possession of my property that they have got among them." "I don't want to say a word," she continued, "for fear that it will prejudice my rights, and as a free American citizen I object to giving my testimony."[55] A proclamation like this—asserting the rights of citizenship at a moment in U.S. history marked by disfranchisement and the denial of citizenship to most African Americans—no doubt reminded the court of her streetcar case.

Despite her reluctance, the judge ordered Pleasant to testify. The details, according to Pleasant, were as follows: In February 1897, she gave Solomons a promissory note for $3,000 on real estate that was worth between $23,000 and $40,000. Then, unbeknownst to Pleasant, Solomons deposited the promissory note in the London, Paris, and American Bank for collection. In October of that same year, Solomons delivered a promissory note to Leo Block, who eventually held the deeds to both the Sutter Street property and Pleasant's Washington Street property.

The case was complicated by Teresa Bell's claim that Pleasant did not own the Sutter Street property. Teresa Bell's attorney, Theodore Z. Blakeman, alleged that Pleasant deeded the Sutter Street property back to Bell in 1892. In her diary entry for June 22, 1899, Teresa Bell wrote, "Mr. Blakeman [her attorney] thinks this case is first class and thinks well of my recovery of Sutter Street. There is no doubt I can show such a fraud as between Pleasant and Solomons." Blakeman attempted to show that Pleasant was in possession of the deed to Sutter Street only for a short time (before Thomas Bell died) and then only for the purpose of raising funds for the Bells. Pleasant was instructed to borrow $11,000 on the property for the Bells "so as to keep their need of money from the public."[56] According to Blakeman (and Bell), Pleasant deeded the property back to Teresa Bell and then stole it from her "while she was acting as housekeeper of the Bell mansion."[57]

If Teresa Bell's diary accurately captures the mood of the courtroom, Pleasant was frustrated and defiant throughout the proceedings. "M.E.P. made a regular circus" of Judge Hunt's courtroom, according to Bell. Pleasant's "circus" had to do with her insistence that her interests were not being represented and her rights as an American citizen were being jeopardized. September 13 proved to be another trying day for Pleasant. According to Teresa, "She looked on the verge of a collapse." Bell takes great pleasure from the day's events, which she assumed to be Pleasant's downfall: "Mammy felt her claw in a trap. She pulled her hat off and put it on, then tied her handkerchief over her head, then over the hat and the head. She didn't know what she was about and the sweat had a polish on her I had never seen there before."[58] Bell's diary once again conjures up a narrative of Pleasant's defeat. In fact, a week after this scenario, the *Chronicle*'s story about the case stated, "Mrs. Teresa Bell Loses." The judge ruled that Pleasant's deeds had been validly conveyed to Solomons, who would be paid what was due him on the promissory note, and the property would be handed over to the assignee "for the benefit of Mrs. Pleasant's creditors."[59]

Pleasant created a stir in yet another department of the Superior Court that same month. This time the case *Bell v. Solomons* appeared in Judge James M. Seawell's courtroom and Pleasant, again challenged the judge and the premise of the case. According to Teresa, "M.E.P. was very much in evidence and was put out of the courtroom" on September 27, 1899. "They are tryin' to fool you Judge," Pleasant stated. Bell recorded in her diary that "Judge Seawell looked at her in disgust and called for a sheriff to put her out."[60] This seems a probable scenario; Pleasant was well known in Superior Court by this time, and many judges probably had developed an impression of her before she appeared in their courtrooms. Seawell could easily have resented directions from a woman, especially a black woman. In fact, black mammies were the subject of a lengthy monologue in Seawell's court in the next few weeks. Teresa's attorney, Blakeman, read a detailed description of the "Black Mammy of the South" and informed the judge that this was the first time he had ever heard of a "black mammy robbing and plundering" her foster family. There are "innumerable cases on record when the Black Mammy had kept a hoard and late in life when that foster child's resources were gone had brought it forth to succor that foster child." But Pleasant was the first greedy, selfish mammy he had ever seen, Blakeman argued.

Judge Seawell "listened with intense mistrust to Mr. Blakeman," wrote

Teresa. But "that 'Black Mammy' picture must have touched a cord in his heart," she wrote, because he seemed favorable to her side. In November, Seawell gave rights to Bell over property that Pleasant had deeded to Boone. Blakeman considered this a victory, but Teresa seemed lukewarm about the decision.[61] Like most of the half dozen cases she was party to that year, Teresa rarely won the victory over Pleasant she envisioned. And although she described Pleasant's appearances in court as disruptive and circus-like, Mary Ellen, nearly ninety years old, mustered her strength and met her courtroom battles head-on.

The courtroom was not the only place Pleasant received publicity in 1899. Earlier that year she had been the subject of an extensive exposé, titled "Queen of the Voodoos," in the Sunday *Chronicle*. The author of the piece, by most accounts, was James E. Brown Jr., one of Pleasant's former employees at the Octavia Street house and the son of James S. Brown, who ran the livery stable Pleasant supported. Teresa's diary reveals that she met regularly with Brown, who seemed anxious to publish his impressions of Pleasant's evil past. Bell wrote, "James E. Brown knows all of these circumstances as he was doing her writing and bookkeeping during many years."[62] Some have described Teresa and Brown as ringleaders of an "anti-Pleasant conspiracy" that developed in the last years of the nineteenth century.[63] It is difficult to discern how much Bell and Brown actually plotted Pleasant's demise, but they appeared to agree about Pleasant's character. Before Brown's article was published, Bell wrote, "James E. Brown came and told me of his articles on MEP, her life and wicked ways in general."[64] When the article appeared, Bell noted that "it told how many colored people she had robbed."[65] Brown told much more than that: He described her voodoo rituals, her character, and her "wonderful influence over men and women." "Whatever effect Mammy's voodoo art may have had upon her victims can never be known," Brown wrote, "but it is certain that she has shown wonderful power of persuasion that compels one to credit her with some sense outside of mere ability to argue."[66]

Published right after her insolvency case, the article also questioned her poverty: "People who are in a position to know say that she is worth considerably more than a quarter of a million dollars. This fact, however, will not help her creditors very much." Brown then related an exchange Pleasant had with a reporter: "She was asked what she intended to do with her creditors. 'Do,' she replied. 'Why, I am jes' sitting looking on. If they find anything, I'll get up and take it away from 'em. But they ain't going to find anything, so I won't need to disturb myself no how.'"[67] Masquerading as a poverty-stricken mammy may indeed have been one of the ways Pleasant tried to hold onto some of her property in the last years of her life. It is also likely that Pleasant had lost access to her wealth; most of it was tied up in pending lawsuits, and very little of her income was liquid.

Pleasant's ploy as the Bell's maid was also exposed in "Queen of the Voodoos." "Her white apron alone, to say nothing of the bunch of keys that always dangled from it, was worth thousands of dollars a year to her in making people believe that she was nothing but the honest old Southern nurse of the story book, and a faithful servant of a millionaire family," wrote Brown. Printed in the Sunday edition of the most widely read paper of the city, this article must have done extensive damage to Pleasant's chances for economic recovery.

Pleasant chose to focus instead on the depletion of the Bell estate by greedy attorneys. On November 9, 1899, the *San Francisco Call* reprinted excerpts from a letter Pleasant wrote to Judge Coffey, who was in charge of Fred Bell's guardianship case. The article, "'Mammy' Writes and Grills the Bench and Bar: Voices Her Opinion of Executors," included her admonition,

> Mr. Bell would have soon silenced those who said I had too much influence. . . . I have a good deal to say about the executors and lawyer for the Bell estate— selling their assets to pay their own debts. I told it to the lawyers and now I have told it you. . . . These are the kind of things I been saying that makes me such a bad woman in the estimation of people that are not straight themselves. I have said to them to the principals themselves, of the two I would rather be a corpse than a coward! . . . Now, this woman who has respect for the right and the truth would like to have you use your influence.[68]

Judge Coffey apparently did not take kindly to Pleasant's request and resented her prominence in the affair. He stated from the bench that Pleasant's role in the Bells' affairs was inappropriate.

She expended much energy on this battle with the judge. When Coffey refused to meet with her and stated that she had too much influence, it prompted her to respond. Although never spelling out the precise nature of her relationship with the Bells, Pleasant remained adamant about the fact that it was none of Judge Coffey's business. "I have always understood that you had a great deal to say about my influence with Mrs. Bell and the children," she wrote to the judge. "Now, Mr. Bell was a gentleman, and he knew what I was there for and I knew what I was there for; he knew what my influence was with his family," she continued. It is worth noting that this is one of the very few times Pleasant remarked on her relationship with Thomas Bell: "He should have known after twenty odd years, and died satisfied with me, and it shows very poor taste for any one after all these years to try and interfere from the bench or elsewhere."[69] Pleasant's efforts to keep the court from questioning her role in the Bell estate were entirely unsuccessful.

Pleasant lived the last five years of her life at Geneva Cottage, her property on San Jose Road (in south San Francisco) and in a house on Webster Street, nearer to the city center, that she also owned.[70] James Brown recalled Pleasant's move from her Octavia mansion to Geneva Cottage: "Driven out of the Bell mansion and seeking an abiding place where she might rusticate till the storm of her insolvency proceedings had blown over, she thought of Geneva Cottage, and taking with her as much of the Bell furniture as she could gather . . . she moved out to the old place."[71] The *San Francisco Examiner* stated that she raised chickens and pigs at Geneva Cottage during these years as part of her effort to feign poverty.[72] This may indeed be the case, as the City Directory of 1900 lists Pleasant's address as 2309 San Jose Avenue, the location of the cottage. In 1901, when Pleasant granted an interview to Isabel Fraser of the *Call* newspaper, however, she was living on Webster Street.

It was in the Webster Street house that Sam Davis, an author, friend, and editor of her autobiography, found Pleasant very ill in December 1901. He described the environment as "very plain quarters" and explained in the introduction to her autobiography that she had requested his presence because "she felt she was dying."[73] Davis also explained that he had offered Pleasant assistance a few years before; "She replied that she was not in any trouble and needed no assistance."[74] In November 1903, Pleasant moved to the home of friends, Olive and Lyman Sherwood, who lived in the same neighborhood, on Filbert Street. On January 11, 1904, at 10 A.M., Pleasant died at the home of her friends. Pleasant's longtime physician, Peter Kearney, signed the death certificate.[75] She was buried in the Sherwood family cemetery in Napa Valley the next day.

Bold headlines announced the death of Pleasant on January 12, 1904. "Mammy Pleasant Will Work Weird Spells No More," proclaimed the *San Francisco Examiner*, "Mysterious Old Negro Women, at 89, Ends a Life of Schemes and Varied Fortune."[76] According to this obituary, Pleasant had a "grim influence" over the family of Thomas Bell, a fact that was not lost on Fred Bell, who soon contested the will. Interestingly, not all the obituaries summed up her life in relation to the Bells. The *Chronicle* admitted that although her name had most recently been linked to Sarah Althea Hill, William Sharon, and Thomas Bell, "her claim to notability goes back a good deal further."[77] Under the subheading "Aided John Brown," this article repeated Pleasant's claim that she funded the raid on Harpers Ferry. Her death was hastened, according to "those who have been nearest her bedside," by "the grief over the ingratitude of those she felt were her chief debtors," and "the primary cause of her death was a broken heart."[78] Even the more sensational story in the *Examiner* described her as "friend of social arbiters" and "men and women who stood and stand high in the world's esteem."[79]

Like so many parts of her life, Pleasant's death caused tremendous dispute and litigation. According to one obituary, Pleasant had signed over her power of attorney to the Sherwoods just before she died; Lyman was a pension attorney himself.[80] In the week before she died Pleasant signed a new will leaving everything she had to the Sherwoods.[81] Lyman Sherwood filed the will for probate on January 15.[82] The confusion over her estate and her will began immediately, and lawsuits appeared inevitable. Less than three weeks after she died, Pleasant's will—dated a week before her death—was challenged by Frederick Bell.[83] Fred accused the Sherwoods of undue influence over Pleasant, who, he claimed, was not of sound mind or body when she made out her final will. Another will, dated December 22, 1902, left the estate to the Bell children and assigned Fred and Marie Bell as executors.[84] Not surprisingly, Fred Bell produced this will and with his attorney, Joseph Rothschild, filed an opposition in court. "We feel confident we can show that the Sherwood will was made under undue influence," Rothschild told the press. He explained, "Sam Davis, an oldtime friend and editor of the Carson *Appeal,* and Fred Bell had long been caring for the old woman, maintaining her at a private home on Webster Street."[85] According to this version, "they had made arrangements to have her moved to a place on Sutter Street when she was induced, a few weeks before her death, to go to the Sherwood home."[86]

Pleasant's estate inspired years of legal proceedings. The contents of the estate itself led to ancillary lawsuits. The lot on Sutter Street, adjacent to the home on Octavia Street, valued at $30,000 to $50,000, and diamond jewelry valued at $150,000—central components of Pleasant's estate—were already subjects of litigation when Pleasant died.[87] The jewelry, bought by Pleasant and kept in a safe deposit box at Donahoe-Kelly Bank, proved to be one of the most sensational parts of the estate. In May 1904, Pleasant's court assignee, now a Mr. W. H. Davis, revived a suit to recover the jewels in her name.[88] Teresa Bell opposed the suit, claiming that Pleasant was "merely her servant" and that the jewels were hers.[89] Reminiscent of the previous battles, Teresa Bell kept up the fight against Pleasant's estate for decades. Indeed, Teresa Bell's legal efforts to recover what she claimed was hers lasted into the 1920s.[90]

It was not until 1910, six years after Pleasant died, that her will was admitted to probate by none other than Judge Coffey, who had presided over so many of Pleasant's legal affairs.[91] All of Pleasant's possessions were left to the Sherwoods, including 114 acres in Sonoma County and the deeds and securities that were left in the safe deposit box at Donahoe-Kelly Bank.[92] No mention was made of the jewels. By that time, Pleasant's estate was valued at around $10,000—a far cry from the hundreds of thousands (or millions) she once owned.

It seems fair to say that by the end of her life, Pleasant had lost most of her property and capital to creditors, lawyers, and competitors. It is also clear that like many who settled in San Francisco and dabbled in gold, silver, and real estate, she made some poor investments and unwise financial decisions. Because of the tangled nature of the Bell and Pleasant finances and because much of what she owned was in other people's names, we will never know the exact amount of Pleasant's estate. Given that Thomas Bell was worth more than $30 million when he died in 1892—and they probably owned stock and property in common—we can surmise that Pleasant was at least a millionaire at certain points in her life.[93] Sam Davis, publisher of her autobiography, was convinced of this, and remarked, "Since she landed in San Francisco . . . she has made and checked out through the local banks over a million dollars."[94] What happened to her wealth is a puzzle for historians; however, it seems likely that she was an agent of both her success and her demise.

African American millionaires made easy targets for those concerned with maintaining white supremacy at the end of the nineteenth century. Mere homeowners and shopkeepers had been singled out for some of Reconstruction's most brutal violence only decades earlier.[95] Pleasant's visibility at the turn of the century was unprecedented for a black woman in any region of the United States: She appeared in court on a weekly basis for years, her name became synonymous with financial scandal, and we can surmise that most judges in the state knew her name. Her stature as a financial wizard and entrepreneur gained her the notoriety that was reserved for robber barons of the era. Indeed, she used some of the same tactics: vertical integration, real estate speculation, and inside trading on Comstock and other mines. Yet Pleasant's notoriety also stemmed from her manipulation of secrets, both financial and social. These kinds of strategies—a direct result of her boardinghouse business—are more difficult to identify and substantiate; they occurred in seemingly private places (dining rooms) but involved public institutions (banks).

It is not without reason that some point to an anti-Pleasant conspiracy in the 1890s: Lawyers, judges, creditors, and associates of the Bells hammered away at Pleasant until they nearly succeeded in ruining her. But to see her as a mere victim of this conspiracy would be to ignore her agency in a long en-trepreneurial career. Pleasant's financial and social strategies—often one and the same—yielded mixed results. During the course of her half-century in California she survived the boom-and-bust Gold Rush economy, the depres-sions of the 1870s and 1890s, the fluctuating silver markets, the changing demand for luxury accommodations, and shifting demographics that affected her clientele and her role as employer. Rather than describing her as helpless because her enterprise had dwindled to $10,000 and part of the Beltane ranch by 1910, it is probably more accurate to say that Pleasant's faculties were failing, and she was unable to hold on to all that she had once commanded. She also paid a price for some of her strategies and investments that proved unsuccessful. Perhaps masking herself as mammy to the Bells in the "House of Mystery" for three decades ultimately backfired. When word of her rich-es seeped out through the press during the many court cases of the 1890s, those with the most to lose (Fred Bell, Teresa Bell, and others) lashed out. Part of this process entailed unraveling the mammy charade.

The codes of racial and gender behavior forbade black women from gain-ing this type of stature, but Pleasant never abided by these conventions. In this way, Pleasant refused to live in the confined world offered to African Americans of her day and created a space—albeit beleaguered—where she could thrive in a style reserved for millionaires.

6

MAKING MAMMY WORK FOR YOU:
MARY ELLEN PLEASANT IN
POPULAR CULTURE

I am a whole theater unto myself.

MARY ELLEN PLEASANT, *Memoirs* (1902)

During her lifetime, Pleasant's image as a baby seller, mammy, voodoo queen, and madam appeared in cartoons, news stories, and headlines. These characterizations also found new life in U.S. popular culture of the twentieth century. Mary Ellen Pleasant has been a central character in at least seven novels, two plays, one television drama, and several films between 1922 and the present.[1] Pleasant's history—as it is woven into American popular culture—changes with the era and the genre.[2] Her birthplace, her color, her body, and her status have been reinvented in every decade of the twentieth century. Pleasant's story continues to attract authors, playwrights, and filmmakers, in part because of her role as a stand-in for America's most beloved stereotypes of black women. And as her story has moved across time, genre, and space, it has underscored the timeless attachment Americans have to these icons of Mammy, Jezebel, and the tragic mulatta.

Representations of Pleasant in print and visual culture often are amalgamations of stock characters and stereotypes of African Americans. The 1884 cartoon in *The Wasp,* for example, printed during the Sharon trials, pictures Pleasant as part mammy, part Jezebel, and full-time baby seller. This illustration, like the versions of Pleasant that appeared after her death, indicates the flexibility of Pleasant's representations within the limited range of images assigned to nineteenth-century African Americans. Although she wears the servant's or mammy's garb, white apron and collar, this cartoon version of Pleasant is not the fat, dark mammy audiences expected. She is slender, she wears a bonnet rather than a handkerchief, her legs are white, and she sports coquettish Victorian slippers. Here and elsewhere, Pleasant's image, like her historical legacy, defies the mammy stereotype without completely abandoning it. These representations of Pleasant also kept Jezebel and the tragic mulatta close to the surface, an ever-present reminder of the fear of miscegenation, hybridity, and border crossings that Pleasant inspired.[3]

Popular culture's romance with Pleasant has been melodramatic. Not only has she figured in melodramatic silent film and sentimental fiction, but the plots, settings, and texture of the novels, plays, and films, even those not formally identified as melodrama, share all the traits most often defined as melodramatic: sentimentality, an attachment to interior space and home, and a tendency to depict emotionally charged scenarios. This association between Pleasant and melodrama should not surprise us, for as Linda Williams so cogently argues, melodrama has been "the fundamental mode by which American mass culture has 'talked to itself' about the enduring moral dilemma of race."[4] Williams reminds us that black and white racial melodrama has leapt from stage to screen to courtroom, each new version "a partial attempt to explain the secret of American national identity in relation to that racial 'Other.'"[5] Melodramatic versions of Pleasant's story in twentieth- and twenty-first-century mass culture and media offer audiences new ways to reconcile the facts of Pleasant's power and her blackness as well as larger questions about the place of black people in the nation's past. Her first starring role in a racial melodrama was in the courtroom during the Sharon trials and later in the "House of Mystery" and the Beltane Ranch during her struggles with the Bell family. These episodes later became favorite reference points for novelists, playwrights, and filmmakers who appropriated Pleasant's real-life melodrama into fictional texts. As a whole, these texts demonstrate the ways in which audiences are both attracted to and repelled by the idea of mammy as a millionaire. Much like the tradition of minstrelsy, representations of Mary Ellen Pleasant reveal what Eric Lott describes as "the dialectical flickering of racial insult and racial envy."[6]

In the 1920s, just twenty years after her death, Mary Ellen Pleasant's legacy inspired a novel, a stage play, and a silent film. In all three genres, Pleasant appeared as a mammy. More than any other stereotype of African Americans—the Coon, the Sambo, or the Jezebel, for example—the mammy has been the most salient. Since the Civil War, the archetype has inspired songs, poems, and visual art. Recent scholarship details the extent of American attachment to mammy's actual existence. As Cheryl Thurber has shown, resurrecting the history of "real" mammies became a staple of the movement for a New South in the early twentieth century. The United Daughters of the Confederacy even presented a bill to the House of Representatives in 1923 to erect a memorial to her in the nation's capital.[7] Sentimental stories about mammy swept the nation between 1890 and 1940, and as Grace Elizabeth Hale explains, mammies—more than any other icon—rooted the New South in the fictions of the good old days of slavery.[8] Deborah Gray White and others have shown that the stereotype of mammy emerged from historical observations of black women's material realities during slavery.[9] But the belief in and celebration of an actual historic figure who was fat, very dark, happy to serve white masters, and subservient continued long after the myths of slavery and this stereotype were exposed.[10] Caricatures of Mammy Pleasant flourished outside of mammy's familiar home in the South, appearing in the American West and as far as London's theater district.

In 1922, untold numbers of Americans and Britons watched an actress depict Pleasant as mammy in the play *The Cat and the Canary,* which opened on Broadway and on the London stage. Mammy Pleasant is listed in the cast of characters in both productions, suggesting the presence of a black character if not an actual historic figure. Just four years later, Charles Caldwell Dobie's 1926 novel, *Less Than Kin,* sold at least 7,000 copies, and although Pleasant's name was changed to "Mammy Parsons," Dobie made it clear in the press, as did book reviewers, that Pleasant inspired his novel. Again, in 1927, audiences witnessed Pleasant as mammy in the silent film *The Cat and the Canary,* which became one of Universal Pictures' greatest successes of the decade. These texts of the 1920s resurrected California's mammy for a national and international public, transforming her into a fictional character for the first time.

The novel *Less Than Kin* (1926) by Charles Caldwell Dobie tells the story of a white child, Adrienne, and her life with Mammy Parsons—the character based on Mary Ellen Pleasant—in Victorian San Francisco. Dobie, born in San Francisco in 1881, made a career out of writing novels and short stories. A journalist by trade, Dobie sold his first story in 1910 and thereafter was a regular contributor to *Harper's, Scribner's,* and other literary magazines. In 1925 and 1926, he wrote a daily column on arts and letters for the *San Francisco Bulletin* under the pen name "The Caliph." Admired for his witty commentary about the city, Dobie became best known for the "San Francisciana" recorded in his books *San Francisco: A Pageant* (1933) and *San Francisco's Chinatown* (1936).

Dobie remembered watching Pleasant conduct her business in San Francisco when he was a child, and these memories informed *Less Than Kin.* He recalled Pleasant as "a black witch" who terrorized the inhabitants of the mansion on Octavia Street.[11] In his 1933 book of recollections, *San Francisco: A Pageant,* Dobie wrote, "I remember her when I was a child. I used to see her going to market every morning with her folded plaid shawl over her shoulder and her spotless white kerchief folded across her breast. Her costume never varied. And she always wore a large hat of coarsely woven straw tied down by rusty black strings." His description of her also referred to Pleasant's mixed ancestry, something he emphasized in his novel. "She had another peculiarity, for an octoroon, particularly. She had one blue eye," he claimed.[12] This image of Pleasant from his childhood, when he feared the "octoroon" woman, translated nicely into fiction, he remarked in one of his radio broadcasts. "So with just her shadowy figure in mind," Dobie explained, "plus gossip of her that I had heard around the family circle, I made up the character of Mammy Parsons for my book."[13]

The novel unfolds at the servant's cottage of Laguna Vista, a run-down estate north of San Francisco, where Adrienne lives with a woman she calls "Mammy," whose name is Selina Parsons. It is clear from the description of Parsons's business success in San Francisco that Selina Parsons is a fictionalized version of Mary Ellen Pleasant. A reviewer for the *New York Times* wrote, "To any one familiar with San Francisco's history it is evident that in Selina Parsons, the dominant figure of the story, he has reconstructed the career of an actual person, the notorious Mammy Pleasance."[14] The reviewer made plain the centrality of Pleasant's history to the text: "By simply lifting this colorful personality out of her authentic environment and by putting her between the covers of his book, Mr. Dobie had a fascinating story ready-made to his hand."[15] This ready-made quality of Pleasant's history appealed to Dobie and the many novelists who followed. Literary agents and publishing houses recognized all the trappings of a marketable story: a black witch, sordid secrets, Gold Rush fortunes, and sexual indiscretions of all types.

The plot of Dobie's novel concerns the secret past that brought a white child and a black woman into this arrangement of cohabitation. This juxtaposition of a white child and black mammy was a familiar and favorite one in the literature of the period.[16] The 1920s witnessed a renewed fascination with the plantation in American arts and letters. But this is not the typical plantation novel, nor is it the comforting black-white dyad so perfectly represented by the Shirley Temple–Bill "Bojangles" Robinson films of the next decade. Instead, readers find something immediately disconcerting in the Parsons character and her control over the white child. Parsons's power emanates from the fact that she knows the secret that explains their connection. The novel traces their relationship as Adrienne moves from trust and fascination to fear and terror. Early in the novel Adrienne realizes that "Mammy *was* a nigger. . . . And that was why Mammy upon occasion told terrifying stories about fig-black people, until she lay in a stupor, with a white foam on her lips."[17] This frightening discovery is followed by one that is equally damning: Adrienne and Mammy Parsons are kin. Adrienne's mother was distantly related to Parsons's former owner and father.

In Dobie's novel, Selina Parsons was the child of a slaveowner named Sinclair (Adrienne's grandfather) and his slave. When Adrienne discovers this, she watches Mammy and vows, "Never, again, under the same roof with this black kinswoman. She would die first."[18] It is the fact of kinship between black and white—miscegenation—that is the most horrifying revelation for Adrienne and, presumably, for the novel's audience. Parsons's power over the child appears daunting and unnatural. The character who represents Mary Ellen Pleasant restricts the white girl's access to the outside world and to her "natural family"—other white members of the Sinclair family. It is not surprising that Dobie chooses to represent Pleasant as a mysterious black mammy who harbors family secrets. Knowing San Franciscans' secrets—their investments, their desires, their indiscretions—was precisely how Pleasant made her fortune. The real-life dramas of the *Sharon v. Sharon* divorce case and her cohabitation with the Bell family provided ample material for Dobie's novel. Pleasant was accused of keeping both Sarah Hill and Teresa Bell from more natural relations with white people.

By today's standards the novel received tremendous publicity. It was reviewed by newspapers across the country: the Philadelphia *Enquirer,* Providence *Journal,* New Orleans *Times Picayune,* Hartford *Courant,* Kansas City *Journal,* and Salt Lake City *Telegram,* to name a few. To herald the book's second printing, Dobie's publisher took out quarter-page ads in *Harper's* and *Atlantic* magazines.[19] Furthermore, as his publisher was quick to remind Dobie, John Day Company spent sixty cents per copy on advertising, a very generous allotment.[20] The book was reissued in 1935 by D. Appleton-Century Company with a new foreword by San Francisco writer Gertrude Atherton.[21]

There were also plans for a feature-length film based on Dobie's book. In a radio program shortly after the publication of *Less Than Kin,* Dobie announced that Hollywood movie star Deanna Durbin would be playing Adrienne but that "Mammy proved a stumbling block. Now if Mammy were Spanish or Indian . . . but then Hollywood draws the color line." Dobie appeared uncharacteristically concerned with racism in the entertainment industry when it cut into his profit. His agent pitched the story to at least five studios. After much haggling with Universal Pictures, however, the studio dropped the film in 1928.[22] The success of another Universal film based on Pleasant's story, *The Cat and the Canary,* which appeared the preceding year, probably squelched interest in Dobie's film.

Playwright John Willard, like Dobie, may have had first-hand impressions of Pleasant. Born in San Francisco in 1885, John A. Willard was the son of an artist named John Willard Clawson, who, according to Helen Holdredge, sketched the Sharon trial.[23] If Holdredge is correct, it is quite possible that Willard grew up hearing stories about Pleasant that he used as inspiration for *The Cat and the Canary*. As an adult Willard had a diverse career working as a miner, pilot, and actor. He appeared in at least eight productions before he wrote and acted in the play that became so successful.[24]

The Cat and the Canary: A Melodrama in Three Acts opened on February 7, 1922, at the National Theatre in New York City. Creating quite a stir on Broadway, the play earned rave reviews.[25] Described in *Life* as "a certified Grade A thriller in which maniacs and voodoo women . . . glide in and out of the rooms of an old house," it quickly became the thriller of the season.[26] "It is the kind of play Poe would have written," claimed the reviewer from the New York *Sun*. The show stayed on Broadway for nearly eight months and opened at the Shaftesbury Theater in London on Halloween of the same year, where it also enjoyed a successful run of eight months.[27] In 1937, during one of the many revivals of the play, the *New York Times* paid particular attention to the character of the "West Indian voodoo woman" in what it called a "spook show revival."[28]

Melodrama was a particularly apt genre for Pleasant's character to make her stage debut; it is sensational, emotional, and often a drama of race relations and identity.[29] *The Cat and the Canary* delivered on all counts. The entire play is set inside the house, and the drama focuses on the women and their fear of a mysterious presence—perhaps the voodoo woman, the character of Pleasant. Family melodramas such as this one concern themselves with the private sphere and foreground female subjectivity and feelings. This drama, like the novel *Less Than Kin,* involved a racial mystery. What was this mammy or voodoo witch doing in the same house with this white family and their friends? The action of the play centered around the reading of Mr. West's will, which had been locked away in his house for twenty years. Mr. West, like Thomas Bell, lived in a huge Victorian mansion, modeled after Pleasant's house on Octavia Street. All the characters have pseudonyms except Pleasant, who is listed in the cast of characters as Mammy Pleasant. Pleasant was the only one in the house when various members of the West family arrived one dark and stormy night for the reading of the will; she had been living there since West's death.[30]

When *The Cat and the Canary* opened on Broadway, the part of Mammy Pleasant was played by Blanche Friderici, a white actress in blackface. She is present in almost every scene, often lurking in the background in her maid's uniform, with a vacant or bewildered look in her eyes. Willard wrote Pleasant's speech in an intermittent black dialect, just enough to assure the audience that she was really black. When the play opens and the attorney asks Mammy whether she has been "faithful to her trust," she replies "I certainly has. I stuck right here guarding the old place all the time."[31] The intimacy between Pleasant and the white characters is reinforced by the close quarters of the "haunted" house. All of the action takes place in two rooms: the library, where the will is first read, and the bedroom of the heir, Annabelle West. As the drama unfolds, it is clear that one of the members of the family is trying to cheat Annabelle out of her money by driving her crazy. There is a clause in the will that prevents the first heir from inheriting the fortune if she is clinically insane. The suggestion that Pleasant may be terrorizing Annabelle runs throughout the drama.

Intimacy between the young, nervous Annabelle and the devious Mammy Pleasant is a standard fixture in *The Cat and the Canary,* both the play and the later film version. Although the play is consciously set in the 1920s—flapper attire included—plantation references abound. In the second act, Annabelle and Pleasant interact as mistress and mammy: Annabelle asks Mammy to help her dress and treats her as servant and confidante. Pleasant appears to know all the secrets of the West family fortune; she is there when it is first discovered that someone broke into the safe to read the will, she seems to have been in the room when the attorney, Mr. Crosby, was murdered, and she was the only one with Mr. West when he died. She is also, for a time, one of the suspects. Annabelle's cousin Paul is the first to realize that one of the family members in the house that night is trying to scare Annabelle into madness in the hope of inheriting the money. Paul suggests, "Give Mammy Pleasant a thought," but Annabelle refuses to consider the possibility that Mammy Pleasant is related to her and a member of the family.[32] In the end, another male cousin is the culprit. But the mere suggestion that Annabelle may be related to her mammy is a powerful supposition in this 1920s drama, raising the question of miscegenation. Like Selina Parsons in *Less Than Kin,* Mammy would have to be a child of white and black ancestry if she were the next heir—and part of the West family. This question of miscegenation in Pleasant's past appears in much of the historical and popular literature about her as well. Drawing on the historical memory of this "real life" mystery may have been part of Willard's plan; it was most definitely part of Dobie's.

This story proved very appealing to the motion picture industry. *The Cat and the Canary* was made into an influential silent film in 1927, and three remakes followed.[33] The 1927 film, which bore the same title and followed the script of the play very closely, was stylized by the acclaimed European director Paul Leni. One of many German émigrés who influenced Hollywood films substantially in the 1920s, Leni had a particular talent for set design.[34]

His attention to the eerie elements of the drama and his use of techniques associated with German expressionism helped to make the film a huge success for Universal Pictures. To this day it is considered a classic of the thriller and mystery genre.[35]

Film critics and historians are fond of this production, dubbing it Leni's best work, a prototype, or a classic of the silent film era. Although much was made of the leading actress of the film, Laura LaPlante, and the cinematic techniques such as severe chiaroscuro lighting, no mention is made of the Mammy Pleasant character in the reviews or film criticism. In this first filmic version of *The Cat and the Canary*, Pleasant is played by a white woman, Martha Wilcox, who is not in blackface but is listed as "Mammy Pleasant" in the film's cast of characters. It was not unusual for blacks to be played by whites in early film history, as the work of D. W. Griffith demonstrates.[36] The legacy of minstrelsy and the restrictions against hiring black performers in Hollywood meant that audiences expected whites to play black characters.[37] Pleasant's blackness is marked not by skin color but by the character's actions and by the special effects of the film: She walks out of shadows, projects her shadow on other characters, and generally spooks the members of the West family. Her movements are reminiscent of Lydia, the tragic mulatta in *The Birth of a Nation*, perpetuating the tradition of Pleasant as an amalgamation of stereotypes.

Mary Ellen Pleasant, in the role of mammy, was a decided success throughout the decade. That certain audiences might have taken comfort in these depictions of Pleasant as mammy in the 1920s makes sense given what we know about the era. The resurgence of the Ku Klux Klan, the anxiety about evolution and whiteness as evidenced by the Scopes Trial, and the rearticulation of the Old South in popular culture all heightened concern over racial classification, hierarchies, and color.[38] As Peggy Pascoe shows in her assessment of miscegenation law of the period, it is not the clarity of racial definitions but their instability that defined this era.[39] The images of a mammy, harking back to the "good old days" of slavery, is part of what audiences found attractive about the Pleasant character in the stage play and film of *The Cat and the Canary* and the novel *Less Than Kin*.

Yet representations of Pleasant did not always conform entirely to the stereotype of mammy. In *Less Than Kin*, for example, Pleasant is Mammy Parsons, but she links Adrienne to a history of miscegenation and is thus sexualized in a way that mammies usually are not. Pleasant's character in this text reprises the oversexed Jezebel and the tragic mulatta as well as the desexualized mammy. Numerous scholars have pointed to the relationship between the sexualization of black women in popular culture and the history of slavery.[40] Conditions of slave women's lives linked them to corporal, lascivious notions before and after the Civil War. Slavery meant, among other things, that black women's skirts often were hiked up to their thighs in the rice fields, their breasts exposed beneath flimsy burlap shifts in the cotton fields, and their bodies stripped and displayed on the auction block.[41]

America's fascination with the tragic mulatta, skin color, and miscegenation prevailed as a bedrock of twentieth-century political, cultural, and intellectual life.[42] It should come as no surprise that much of the twentieth-century popular culture about Mary Ellen Pleasant pivots on the question or problem of her color, her race mixing, and her parentage. Her refusal to hide her relationship to white men and women was a central theme of her life, as the Sharon and Bell trials made clear.

Fixation on skin color and miscegenation figures prominently in *Less Than Kin*. Pleasant's character (Parsons) has what Dobie repeatedly calls "jungle blood." Try as she might, Parsons can never escape the fact of her blackness even though she is related to the white Sinclairs: "In spite of her light coloring, in spite of her patrician features, in spite of her straight hair, some subtle tint of the dark taint within her crept to the surface to damn her, forever."[43] The Parsons character, though obviously of a certain stature, can never be a real Sinclair. "There was something cool about her," writes Dobie, "a chilled strain that somehow congealed the ripe jungle blood in her veins."[44] Another character in *Less Than Kin,* Dustin Huntley, a friend of the Sinclair family, wonders about Parsons' skin color: "Only her faintly dark coloring betrayed her negro blood. Her lips were thin and tight lipped with a Saxon determination, her brow high and wider than her lower face, her nose strong and clean and Roman. But in her eyes . . . were hidden fathomless pools, murky and haunted like a harried thing; eyes in which the jungle and the slave-ship and the human market-place spoke; eyes capable of all gentleness and cruelty and degradation."[45] Huntley found it hard to believe that this nice black mammy was really a thief, a blackmailer, and a "procuress" like everyone said.

Mixed blood marked Pleasant as a mulatta, but a penchant for dubious sexual practices clearly recalls the Jezebel myth. In much of the fiction and folklore, Pleasant's character has adulterous relationships with black and white men. Some have also implied that she made "sapphic" gestures toward young white women. One author of a study on Sharon's divorce suggested that at precisely the time Pleasant "felt rich and powerful," her memoirs reveal "errant words and phrases that suggest something *outré* in her relationships with young ladies."[46] In addition to being too friendly with women, she is accused of enticing, tricking, and teasing men. This also falls squarely within the tradition of the Jezebel who often tricks men into having sex with her and then seizes their wealth or power. Most caricatures of Pleasant in popular culture suggest that Pleasant's greatest sin—to both nineteenth- and twentieth-century observers—may have been her refusal to play the role of man's helpmate. Indeed, most representations imply that Pleasant had more interest in helping women than she did in helping men.[47]

Notions about black sexuality and power shifted in important ways after the cultural and political movements of the 1960s. Just as stereotypes of African Americans shifted dramatically during Reconstruction, the feminist and black power movements were the catalysts for new fears of black people as dangerous, armed, and politically threatening. At the same time, scholars pressured the academy to include the histories of white women and people of color. It became more feasible to reclaim black heroines and write them into history. Responding to this changing political landscape, writers and artists retrieved Pleasant's legacy and introduced her to new generations of readers. The issues of gender, sex, and color continued to predominate in the literature about Pleasant, but authors of the post–civil rights era take drastically different approaches. Whether Pleasant could be a heroine, given her often scandalous past, was a question novelists would take up in one form or another. Novels that reshape the Pleasant story have been published in each of the last three decades.

Frank Yerby's novel *Devilseed,* published in 1984, marked the end of his prolific career. Yerby had written thirty novels on a range of topics before publishing this one about Gold Rush San Francisco. His novels, most of them historical, are set all over the world: from the kingdom of Dahomey in West Africa to ancient Greece to Moorish Spain. In 1944 Yerby won the O. Henry Memorial Award for his short story "Health Card," and in 1946 his first novel, *The Foxes of Harrow,* became an instant bestseller. Yerby experienced phenomenal success as a novelist and, according to one source, was for a time the wealthiest black writer in history.[48] By the 1960s Yerby had acquired a reputation as "the prince of pulpsters," writing what he called costume novels.[49] *Devilseed* features French whore and social climber Mireille Duclos, and her competition, Mary Ellen Pleasant, as its leading characters. Like his previous novels, this one shows Yerby's interest in historical settings as well as sexual drama.

Pleasant appears not as a mammy or Jezebel per se but as a social and financial power broker. The character of Mireille bears a slight resemblance to Sarah Althea Hill (Senator Sharon's mistress), but she becomes Pleasant's rival, not her protégé. The novel is a mélange of fictional characters and ones, like Pleasant, who are modeled after historic figures of Gold Rush San Francisco. Details about Pleasant's life are sprinkled throughout the raunchy story line, and Thomas Bell and Teresa Bell are also mentioned by name, as are many of Pleasant's homes and properties. In particular, the book resurrects Pleasant's role as a madam.

Mireille first meets Pleasant when she is summoned to the best known of Pleasant's boardinghouses at 920 Washington Street. Pleasant has hatched a scheme to get waterfront property from Mireille and make it look as though she is doing her a favor. When Mireille asks Pleasant whether she "operates an employment agency for quadroon tarts or a nest of spies," Pleasant answers, "A little of both."[50] Jasmine, Mireille's maid and a quadroon prostitute, explains Pleasant's background to her inquiring boss: "Her's a little darker than you or me, but not much. She's been passing all her life. . . . The truth was they couldn't figger out what she was, and they was betting she was Eyetalian or Greek or some other o' them dark-complexion foreigners. . . . Her papa was a white man, and her mama was a quadroon from Haiti."[51] As in the earlier novels, color is central to the story, and the characters in *Devilseed* are explicit about the fact that Pleasant's father was white. This version of Pleasant's background does not make her exceptional in Yerby's San Francisco, which is populated with persons of all colors, races, and ethnic backgrounds. In fact, miscegenation and other forms of illicit sexual activity are one of Yerby's central preoccupations.

In Yerby's text, however, Pleasant is no more unpleasant or sexualized than the rest of her contemporaries. In the introduction to another novel, Yerby states that he did not make black characters "either more or less than what they were."[52] The same can certainly be said for *Devilseed;* black characters are not romanticized or even admirable. Yerby's San Francisco is rough and nasty, and so is everyone in it. Pleasant is not the reincarnation of evil— although several characters including Mireille refer to her as the wickedest woman of San Francisco—she is but one character in a cast of thousands, all with dubious backgrounds and intentions.

What does make Pleasant exceptional in this cast—and in African American history—is her success. The maid explains, "She owns three first-class boardinghouses—exclusive supper clubs, really, serving th' best damn food in town. A saloon on Sansome Street, a livery stable, three laundries, and more waterfront property than you can shake a stick at."[53] The narrative follows Mireille's quest to become as powerful as Pleasant. "I like you," she says to Mary Ellen. "You're all I've always wanted to be—and failed. Mistress of yourself. And of—the world."[54]

What Pleasant does not have, in this narrative, is the demeanor of a mammy. In fact, notes Mireille, Pleasant "had not one mammy-like characteristic to her name: neither warmth, nor sentimentality, nor even—love."[55] It is this heartlessness, not the color of her skin, that renders Pleasant unlike her female contemporaries in the novel. Yerby rewrites the legend of Pleasant as mammy, choosing instead to portray her as a relentless operator. *Devilseed* makes much of Pleasant's supposed career as a baby seller—hardly the kind of activity a stereotypical mammy would engage in. Once again, this picks up on scenes from "real life"—she was accused of being a baby seller in the Sharon divorce trial while trying to convince the judge that Sharon and Hill were married. In *Devilseed,* Pleasant helps Mireille convince a wealthy judge that she is pregnant with his child to procure the judge's fortune. By the end of the novel the two characters are competing for enormous profits in quicksilver mining, referencing the fights between Pleasant and Teresa Bell in the 1890s. When Mireille causes Pleasant to lose her fortune, Pleasant sells Mireille's teenage daughter into the opium and sex dens of San Francisco's Chinatown.

In this novel, the character of Mary Ellen Pleasant engages in heartless deeds, not because she is a voodoo queen with African blood, as in *Less Than Kin,* but because like most of her male contemporaries, she is out for profit. It is a much more accurate depiction of Pleasant's technique. Yerby does not paint Pleasant as a leader of black people; the other black characters in *Devilseed* fear her or work for her. Mireille's coach driver, James Swithers, for example, is one of Pleasant's spies who functioned as a sort of double agent spying on the two women; he probably is modeled after the black waiters and porters Pleasant employed in her boardinghouses. In one telling passage, Swithers explains how Pleasant's use of black labor outwits her elite, white clientele: "I reckons some of them gentlemens what eats in Madame Pleasant's boardinghouses must of run off at th' mouf in front of them nigger waiters of hern. Most whitefolks plumb fergits that black barbers and waiters and sichlike ain't sticks o' furniture. Madame Pleasant is got hern trained. Them fellas kin tell a real hot stock market tip, fer instance, from one that ain't worth much."[56] Yerby's refusal to romanticize black characters yields curious results in his characterization of Pleasant. First, she appears unlike the other female characters in the novel, who are sex-obsessed, and like the male elite, who are power-obsessed. Pleasant is the only female character who is not constantly engaged in some sort of illicit sexual activity. Pleasant is "other" not because of her gender, her sexual proclivities, her race, color, or penchant for voodoo; her otherness stems from her association with so-called masculine traits, especially her love for profit and her detachment from emotional matters. It is her refusal to play helpmate, again, that Yerby chooses to emphasize. Pleasant's characterizations in *Less Than Kin* and *Devilseed,* though separated by sixty years, are pre-occupied with matters of sexual relations, color, power, and trickery—all favorite concerns of Jezebels and typical of racial melodrama. In Yerby's and Dobie's texts, she is governed by her will to control men and manipulate family dynamics, traits that are reminiscent of a plantation Jezebel. These authors locate Pleasant's otherness in her sexual and economic power and her ability to disarm male authority.

Restoring and recreating Pleasant's legacy in the face of persistent stereotypes is the purpose behind *Free Enterprise,* published in 1993. Michelle Cliff's rendering of Pleasant reveals an extraordinary figure, but of a very different ilk than the previous representations. Like Yerby, Cliff is clearly aware of the myths that have shaped Pleasant's legacy. She is particularly interested in the way in which the stereotypes of voodoo queen, mammy, and Jezebel have overshadowed Pleasant's role in the abolitionist movement. Cliff explains in an interview what it was about Pleasant that attracted her: "Pleasant defeats every stereotype of an African-American woman in the nineteenth century: she was a successful businesswoman, an entrepreneur; she was always a revolutionary, and she never gave up the cause, even after the failure of the raid on Harpers Ferry."[57] A writer of fiction, prose, and poetry, Cliff has long been interested in the myths and silences surrounding black women's history. In a 1979 article, "The Resonance of Interruption," Cliff addresses the difficulties of locating black women's words given the interruptions and constraints of their lives.[58] In *Free Enterprise,* the author turns her attention to the invisible women of the abolitionist movement. She gives voice to black women of the past and attempts to break down the genres that have ignored or concealed this history: "I can't stand the idea of the novel here, the history there, the biography there. I can't see why these things can't be mixed up. We have to bring our imagination to our history, because so much has been lost."[59]

Free Enterprise is about the enterprise of freedom—the abolitionist movement—and Mary Ellen Pleasant is one of the central figures of the novel and of the movement, as Cliff depicts it. A testimonial to the histories of "lost" black women, the novel carefully connects Pleasant's story to those of her contemporaries: Harriet Tubman, Frances Ellen Watkins Harper, and Mary Ann Shadd Cary. Pleasant is introduced to the reader in a scene at Boston's Tremont Temple in 1858 at a Frances E. W. Harper lecture. In a series of letters, flashbacks, and memories, Cliff reveals Pleasant's history—a past that has been neglected by the official recorders.

In Cliff's novel, Pleasant bemoans the version of the past that "has been printed, bound, and gagged, resides in schools, libraries, the majority unconscious. Serves the common good. Does not cause trouble."[60] "There would soon enough be no one who knew the real story," Cliff writes. To remedy this historical amnesia, *Free Enterprise,* like *Devilseed,* is peppered with recognizable elements from Pleasant's past: her boardinghouses, her association with John Brown, and her San Francisco businesses. Fictionalized conversations reveal a tough capitalist who has abolitionist zeal. Cliff creates a Pleasant who is dedicated to the enterprise of freedom, the memory of fellow abolitionists and of John Brown's raid in particular: "The failure of their enterprise haunted her. At times a bitterness burned inside her, threatening to rise in her gullet and cut off her breath. She placed the origin of the burning in October 1859, when Harriet Tubman had been disregarded and Captain Brown seized the (wrong) day." Harriet Tubman had warned against the attack at Harpers Ferry on that particular day, as Cliff describes it, but Brown had proceeded and died during the raid. Pleasant's collaboration "has gone undetected" and "will go to her grave with her."[61]

This description of John Brown's raid—in which Tubman's word is ignored—is not part of the historical record. And although there is evidence to support the claim that Pleasant was in Chatham and involved in the planning of the raid (see chapter 2) there is no such evidence that Tubman was also involved in the raid. This question of evidence is, of course, part of Cliff's larger point: If women are erased from official versions, how do we know that they were not there?[62]

Cliff's desire to render Pleasant as a black feminist icon works well in her depiction of the abolitionist movement. But reclaiming Pleasant the capitalist is equally important to the author: "She is a woman who travels first-class. She is a successful businesswoman in San Francisco, hotel keeper in that wide-open city, entrepreneur and woman of property, investor in the opening of the West: woman of the year with just the right amount of mystery to keep the sharks at bay."[63] Cliff makes no apology for Pleasant's financial ventures. But because slavery is essential to the development of industry, capitalism, and the West—indeed, free enterprise in the nineteenth century relies on it—being a first-class businesswoman meant one necessarily dabbled in the wrong kind of enterprise. The contradiction of entrepreneurial success and freedom fighting—so much a part of Pleasant's day-to-day life—is precisely what Cliff means to explore.[64] As she explains, the novel is "really about how people connected and worked as resisters and collaborators to the slave trade."[65]

Pleasant's fictionalized conversations with John Brown show how this writer grapples with the marriage of freedom and slavery. In *Free Enterprise,* Pleasant argues with Brown about the importance of African Americans owning property. Cliff's Pleasant writes, "I worried, as I told him, that he saw our people's experience as somehow ennobling; that we were *better* than capitalism, since we had been crucified by it."[66] Brown asks Pleasant, in another telling exchange, "But, my dear friend . . . why is private property so important to you?" Pleasant responds, "Because in this world, Captain, property ownership equals power. And in this world, I cannot and do not wish to contemplate the next, we need as much power as we can get. We are not an otherworldly people, Captain. We are of this world and this time."[67] It is here that Cliff captures, in an imaginative way, the dilemma faced by African Americans during Reconstruction: Turning away from the state and the system that enslaved them, refusing to own property, and refusing to vote were not viable options. Nor, as Cliff correctly asserts, were they an option that Mary Ellen Pleasant would have ever considered.

In many ways *Free Enterprise* is intended to counter the earlier narratives—specifically Helen Holdredge's *Mammy Pleasant*—that have stood for the history of Mary Ellen Pleasant. It is in this capacity that Cliff is at her best. Cliff strikes out against the simplistic association of Pleasant with mammy and records a more nuanced—and accurate—reading of the significance of the stereotype:

> Of course, she was careful, knowing that commerce was not considered her concern. [Pleasant] began her empire building by embodying Mammydom, as much as she grated against the word, the notion. . . .
>
> To further quell any unease that she was stepping across, over, and through, Mary Ellen Pleasant dressed as a dignified, unobtrusive houseservant, no handkerchief head, but black alpaca dress, white apron, lace cap.
>
> So she could move among them easily, in and out of any station they required. Disguised.[68]

As a celebration of Pleasant's contradictory status as revolutionary and capitalist, *Free Enterprise* triumphs. Others have applauded this aspect of the novel. Literary scholar Deborah McDowell explains, "To her credit, [Cliff] has not written a morality play in which the wolf of free enterprise downs the lamb of political dissent."[69] Indeed, in Cliff's novel, "the wolf and lamb can and must lie down together."[70] Cliff creates a freedom fighter who understands the market economy—a far cry from Dobie's Mammy Parsons and Holdredge's Mammy Pleasant.

To a certain extent Cliff romanticizes Pleasant's capitalist endeavors. It is a capitalism that can serve feminist, antiracist agendas. Yet both Cliff's and Yerby's texts point to the difficulty of grappling with the contradictions of Pleasant's life. Their work reminds us that although "the end of the innocent notion of the essential black subject" is upon us, according to Stuart Hall, refashioning the "new black subject" in all her complexities is a difficult task indeed.[71]

The latest novels, *Pale Truth* (2000) and *Sister Noon* (2001), follow in the tradition of Helen Holdredge; Pleasant is associated with voodoo and someone to be feared. These authors revive myths that Holdredge perpetuated while weaving a good story and borrowing tidbits from the historical record. One cannot fault them for such efforts, although these texts are decidedly less complicated and less concerned with the contradictions of Pleasant's life than Michelle Cliff's. *Pale Truth*, the first in a historical trilogy celebrating California's past, opens with the birth of light-skinned Mary Ellen to her voodoo queen mother Delila. Her baby "had the strangest eyes she had ever seen. . . . One eye appeared to be green, the other blue or black."[72] The melodramatic text sticks close to the narrative of Pleasant's story as Holdredge describes it, covering Pleasant's life from birth to 1853. Described as a "certainly historically accurate novel" and "hardly subtle" by reviewers, it includes dramatic retellings of life on a Georgia plantation, Pleasant's journey to San Francisco, and her early days in the city passing as a white woman.[73] Racial melodrama greets the reader at every turn. Nearly fifty years after *Mammy Pleasant* was heralded by some as a definitive source on the San Francisco entrepreneur, *Pale Truth*, a novel filled with unsubstantiated versions of Pleasant's past, is again being celebrated as historically accurate. This text reminds readers of the new century that the blurring of fact and fiction is the most salient characteristic of the story of Pleasant.

Karen Joy Fowler's connection to Helen Holdredge is more explicit than previous authors'; Fowler mentions the Holdredge collection in her acknowledgments, and she published with G. P. Putnam's Sons, who in 1953 released *Mammy Pleasant* and in 1954 *Mammy Pleasant's Partner*. *Sister Noon* takes place in the 1890s, when Pleasant is at the peak of her powers. It opens with a flashback to the 1850s, when Mary Ellen Pleasant attended a ball passing as a white woman, but by the end of the evening she has told the guests the truth about her color, ending the racial masquerade. Again, much attention is paid to Pleasant's coloring and the secrets she harbors about others. Fowler makes the mysteries of Pleasant's past a central component of the novel, consistently referring to different beliefs, versions of the same event, and the press coverage about her. "How did a colored woman, an ex-slave, come to have so much money and influence, San Francisco asked itself, and gave itself three possible answers," writes Fowler.[74] The three answers in *Sister Noon* are quite plausible: that she rose to power and prominence through cooking, "a system of carefully managed secrets," or voodoo.[75] Of these possibilities, voodoo seems to be the most popular choice for Pleasant's fictional contemporaries.

One of the curiosities of these recent depictions of Pleasant is the way in which they have chosen voodoo as the preferred explanation of Pleasant's power. If racial melodrama has served to underscore the nation's uneasy relation to the racial "other," these novels suggest that Pleasant continues to reside in the farthest reaches of otherness, where black people use voodoo. As a character in *Sister Noon* defines it, voodoo is "black arts aimed at the destruction of the white race."[76] To Fowler's credit, she is also taking aim at the myths about voodoo, and her white characters busy themselves with all forms of the occult. After eighty years of stage, film, and fiction, we once again return to a dark house with a scary mulatta witch named Mammy.

Between 1922 and 2002, more than a dozen novels, films, and stage plays adopted Pleasant's story as their centerpiece. Clearly, Pleasant and her legacy captured the imagination of authors, directors, and playwrights. The ways Pleasant is represented in fiction, drama, and film shift dramatically over the course of the twentieth century but often return us to the same themes in a melodramatic vein. From a well-dressed African-blooded voodoo queen to an enterprising freedom fighter and entrepreneur, Pleasant's character has been molded into new forms to fit new social and material realities.

For Charles Dobie, writing in the 1920s, Pleasant brought danger and sin to the lives of innocent victims in nineteenth-century San Francisco. His novel reached large audiences at a time of reactionary race politics, and it helped to reinforce the stereotype of Pleasant as savage and otherworldly. A resident of San Francisco, Dobie promoted his version of Pleasant's past in a newspaper column and on the radio, claiming an "authentic" knowledge of his protagonist. Pleasant is immortalized as a mammy-gone-wrong in *Less Than Kin* and *The Cat and the Canary*. In these texts, however, Pleasant also appears as a Jezebel. In the post–civil rights era, two novels by black authors subvert earlier legends and versions of Pleasant's past. As we have seen, Yerby and Cliff do replace old mythology, albeit in very different ways. Yerby creates an emasculating black woman who has more in common with the Gilded Age robber barons than with her black employees and protégées. In Cliff's *Free Enterprise*, Pleasant has been transformed into a feminist, gun-toting abolitionist with a bankroll.

These fictionalized versions of Mary Ellen Pleasant rely on her own performative strategies: She did indeed appear differently to different audiences in her own life.[77] When necessary she could "embody Mammydom," and she could just as easily travel first class. What these fictional versions of Pleasant tell us is that her life challenged the boundaries that defined and controlled African American women in the nineteenth century. Pleasant does not conform neatly to common stereotypes: the heroic slave, the devoted mammy, the two-bit floozy. Perhaps that is why novelists more so than historians have found her twisted legacy so enticing.

CONCLUSION
Revisioning Mary Ellen Pleasant

What should one care whose heart is good and whose acts have
been right and who does not look back with regrets for the past?
MARY ELLEN PLEASANT, *Memoirs* (1902)

Pleasant's life ended at the dawn of the twentieth century. She witnessed
sweeping changes during the fifty years she spent in California: the Civil War,
the development of the West's largest city, the transformation of the landscape from the Gold Rush to the railroads, and what one scholar has called
the incorporation of America.[1] Pleasant's labor and entrepreneurship in some
ways were characteristic of western women's experiences: She managed
boardinghouses, profited from the earnings of miners and railroad moguls,
and participated in movements and institutions that transformed the West's
public life. However, being an African American meant that Pleasant operated in and out of myriad social and political domains. Traveling in and
among Bonanza Kings, black ministers, Confederate judges, and Irish working women, among others, Pleasant crossed boundaries of all description.
Pleasant's ability to move in a wide circle of California society made her both
valuable and dangerous to many.

Black business leaders in the nineteenth century often faced insurmountable odds. Access to credit, building permits, and investment institutions
were denied African Americans as a matter of course. Pleasant overcame
these and others barriers that were put in her way. Her career as both abolitionist and capitalist places her in a group of women such as Maggie Lena
Walker and Madame C. J. Walker who combined business savvy with a
commitment to racial progress.[2] But for an African American woman to be
making money in ways not becoming her sex was something that many
found troublesome. Although Pleasant maintained her contact with abolitionist David Ruggles over the years, we can only wonder whether other
members of the black elite welcomed her into their ranks. It appears that
they did, given the praises heaped on her in the black newspapers in the

1870s. However, race *and* gender always shaped Pleasant's access to capital and to the sites of political and social power.

Pleasant's wealth resulted in part from her knowledge of the elite and their habits and from her connections to the working class. She was known for filling jobs at the Palace Hotel and staffing numerous local institutions with black workers. Pleasant's mobility across class boundaries proved valuable in her economic ventures, such as boardinghouses and laundries. The wealthiest men in the West—Charles Crocker, Collis P. Huntington, Mark Hopkins, and Leland Stanford—accumulated their wealth by successfully exploiting vast numbers of workers in the construction of the Central Pacific Railroad. Pleasant used the same strategies on a smaller scale to diversify and operate her businesses, from her laundries to her ranch.

Pleasant's success resulted in part from her ability to understand the workings of what have traditionally been considered the public and private spheres. Dealing in sexual secrets clearly was part of her enterprise. The Sharon trials provide a glimpse of this strategy. Whether Pleasant worked as a madam or merely made matches that she profited from, these activities in the private realm helped her amass her fortune. She capitalized on one of Victorian America's chief obsessions: controlling and monitoring sexuality.[3]

Whereas many of the nineteenth-century women who occupied public urban space were either prostitutes or reformers, Pleasant was neither.[4] Yet she reshaped social and political spaces in much the same way as female reformers of the era. By speaking in public, especially courtrooms, Pleasant made it possible for other women to do so. By challenging racist streetcar practices during Reconstruction, Pleasant contributed to national efforts to eradicate Jim Crow practices. She had little in common with the best-known arbiters of racial uplift, most of whom were members of elite black communities in the East and South; nevertheless, Pleasant embraced its central tenets.[5] Hiring working-class African Americans in her enterprises and embodying the successful black business mogul Booker T. Washington heralded, Pleasant championed racial uplift on the nation's West Coast.

Denied the franchise, nineteenth-century black women often expressed their political concerns outside of political parties and traditional arenas. Some recent scholarship in African American history locates women's activism in black churches and benevolent organizations.[6] However, Pleasant found multiple arenas in which to articulate her critique of white male hegemony. In numerous instances Pleasant used the courtroom to communicate the personal injury she experienced at the hands of lawyers, judges, and creditors. Her insistence on citizenship at the height of the antiblack backlash in the Gilded Age marked her as an outspoken race woman in the tradition of Ida B. Wells Barnett.

Well aware of the suspicion she caused, Pleasant tried to placate her enemies at the end of her life. Her autobiography reveals her ever-vigilant efforts at self-representation: "What should one care whose heart is good and whose acts have been right and who does not look back with regrets for the past? I have given all I had to others, and when I attached myself to any one as a friend, I have remained to the end. I do not harbor a vindictive thought against the people who have betrayed my friendship or maligned me, and, in going down to my grave, I forgive them all."[7] Pleasant's legacy, though not controlled by those who maligned her, has clearly been shaped by those fascinated with or afraid of her. This preoccupation with the legends about her life has shaped the historiography. In the last century, Pleasant has become a figment of imagination as much as a figure of history.

Coming to terms with her life as an abolitionist, activist, entrepreneur, philanthropist, and litigant means coming to terms with the multiple versions of her legacy. Because Pleasant's life has been the subject of contradictory narratives in newspapers, courtrooms, silent films, and diaries, her history is also the story of these narratives and why certain ones predominate.[8] The version of Pleasant as the faithful servant or mammy is the one that becomes more and more prevalent both in her own lifetime and in twentieth-century popular culture. There are several reasons for this. In the first place, Pleasant imposed this definition on herself in public spaces in San Francisco as she was repeatedly called to defend herself and her right to her own property. Second, as her enterprise increased, so did the need to disguise it.

The zenith in Pleasant's career coincided with the most brutal attacks on African American rights, properties, and bodies since slavery. As shapers of white supremacy whittled away at civil rights at the end of the nineteenth century, white ethnic workers in California also fought to distinguish themselves from black, Asian, and Mexican workers. As recent scholars have articulated, the fictive category of whiteness was successfully constructed in nineteenth-century law, practice, custom, and popular culture in opposition to blackness.[9] The need to cast Pleasant as mammy reflects this need to racialize the political and cultural landscape as class relations shifted and the West industrialized.

The characterization of mammy worked to disguise her entrepreneurial success at times, but ultimately Pleasant stepped too far from the mammy stereotype to mask her enterprise. Despite copious efforts on the part of Holdredge and other mythmakers, Pleasant's history cannot be reduced to a single identity or legend. In 1902, an ailing Mary Ellen Pleasant sequestered herself in her home in San Francisco and told one of her friends, "I have been accused of many things, and under the load of accusation I have held my tongue. I have never been given to explaining away lies. And you can't explain away the truth."[10] And with that, she left her biographers their greatest clue and their greatest challenge.

NOTES

Introduction

1. Darlene Clark Hine, "Lifting the Veil, Shattering the Silence: Black Women's History in Slavery and Freedom," in *The State of Afro-American History: Past, Present, and Future,* ed. Darlene Clark Hine (Baton Rouge: Louisiana State University Press, 1986), 223–49.

2. For example, see William Sherman Savage, *Blacks in the West* (Westport, Conn.: Greenwood Press, 1976), 133–34; William Loren Katz, *The Black West* (Seattle: Open Hand Publishing, 1987), 138–39; William Loren Katz, *Black People Who Made the Old West* (Trenton, N.J.: Africa World Press, 1992), 90; Kenneth G. Goode, *California's Black Pioneers* (Santa Barbara, Calif.: McNally and Loftin, 1974), 65, 87–88; Joann Levy, *They Saw the Elephant: Women in the California Gold Rush* (San Francisco: Anchor Books, 1990), 210–11; Ronald Dean Miller, *Shady Ladies of the West* (Los Angeles: Westernlore Press, 1964), 64–67.

3. Herbert Asbury, *The Barbary Coast* (New York: Alfred A. Knopf, 1933), 11; Eugene B. Block, *The Immortal San Franciscans: For Whom the Streets Were Named* (San Francisco: Chronicle Books, 1971), 94–96; James D. Hart, *A Companion Guide to California* (New York: Oxford University Press, 1978), 333; Joan M. Jensen and Gloria Ricci Lothrop, *California Women: A History* (San Francisco: Boyd and Fraser, 1987), 37. See also W. Sherman Savage and Rayford W. Logan, "Mary Ellen Pleasant," in *Dictionary of Negro Biography,* ed. Rayford W. Logan and Michael R. Winston (New York: W. W. Norton, 1982), 495–96; W. Sherman Savage, "Mary Ellen Pleasant," in *Notable American Women,* ed. Edward T. James (Cambridge, Mass.: Belknap Press, 1971), 75–77.

4. W. E. B. Du Bois, *The Gifts of Black Folk* (Boston: Stratford, 1924).

5. For an insightful discussion of this phenomenon, see Michel-Rolph Trouillot, *Silencing the Past: Power and the Production of History* (Boston: Beacon Press, 1995).

6. On black entrepreneurship, see Juliet E. K. Walker, "Racism, Slavery, and Free Enterprise: Black Entrepreneurship in the United States," *Business History Review* 60 (Autumn 1986): 343–82.

7. Nell Irvin Painter, "Representing Truth: Sojourner Truth's Knowing and Becoming Known," *The Journal of American History* 81:2 (September 1994): 471.

8. Mary Ellen Pleasant, "Memoirs and Autobiography," *The Pandex of the Press* 1 (January 1902): 4.

9. Ibid.

10. Ibid.

11. Ibid.

12. *The Pandex of the Press* 1:2 (February 1902): 94.

13. Pleasant, "Memoirs," 1.

14. Ibid., 4.

15. Lerone Bennett posits that most of her diaries were taken from her home, which was ransacked upon her death in 1904. Bennett, "An Historical Detective Story: The Mystery of Mary Ellen Pleasant, Part II," *Ebony* (May 1979): 86. Curators in San Francisco are still approached by researchers who claim to be on the trail of the missing diaries, but none have surfaced yet.

16. Isabel Fraser, "Mammy Pleasant: The Woman," *San Francisco Call* (July 9, 1901): 2.

17. On the role of mammy in U.S. history and culture, see Grace Elizabeth Hale, *Making Whiteness: The Culture of Segregation in the South, 1890–1940* (New York: Pantheon Books, 1998); Cheryl Thurber, "The Development of the Mammy Image and Mythology," in *Southern Women: Histories and Identities,* ed. Virginia Bernhard et al. (Columbia: University of Missouri Press, 1994); Patricia A. Turner, *Ceramic Uncles and Celluloid Mammies: Black Images and Their Influence on Culture* (New York: Anchor Books, 1994); Kenneth W. Goings, *Mammy and Uncle Mose: Black Collectibles and American Stereotyping* (Bloomington: Indiana University Press, 1994).

18. Holdredge was born in Duluth, Minnesota in 1898 and educated in private schools in Portland. She attended the University of Oregon. Before writing *Mammy Pleasant,* she had been an opera singer, radio singer, and illustrator. It was in the writing of fictionalized biography, however, that she became most successful. She devoted more than thirty years to collecting information about Pleasant and writing her books. Holdredge lived in Sacramento, California for much of her adult life, but she combed the entire country for clues about Pleasant and her associates. She died in 1986.

Another author, Susheel Bibbs, recently published a book about Marie LaVeau, Mary Ellen Pleasant, and "the unique religious heritage (Voodoo) which inspired them both." Susheel Bibbs, *A Heritage of Power: Marie LaVeau, Mary Ellen Pleasant* (San Francisco: MEP Publications, 1998); see also the catalog published in conjunction with the exhibit at the California State Capitol Museum, Susheel Bibbs, "Mary Ellen Pleasant, 1817–1904: Mother of Human Rights in California" (San Francisco: MEP Publications, 1996).

19. Helen Holdredge Notebook, #26, no date, MEP Coll., SFPL. Holdredge explains that a San Francisco bookstore owner "appeared on television with the gal-

leys and stirred up a great deal of excitement, the first printing had been sold out before delivery by the publisher."

20. *Saturday Review* 36:12 (November 14, 1953) and *New York Times*, November 29, 1953.

21. *New York Times*, November 29, 1953.

22. William B. Secrest Sr. finds the same inventions in Holdredge's "biography" of San Francisco detective Isaiah Lees, *The House of the Strange Woman* (San Carlos, Calif.: Nourse, 1961). See William B. Secrest Sr., "The Strange Book of Helen Holdredge," *The Californians* 12:5 (1995): 42–49.

23. Helen Holdredge, *Mammy Pleasant's Partner* (New York: G. P. Putnam's Sons, 1954); Helen Holdredge, *Mammy Pleasant's Cookbook* (San Francisco: 101 Productions, 1970); Helen Holdredge, *The House of the Strange Woman* (San Carlos, Calif.: Nourse Publishing, 1961); Holdredge also wrote two other fictionalized biographies; see *Firebelle Lillie* (New York: Meredith Press, 1967); and *The Woman in Black: The Life of Lola Montez* (New York: G. P. Putnam's Sons, 1955).

24. Helen Holdredge Notebook, #26, no date, MEP Coll., SFPL.

25. Helen Holdredge, *Mammy Pleasant* (New York: G. P. Putnam's Sons, 1953), v.

26. Helen Holdredge notebook #26, no date, MEP Coll., SFPL.

27. Ibid.

28. Toni Morrison, *Playing in the Dark: Whiteness and the Literary Imagination* (Cambridge, Mass.: Harvard University Press, 1992), 5.

29. The Cold War and the immediacy of the civil rights movement may also have contributed to the popularity of Holdredge's text. Locating evil in the body of a sinister black woman as Holdredge does in *Mammy Pleasant* fits nicely with the 1950s strategy of finding the enemy within. For example, see Stephen J. Whitfield, *The Culture of the Cold War* (Baltimore, Md.: Johns Hopkins University Press, 1991).

30. For example, see Obituary, *San Francisco Call,* January 12, 1904, p. 16; Obituary, *San Francisco Chronicle,* January 12, 1904, p. 9.

31. Albert J. Raboteau, *Slave Religion: The "Invisible Institution" in the Antebellum South* (New York: Oxford University Press, 1978).

32. Ibid.

33. For example, see Karen McCarthy Brown, "Women's Leadership in Haitian Vodou," in *Weaving the Visions: New Patterns in Feminist Spirituality,* ed. Judith Plaskow and Carol P. Christ (San Francisco: Harper and Row, 1989): 226–34.

34. Lawrence W. Levine, *Black Culture and Black Consciousness: Afro-American Folk Thought from Slavery to Freedom* (New York: Oxford University Press, 1977).

35. Holdredge, *Mammy Pleasant,* 9.

36. Ibid., 24.

37. Folklorist Patricia Turner suggests that rumors often function as tools of resistance in black communities. See Patricia A. Turner, *I Heard It through the Grapevine: Rumor in African-American Culture* (Berkeley: University of California Press, 1993). For another historical study that traces rumor in black communities, see Spencie Love, *One Blood: The Legend of Charles Drew* (New York: Norton, 1996).

Love demonstrates that the rumor that Drew was denied a blood transfusion—a technology that he helped to develop—reveals much about the power whites had in the Jim Crow South.

38. Douglas Henry Daniels, *Pioneer Urbanites: A Social and Cultural History of Black San Francisco* (Philadelphia: Temple University Press, 1980).

39. William S. McFeely, *Frederick Douglass* (New York: Norton, 1991), 86–87. On Pleasant and the African American Meeting House, see African Baptist Church, ledger, Nantucket Historical Association.

40. New studies take a more critical approach to the study of African Americans in the West. For example, see Albert S. Broussard, *Black San Francisco: The Struggle for Racial Equality in the West, 1900–1954* (Lawrence: University Press of Kansas, 1993); Quintard Taylor, *In Search of the Racial Frontier: African Americans in the American West, 1528–1990* (New York: Norton, 1998); Lawrence B. de Graaf, Kevin Mulroy, and Quintard Taylor, eds., *Seeking El Dorado: African Americans in California* (Los Angeles: Autry Museum of Western Heritage, 2001).

41. Beverly J. Stoeltje, "A Helpmate for Man Indeed: The Image of the Frontier Woman," *Journal of American Folklore* 88:347 (January–March 1975): 25–41. Scholars of western women's history have worked arduously to address this problem; see Joan M. Jensen and Darlis Miller, "The Gentle Tamers Revisited: New Approaches to the History of Women in the American West," *Pacific Historical Review* 49 (May 1980): 173–212; Susan Armitage and Elizabeth Jameson, eds., *The Women's West* (Norman: University of Oklahoma Press, 1987); Elizabeth Jameson and Susan Armitage, *Writing the Range: Race, Class, and Culture in the Women's West* (Norman: University of Oklahoma Press, 1997). For an eloquent summation of the challenges and possibilities of the study of gender in the West, see Susan Lee Johnson, "'A Memory Sweet to Soldiers,': The Significance of Gender in the History of the American West," *Western Historical Quarterly* 24 (November 1993): 495–517.

42. Juliet E. K. Walker, *The History of Black Business in America: Capitalism, Race, Entrepreneurship* (New York: Prentice Hall, 1998), 145.

43. Loren Schweninger, *Black Property Owners in the South, 1790–1915* (Urbana: University of Illinois Press, 1990), 87.

44. A'Lelia Perry Bundles, *On Her Own Ground: The Life and Times of Madam C. J. Walker* (New York: Scribner, 2001); Walker, *The History of Black Business,* 208–11. Walker points out that although Madam C. J. Walker has been celebrated as the first female millionaire of any race, it was probably a black woman named Annie Minerva Turnbo-Malone (1869–57), who also marketed black hair products. Walker, *The History of Black Business,* 208.

45. For example, see Tera W. Hunter, *To 'Joy My Freedom: Southern Black Women's Lives and Labors after the Civil War* (Cambridge, Mass.: Harvard University Press, 1997); Elizabeth Clark-Lewis, *Living In, Living Out: African American Domestics in Washington, D.C., 1910–1940* (Washington, D.C.: Smithsonian Institution Press, 1994); Jacqueline Jones, *Labor of Love, Labor of Sorrow: Black Women, Work, and the Family from Slavery to the Present* (New York: Basic Books, 1985).

46. Walker, *The History of Black Business,* 146.

47. This figure is derived from census data compiled by Lawrence B. de Graaf in his seminal article, "Race, Sex, and Region: Black Women in the American West, 1850–1920," *Pacific Historical Review* 49 (May 1980): 285–313.

48. Walker, *The History of Black Business,* 151.

49. *The Cleveland Gazette,* November 29, 1884.

50. On the issue of silence in black women's history, see Evelyn Brooks Higginbotham, "Beyond the Sound of Silence: Afro-American Women in History," *Gender and History* 1 (Spring 1989): 50–67; Darlene Clark Hine, "Rape and the Inner Lives of Black Women in the Middle West: Preliminary Thoughts on the Culture of Dissemblance," *Signs* 14:4 (Summer 1989): 912–20.

51. For example, see Winthrop D. Jordan, *Tumult and Silence at Second Creek: An Inquiry into a Civil War Slave Conspiracy* (Baton Rouge: Louisiana State University Press, 1993). For a refreshing study of African American history, biography, and historical silences, see also Nick Salvatore, *We All Got History: The Memory Books of Amos Webber* (New York: Random House, 1996).

52. For example, see Tillie Olsen, *Silences* (New York: Dell, 1979); Michelle Cliff, "The Resonance of Interruption," *Chrysallis* 8 (Summer 1979): 29–37.

53. Deborah Gray White, "Mining the Forgotten: Manuscript Sources for Black Women's History," *Journal of American History* 74 (June 1987): 237–42.

Chapter 1: Nantucket

1. Helen Holdredge, *Mammy Pleasant* (New York: G. P. Putnam and Sons, 1953); Susheel Bibbs, "Mary Ellen Pleasant: Mother of Civil Rights in California," *Historic Nantucket* 44:1 (1995): 9–13; Charlotte Dennis Downs Interviews, MEP Coll., SFPL.

2. In "The Mammy Pleasant Legend," J. Lloyd Conrich remarks, "Some versions of the legend say that Mammy's father was the white owner of a plantation. . . . Some tales say that Mammy's parents were both slaves, while others claim they were free and well to do. The only definite conclusion that one can come to after exhaustive research on the circumstances surrounding the birth of Mammy Pleasant is that we don't know the truth at all." J. Lloyd Conrich, "The Mammy Pleasant Legend," unpublished manuscript, no date, California Historical Society, 17.

3. For the purpose of clarity, I will refer to Mary Ellen Pleasant as Mary Ellen or Pleasant throughout the chapter although in this early period she probably went by the name Mary Williams or Ellen Williams.

4. For an example of slaves who disguised themselves to escape, see the chapter on William and Ellen Craft in R. J. M. Blackett, *Beating against the Barriers: The Lives of Six Nineteenth-Century Afro-Americans* (Baton Rouge: Louisiana State University Press, 1986), 86–137.

5. Louis R. Harlan, *Booker T. Washington: The Making of a Black Leader, 1856–1901* (New York: Oxford University Press, 1972), 245–52. On the significance of African American history and memory, see David Blight, "'For Something beyond

the Battlefield': Frederick Douglass and the Memory of the Civil War," *The Journal of American History* 75:4 (March 1989): 1156–78; Robert E. McGlone, "Rescripting a Troubled Past: John Brown's Family and the Harpers Ferry Conspiracy," *The Journal of American History* 75:4 (March 1989): 1179–1200.

6. Mary Ellen Pleasant, "Memoirs and Autobiography," *The Pandex of the Press* 1 (January 1902): 5.

7. Ibid.

8. U.S. Bureau of the Census, *Third Census of the United States* (Washington D.C., 1812).

9. On Nantucket history, see Edward Byers, *The Nation of Nantucket: Society and Politics in an Early American Commercial Center, 1660–1820* (Boston: Northeastern University Press, 1987); Nathaniel Philbrick, *"Away Off Shore": Nantucket Island and Its People, 1602–1890* (Nantucket, Mass.: Mill Hill Press, 1994).

10. On Douglass, see Anthony S. Parent Jr. and Susan Brown Wallace, "Childhood and Sexual Identity under Slavery," in *American Sexual Politics: Sex, Gender and Race Since the Civil War,* ed. John C. Fout and Maura Shaw Tantillo (Chicago: University of Chicago Press, 1993), 19–57.

11. Gary B. Nash, *Forging Freedom: The Formation of Philadelphia's Black Community, 1720–1840* (Cambridge, Mass.: Harvard University Press, 1988); W. E. B. Du Bois, *The Philadelphia Negro: A Social Study* (New York: Schocken Books, 1967); Julie Winch, *Philadelphia's Black Elite: Activism, Accommodation, and the Struggle for Autonomy, 1787–1848* (Philadelphia: Temple University Press, 1988).

12. Helen Holdredge, *Mammy Pleasant*, 8.

13. Ibid.

14. Records from the Ursuline Convent Archives do not confirm the presence of Mary Ellen in the early nineteenth century. It could be that she was using a pseudonym, but at this point no documentation exists that proves she was taken to New Orleans.

15. U.S. Bureau of the Census, *Fourth Census of the United States, 1820* (Washington, D.C., 1821), *Fifth Census of the United States, 1830* (Washington, D.C., 1832).

16. Downs says, "I was in and out of the Bell house [Pleasant's home on Octavia Street] from the time it was built and before that at Mammy's boardinghouse at Washington." Charlotte Dennis Downs Interview, #26, April 16, 1950, MEP Coll., SFPL (Downs was 88 in 1950). Downs explains that her father went into the livery business with James E. Brown. Their business opened on the corner of Sansome and Washington in 1854. George Dennis married the eldest daughter of Brown, Mary Ann, and they had ten children, including Charlotte. Charlotte married a sailor named John Downs. This meant that Charlotte was also related to the influential Brown family: She was the grandniece of Pleasant's contemporary James S. Brown and the niece of Pleasant's later enemy James E. Brown.

17. Ibid. On Dennis Sr., see Rudolph M. Lapp, *Blacks in Gold Rush California* (New Haven, Conn.: Yale University Press, 1977), 98, 188; see also Lindsay Camp-

bell, "Gambling in San Francisco in the Days of Gold as Seen by a Slave," *San Francisco Sunday Call,* July 16, 1911.

18. This particular autobiography has since been lost, although in her notebooks Holdredge claimed to have read it.

19. Charlotte Dennis Downs Interview, #24, no date, MEP Coll., SFPL.

20. Many report that Pleasant's house was ransacked after she died and her diaries were stolen; see Bennett, "An Historical Detective Story."

21. U.S. Bureau of the Census, *Sixth Census of the United States, 1840* (Washington, D.C., 1842); see also Janet B. Hewett, *Georgia Confederate Soldiers, 1861–1865, Name Roster,* Vol. 2. (Wilmington, N.C.: Broadfoot Publishing Company, 1998).

22. For example, see Ronald Vern Jackson et al., eds., *Early America Series: Early Georgia, 1733–1819* (Bountiful, Utah: Accelerated Indexing Systems, n.d.); Alvaretta Kenan Register, ed., *Index to the 1830 Census of Georgia* (Baltimore, Md.: Genealogical Publishing Company, 1974); Ronald Vern Jackson et al., eds., *Georgia 1850 Census Index* (Bountiful, Utah: Accelerated Indexing Systems, n.d.).

23. On the significance of color in the nineteenth century, see James Oliver Horton, *Free People of Color: Inside the African American Community* (Washington, D.C.: Smithsonian Institution Press, 1993), chapter 6. On miscegenation and popular culture, see William L. Van DeBurg, *Slavery and Race in American Popular Culture* (Madison: University of Wisconsin Press, 1984), 63–65.

24. As quoted in J. A. Rogers, *Sex and Race,* Vol. 3 (New York: Author, 1944), 310–11.

25. Charles Caldwell Dobie, *San Francisco: A Pageant* (New York: Appleton-Century, 1933), 317.

26. Helen Holdredge to A. A. Smyser, Nov. 3, 1976, California Historical Society.

27. Holdredge claims that San Franciscan Isiah Lees owned the photograph and that upon his death it was sold to a Nevada historian. The image eventually became the property of Joseph Henry Jackson, editor of the *San Francisco Chronicle,* who let Holdredge make a copy. California Historical Society.

28. Lois Taylor to Helen Holdredge, April 11, 1977, California Historical Society.

29. Helen Holdredge to A. A. Smyser, Nov. 3, 1976, California Historical Society. In this letter Holdredge writes, "In 1880 Mammy was invited to the Palace Hotel to meet King Kalakaua of Hawaii. It was the custom in San Francisco to always send an invitation to any major affair. She invariably sent 'regrets' but on this occasion she wanted to attend because she wished to ask the king if it was true that she closely resembled the Dowager Queen Emma of Hawaii. He obviously thought she did because when he left for Hawaii he carried with him a negative plate of Mammy's full-length portrait."

30. Leon Litwack, *North of Slavery: The Negro in the Free States, 1790–1860* (Chicago: University of Chicago Press, 1961); James O. Horton and Lois E. Horton, *In Hope of Liberty: Culture, Community and Protest among Northern Free Blacks, 1700–1860* (New York: Oxford University Press, 1997).

31. Holdredge, *Mammy Pleasant,* 12–13; Carter G. Woodson, "The Negroes of Cincinnati prior to the Civil War," *The Journal of Negro History* I (January 1916): 1–22; Holdredge claims that Pleasant attempted to pass as white, working as a bonded servant for the Williamses. This seems unlikely because Price was a plantation owner. In any case, Pleasant left so few clues about this early period, most details of her childhood remain unknown.

32. J. Hector St. John de Crèvecoeur, *Letters from an American Farmer and Sketches of Eighteenth-Century America,* edited with an introduction by Albert Stone (New York: Viking Penguin, 1981), 165.

33. Mary Ellen Pleasant, "Memoirs," 5. We can be fairly sure that Pleasant arrived in the 1820s. If, as she claimed, she arrived when she was six, it would be 1820 (if her birth year is 1814). If she was eleven, as Holdredge believed, it could have been as late as 1825. Many years later, Pleasant testified on the witness stand that she was married on Nantucket in 1846. From her description and others, it seems likely that she spent several years on the island, perhaps as many as twenty.

34. "The Life Story of Mammy Pleasance," *San Francisco Examiner,* October 13, 1895; see also Helen Holdredge Notebook, #26, n.d., MEP Coll., SFPL.

35. "The Life Story of Mammy Pleasance."

36. Daniel Vickers, "Nantucket Whalemen in the Deep-Sea Fishery: The Changing Anatomy of an Early American Workforce," *The Journal of American History* 72 (September 1985): 277–96.

37. Ibid.

38. Nathaniel Philbrick, "'Every Wave Is a Fortune': Nantucket Island and the Making of An American Icon," *The New England Quarterly* (September 1993): 434–47.

39. Frederick Douglass, *My Bondage, My Freedom* (Salem, N.H.: Ayer Co., 1984 ed., 1855), 345.

40. Byers, *The Nation of Nantucket,* chapter 5.

41. Jean R. Soderlund, *Quakers and Slavery: A Divided Spirit* (Princeton, N.J.: Princeton University Press, 1985). In 1733, a Nantucketer named Elihu Coleman wrote an antislavery pamphlet distributed widely in the colonies. Yet Coleman's pamphlet did not signal uniformity among the Quakers at large. In fact, abolition proved to be a flashpoint of debate in eighteenth-century yearly meetings across the eastern seaboard and Delaware Valley. Soderlund explains that Coleman had to receive special permission from the New England Yearly Meeting to publish his antislavery pamphlet. Quakers in pre-Revolutionary New England were by no means unequivocally antislavery. Soderlund, 23. On Massachusetts and abolition, see Lorenzo Greene, *The Negro in Colonial New England* (Washington, N.Y.: Kennicat Press, 1966).

42. On the history and significance of black sailors, see W. Jeffrey Bolster, *Black Jacks: African American Seamen in the Age of Sail* (Cambridge, Mass.: Harvard University Press, 1997); W. Jeffrey Bolster, "'To Feel Like a Man': Black Seamen in the Northern States, 1800–1860," *Journal of American History* 76 (March 1990): 1173–99.

43. Barney Census, 1820.

44. On the American Revolution and Nantucket's political history, see Byers, *The Nation of Nantucket,* especially 201–28; Philbrick, *"Away Off Shore."*

45. Isabel Kaldenbach-Montemayor, "Blacks on the High Seas," unpublished paper, Nantucket Historical Association. Kaldenbach-Montemayor disputes the notion that black islanders arrived on the Underground Railroad, noting that the largest increase in the black population occurred between 1830 and 1840, from 279 to 578 (24).

46. Michael Sokolow notes that 412 black men and women lived in Salem, Massachusetts in 1850, making Salem the town with the third largest black population in the state (after Boston and New Bedford). Michael Sokolow, "'New Guinea at One End, and a View of the Alms House at the Other': The Decline of Black Salem, 1850–1920," *The New England Quarterly* (June 1998): 204–28. See also Leonard P. Curry, *The Free Black in Urban America, 1800–1850: The Shadow of a Dream* (Chicago: University of Chicago Press, 1981).

47. Lorin Lee Cary and Francine C. Cary, "Absalom F. Boston, His Family, and Nantucket's Black Community," *Historic Nantucket* 25:1 (Summer 1977): 20.

48. In the 1840s, to protest the integration of its schools, some white islanders complained about the "animalness" of Guinea's residents. See Kristi Kraemer, "Background and Resolution of the Eunice Ross Controversy," *Historic Nantucket* 29:1 (July 1981): 17. For an example of the racial attitudes of white residents, see Mary Eliza Starbuck, *My House and I: A Chronicle of Nantucket* (Boston: Houghton Mifflin Company, 1929), 75–86; "Residents of 'Guinea' Fifty Years Ago," Nantucket *Inquirer and Mirror,* January 16, 1913.

49. Captain Paul Cuffe attended local and regional Quaker meetings beginning in 1808. On Cuffe, see Rosalind Cobb Wiggins, *Captain Paul Cuffe's Logs and Letters, 1808–1817: A Black Quaker's "Voice from within the Veil"* (Washington, D.C.: Howard University Press, 1996); Bolster, *Black Jacks.*

50. A definitive study of the African Church/School, now called the African Meeting House, has yet to be written. However, the building was acquired by Boston's Museum of Afro-American History and has been restored. See Edouard A. Stackpole, "A Plan Has Been Established for the Restoration of the Old African Baptist Church on Nantucket," *Historic Nantucket* (1988); "Landmark in Nantucket's Black History Restored," *New York Times,* January 12, 1997. On the history of the school in particular, see Barbara Linebaugh, *The African School and the Integration of Nantucket Public Schools, 1825–1847* (Boston: African-American Studies Center, Boston University, 1978).

51. African Baptist Church, ledger, Nantucket Historical Association.

52. Evelyn Brooks Higginbotham, *Righteous Discontent: The Women's Movement in the Black Baptist Church, 1880–1920* (Cambridge, Mass.: Harvard University Press, 1996).

53. Cary and Cary, "Absalom F. Boston"; Gloria Davis Goode, "African-American Women in Nineteenth-Century Nantucket: Wives, Mothers, Modistes, and Visionaries," *Historic Nantucket* 40:3 (Fall 1992): 76–78.

54. Pleasant, "Memoirs," 6.

55. Ibid.

56. Crèvecoeur, *Letters from an American Farmer and Sketches of Eighteenth-Century America* edited with an introduction by Albert Stone (New York: Viking Penguin, 1981), 127. On Crèvecoeur, see also Nathaniel Philbrick, "The Nantucket Sequence in Crèvecoeur's *Letters from an American Farmer,*" *The New England Quarterly* (September 1991): 414–32. On education, see Litwack, *North of Slavery;* Horton and Horton, *In Hope of Liberty;* Curry, *The Free Black in Urban America.*

57. Pleasant, "Memoirs," 5.

58. As quoted from Pleasant's unpublished memoir, in Bibbs, "Mary Ellen Pleasant," 9.

59. The *Nantucket Inquirer* of this era advertises several shops that trade in "cash or sperm oil."

60. Nathaniel Philbrick, *"Away Off Shore,"* 57.

61. Lisa Norling, *Captain Ahab Had a Wife: New England Women and the Whalefishery, 1720–1870* (Chapel Hill: University of North Carolina Press, 2000), 42. Norling is careful to note that the fact that women engaged in commercial activity in this era is not unusual. "What may have been singular about the Nantucket case was the way in which the location and range of the overlap between the male and female economies ebbed and flowed with the contraction and expansion of the island's maritime industries" (42).

62. Eliza Barney diary, n.d., Nantucket Historical Association.

63. Phebe Ann Hanaford, *Daughters of America, or Women of the Century* (Augusta, Maine: True and Co., 1883), 586–87; Otelia Cromwell, *Lucretia Mott* (Cambridge, Mass.: Harvard University Press, 1958), 5. Much of the secondary literature about the island recounts this belief. For example, see A. B. C. Whipple, *Vintage Nantucket* (New York: Dodd, Mead, and Company, 1978), especially chapter 8, "Matriarchy," where Whipple writes, "Nantucket seems to have produced and nurtured as hardy, self-sufficient and enterprising a lot of women as any in the world, except possibly the Amazon" (155). The tradition of women managing shops did not begin in the antebellum period; Kezia Coffin operated a thriving store before the American Revolution. She was later charged with aiding and abetting the enemy, accused of entertaining raiders in her warehouse. Coffin was temporarily imprisoned and died in 1798. See Philbrick, *"Away Off Shore,"* 123–33.

64. Ibid.

Chapter 2: She Was a Friend of John Brown

1. One source claimed she settled in Philadelphia, not Boston. See "The Life Story of Mammy Pleasance," *San Francisco Examiner,* October 13, 1895.

2. Other accounts say she left for Philadelphia to be with Mary Hussey's granddaughter, Phebe, and her husband, Edward Gardner. See *San Francisco Examiner,* October 13, 1895.

3. Wendy Gamber is careful to note that this independence was precarious at best. See Wendy Gamber, *The Female Economy: The Millinery and Dressmaking Trades, 1860–1930* (Urbana: University of Illinois Press, 1997).

4. Helen Holdredge, *Mammy Pleasant* (New York: G. P. Putnam and Sons, 1953), 17.

5. Ibid.

6. For example, see Sue Bailey Thurman, *Pioneers of Negro Origin in California* (San Francisco: Acme Publishing Co., 1971), 47; Delilah L. Beasley, *The Negro Trail Blazers of California* (Los Angeles: Times Mirror Printing and Binding House, 1919), 97; Lerone Bennett, "An Historical Detective Story: The Mystery of Mary Ellen Pleasant, Part II," *Ebony* (May 1979): 74. He is even referred to by different names in the same article. See Edna Bryan Buckbee, "The Boys Called Her 'Mammy' Pleasant," *The Pony Express* (October 1953): 1–14.

7. Bennett, "An Historical Detective Story, Part II," 74.

8. According to Bennett's document, "The governor, [Pleasant] said, bought [Smith's] mother and children and sent them to Ohio, where the sons learned trades and migrated to Pennsylvania and other Northern states. And although the family was fair enough to 'pass,' the mother voluntarily identified with Blacks." Ibid.

9. I have chosen to leave the names as they appear in the document or text. If Mary Ellen is referred to as "Pleasants" or "Plaissance" or "Pleasance" in a document, I have not changed the spelling.

10. William Willmore Jr. Interview, MEP Coll., SFPL; Helen Holdredge claimed that Pleasant went back to New Orleans at this point in her life. According to this scenario, Pleasant was soon in the hands of high priestess of the voodoo queens: Marie Laveau. Holdredge—not known for her accurate portrayal of Africanisms—delights in the treacherous spells Pleasant learned from Laveau and makes much of Pleasant's power over other black people, thanks to her voodoo training. Holdredge, *Mammy Pleasant*, 28.

11. J. Lloyd Conrich, "The Mammy Pleasant Legend," unpublished manuscript, California Historical Society, no date, 19.

12. Ibid., 20.

13. Holdredge, *Mammy Pleasant*, 21–23; Charlotte Dennis Downs Interviews, MEP Coll., SFPL.

14. U.S. Bureau of the Census, *Sixth Census of the United States, 1840* (Washington, D.C., 1842).

15. See Sam Davis, "How a Colored Woman Aided John Brown," *The Inquirer and Mirror*, December 26, 1901.

16. *San Francisco Examiner*, October 13, 1895.

17. For example, see Bennett, "An Historical Detective Story, Part II," 72; Holdredge, *Mammy Pleasant*, 18–23.

18. U.S. Bureau of the Census, *Sixth Census of the United States, 1840*. There are only three James Smiths listed in Boston; two are white and one is a free colored man between the ages of twenty-four and thirty-six.

19. Suffolk County Probate Index, 1643–1894, Massachusetts Archives and Records Preservation.

20. Buckbee, "The Boys Called Her 'Mammy' Pleasant," 3.

21. W. E. B. Du Bois, *The Gifts of Black Folks* (Boston: Stratford, 1924), 271.

22. *San Francisco Examiner,* October 13, 1895; Holdredge notebook, #4, no date, MEP Coll., SFPL.

23. J. D. B. DeBow, ed., *Statistical View of the United States: . . . Being a Compendium of the Seventh Census to Which Are Added the Results of Every Previous Census, Beginning with 1790 . . .* (New York: Gordon and Breach Science Publishers, 1970 [1850]), 164. The census data tabulated in Table 175 of this volume indicate that in 1850, the average wages to a California day laborer or unskilled worker amounted to $5 a month without board, or $60 a year. Monthly wages to a carpenter in California, a skilled worker, amounted to $7.60, or $91.20 per year. It should be noted that wages outside California were much lower because of the inflation of the Gold Rush economy. In the District of Columbia and in the state of Connecticut, for example, average monthly wages to day laborers without board were $0.98, making their annual wages $11.76.

24. *Population Schedules of the Seventh Census of the United States, 1850* (Washington, D.C.: National Archives and Records Service).

25. Douglass first took refuge at the home of David Ruggles in New York, who suggested he might find New Bedford more hospitable for fugitive slaves. Pleasant would come to know the son of the David Ruggles in San Francisco, so it is quite likely that she knew his father as well. See Frederick Douglass, *Narrative of the Life of Frederick Douglass* (Cambridge, Mass.: Harvard University Press, 1988 [1845]), 323–26, for a description of New Bedford in the 1840s.

26. Frederick Douglass reports that "not fewer than forty" men left New Bedford for California, and, "not one of the company of colored persons from New Bedford expresses any regret." *The North Star,* November 30, 1849.

27. *Pleasants v. North Beach and Mission Railroad Company,* Appeal, 1867, California State Archives; "Helen Holdredge letter to Edward Stackpole," April 9, 1951, Nantucket Historical Association. This letter, like many of Holdredge's notebooks, indicates that Holdredge had access to Pleasant's diaries or letters that are now missing or destroyed.

28. On the friendship between Frederick Douglass and the Gardner family (Anna, in particular), see William S. McFeely, *Frederick Douglass* (New York: W. W. Norton, 1991), 87–98; see also Anna Gardner, "The Antislavery Phase of Our Island's History," Nantucket *Inquirer and Mirror,* July 11, 1895.

29. According to Lerone Bennett, John Pleasant "occupied a shadowy and indistinct role in the Pleasant play." He also surmised "Black or White, known or unknown, poor or rich, there was apparently only one role for a man in her life—and that was a supporting role behind the scenes." Bennett, "An Historical Detective Story, Part II," 74.

30. Charles P. Kimball, *San Francisco City Directory: 1821–1894* (San Mateo,

Calif.: D. I. Lamphier, 1997). According to *The Elevator,* May 5, 1865, John Pleasant also lived on Cleary Street. In the city directory of 1875 he lists the house on Old San Jose Road as his dwelling.

31. As W. Jeffrey Bolster points out, "The relative rise in seacooks' pay was one of the few changes within the maritime industries that benefited blacks as the nineteenth century progressed." W. Jeffrey Bolster, *Black Jacks: African American Seamen in the Age of Sail* (Cambridge, Mass.: Harvard University Press, 1997), 168.

32. Nell Irvin Painter, *Sojourner Truth: A Life, a Symbol* (New York: Norton, 1996); Jane Rhodes, *Mary Ann Shadd Cary: The Black Press and Protest in the Nineteenth Century* (Bloomington: Indiana University Press, 1998); Hazel Carby, *Reconstructing Womanhood: The Emergence of the Afro-American Woman Novelist* (New York: Oxford University Press, 1987), 62–94.

33. Shirley J. Yee, *Black Women Abolitionists: A Study in Activism, 1828–1860* (Knoxville: University of Tennessee Press, 1992); Jean Fagan Yellin, *Women and Sisters: The Antislavery Feminists in American Culture* (New Haven, Conn.: Yale University Press, 1989); Jean Fagan Yellin and John C. Van Horne, eds., *Abolitionist Sisterhood: Women's Political Culture in Antebellum America* (Ithaca, N.Y.: Cornell University Press, 1994). On the limits of nineteenth-century female behavior more generally, see Mary P. Ryan, *Women in Public: Between Banners and Ballots, 1825–1880* (Baltimore, Md.: Johns Hopkins University Press, 1990); Mary Kelley, *Private Woman, Public Stage: Literary Domesticity in Nineteenth-Century America* (New York: Oxford University Press, 1984).

34. The 1860 U.S. Census lists both Mary Ellen and John as residents at the home of Selim Woodworth (see chapter 3), and the 1870 census lists them both at 920 Washington Street, Pleasant's boardinghouse.

35. For example, see Cloyte Murdock, "America's Most Fabulous Black Madam," *Ebony* 9 (April 1954): 46–55.

36. That Lizzie had the surname of Pleasant's first husband might indicate that Lizzie was conceived before John Pleasant and Mary Ellen were married in 1847. Helen Holdredge claims Elizabeth was born in 1851 in Boston, where Mary Ellen was living temporarily, to hide from slavecatchers. Holdredge, *Mammy Pleasant,* 25.

37. Interview with William Willmore, #26, March 1938, MEP Coll., SFPL.

38. *The Elevator,* April 14, 1865.

39. Holdredge, *Mammy Pleasant,* 25.

40. J. Kingston Pierce, *San Francisco: You're History!* (Seattle: Sasquatch Books, 1995), 234.

41. Interview with William Willmore Jr., #26, March 1938, MEP Coll., SFPL.

42. Deborah Gray White, *Ar'n't I a Woman: Female Slaves in the Plantation South* (New York: Norton, 1985). For a visual representation of this phenomenon, see Marlon Riggs, director/producer, *Ethnic Notions* (Berkeley: California Newsreel, 1989).

43. Malcolm J. Rorbaugh, *Days of Gold: The California Gold Rush and the American Nation* (Berkeley: University of California, 1997), 73. An 1892 article in the

Nantucket *Inquirer and Mirror* states, "No place contributed more liberally in proportion to its population than Nantucket." Nantucket Historical Association, no date.

44. Edouard A. Stackpole Collection, Nantucket Historical Association.

45. *San Francisco Examiner,* October 13, 1895.

46. Interview with James Allen Francis Jr., #24, no date, MEP Coll., SFPL. Another source dates her arrival as January 12, 1849, perhaps a date given to an interviewer by Pleasant herself. *San Francisco Examiner,* October 13, 1895.

47. Louis J. Rasmussen, *San Francisco Ship Passenger Lists: Names of Passengers Arriving by Vessels into the Port of San Francisco, 1850–1875,* Vol. 3 (Colma, Calif.: San Francisco Historic Records, 1966).

48. James P. Delgado, *To California by Sea: A Maritime History of the California Gold Rush* (Columbia: University of South Carolina Press, 1990). Ships leaving from southern ports usually traveled through Panama, perhaps giving credence to Francis's recollection that his father and Pleasant left from New Orleans.

49. Edouard A. Stackpole Collection, newspaper clipping, April 13, 1853; *Names and Sketches of Nearly Two Thousand of the Richest Men of Massachusetts,* 2nd ed. (Boston: 21 Cornhill, 1852), Nantucket Historical Association.

50. Delgado, *To California by Sea,* 65–66.

51. *The North Star,* November 30, 1849. Frederick Douglass was by no means alone in his celebration of California as a place of freedom during the Gold Rush years. Eliza W. Farnham, social worker and domestic feminist, described the state as "the world's nursery of freedom." Eliza W. Farnham, *California: In-Doors and Out* (New York: Dix, Edwards, and Co., 1856), 327.

52. For example, see Leon F. Litwack, *North of Slavery: The Negro in the Free States, 1790–1860* (Chicago: University of Chicago Press, 1961.

53. For example, see Tomás Almaguer, *Racial Fault Lines: The Historical Origins of White Supremacy* (Berkeley: University of California Press, 1994); Lisbeth Haas, *Conquests and Historical Identities in California, 1769–1936* (Berkeley: University of California Press, 1995); Sucheng Chan, "A People of Exceptional Character: Ethnic Diversity, Nativism, and Racism in the California Gold Rush," *California History* (Summer 2000): 44–85.

54. William Loren Katz, *Black People Who Made the Old West* (Trenton, N.J.: Africa World Press, 1992), 73. It is ironic that Katz draws this conclusion in a chapter on San Francisco entrepreneur William Leidesdorff, who passed as white. Mexico outlawed slavery twenty-three years before the 1846 conquest; see Rudolph M. Lapp, *Blacks in Gold Rush California* (New Haven, Conn.: Yale University Press, 1977), 126.

55. This belief often is attributed to W. Sherman Savage, although many others have subscribed to it. For example, see William Sherman Savage, *Blacks in the West* (Westport, Conn.: Greenwood Press, 1976); Kenneth L. Kusmer, "The Black Urban Experience in American History," in *The State of Afro-American History: Past, Present, and Future,* ed. Darlene Clark Hine (Baton Rouge: Louisiana State University Press, 1986), 91–129.

56. Most scholars, such as Douglas Daniels, are careful to qualify their remarks.

Daniels points to job discrimination in San Francisco and numerous examples of racism in the West. Daniels, *Pioneer Urbanites: A Social and Cultural History of Black San Francisco* (Philadelphia: Temple University Press, 1980), 21.

57. Ibid. The 1852 figure is from the state census. The ratio of black men to black women, according to Douglas Daniels's calculations, was 261 per 100 in 1860, and it was presumably more askew eight years earlier.

58. Rorbaugh, *Days of Gold,* 94.

59. Pleasant, "Autobiographical Segments," as quoted in Bennett, "An Historical Detective Story, Part II," 74.

60. For more information on early banking in the state and Wells Fargo in particular, see Robert J. Chandler, "Integrity Amid Tumult: Wells, Fargo and Co.'s Gold Rush Banking," *California History* 70:3 (Fall 1991): 258–77.

61. DeBow, *Statistical View of the United States,* 164.

62. Ibid.

63. Edith Eleanor Sparks, "Capital Instincts: The Economics of Female Proprietorship in San Francisco, 1850–1920" (UCLA diss., 1999), 122–25.

64. U.S. Bureau of the Census, *Population of the United States in 1860* (Washington, D.C., 1864), 22–27. Douglas Daniels comes up with a different figure, citing a 187:100 ratio of men to women in 1860, using the census and city directories. He also notes that for African Americans the ratio is 261 men for every 100 women. Daniels, *Pioneer Urbanites,* 21.

65. For two insightful accounts of the complexity of gender and gender relations during the Gold Rush, see Susan Lee Johnson, *Roaring Camp: The Social World of the California Gold Rush* (New York: W. W. Norton, 2000), and Brian Roberts, *The California Gold Rush and Middle-Class Culture* (Chapel Hill: University of North Carolina Press, 2000).

66. For example, see *The San Francisco Call,* May 7, 1899.

67. Herbert Asbury, *The Barbary Coast* (New York: Alfred A. Knopf, 1933), 11.

68. Michael Bargo, "Women's Occupations in the West in 1870," *Journal of the West* 32:1 (January 1993): 30–45. Unfortunately, as this article points out, the 1870 census did not give data on occupations by race.

69. Holdredge, *Mammy Pleasant,* 37. Thomas Mosler is the man Pleasant chose as her lover, according to Holdredge. "Fidelity had not concerned Mary Ellen when she had been married to Smith and it did not concern her now. . . . Her affection for her lover was shallow in the extreme but she liked him for his physical beauty, his fine rugged face and his virility" (38).

70. Holdredge claims that Pleasant worked for a Captain Thomas Johns, cooking in his "bachelor's establishment," and, beginning in 1857, for Selim and Fred Woodworth. After the Woodworths left the city, "Mary Ellen temporarily kept house for Charles and Walter Mintern, owners of the Sacramento River steamers, and Ben Hartshorn, who owned Colorado Navigation Company and Charles Cunningham (owner of Cunningham Wharf). About September 1857 she returned to the Woodworths." Helen Holdredge Notebook, #4, no date, MEP Coll., SFPL.

71. Interview with James Allen Francis Jr., #24, March 6, 1950, MEP Coll., SFPL.

72. Asbury, *Barbary Coast,* 12.

73. Johnson, *Roaring Camp,* 125.

74. Sparks, "Capital Instincts," 65. Sparks details this shift in the laundry business and its relationship to the anti-Chinese movement.

75. The anti-Chinese movement chipped away at these economic gains, and Chinese men were replaced by European and European American men around the turn of the century. Sparks, "Capital Instincts," 62–72; Paul Ong, "An Ethnic Trade: The Chinese Laundries in Early California," *Journal of Ethnic Studies* 8:4 (Winter 1981): 95–113; Johnson, *Roaring Camp,* 125–27.

76. Helen Holdredge notebook, #4, no date, MEP Coll., SFPL.

77. Susheel Bibbs, "Mary Ellen Pleasant: Mother of Civil Rights in California," *Historic Nantucket* 44:1 (1995): 11.

78. On the transatlantic abolitionist movement, see R. J. M. Blackett, *Building an Anti-Slavery Wall: Black Americans in the Atlantic Abolitionist Movement, 1830–1860* (Ithaca, N.Y.: Cornell University Press, 1983). On Nantucket migration to California, see Rohrbough, *Days of Gold,* 73, 85.

79. Interview with William Willmore Jr., March 1938, #26, MEP Coll., SFPL. There were many New Bedford abolitionists and ex-whalers who settled in San Francisco. It is highly probable that Pleasant did indeed have a network of New Bedford friends and associates on whom she relied. In 1851, the *New Bedford Mercury* encouraged free blacks and fugitive slaves to head west. On the New Bedford community in California, see Lapp, *Blacks in Gold Rush California,* 18–19.

80. Rudolph M. Lapp, "Negro Rights Activities in Gold Rush California," *California Historical Society Quarterly* 45 (March 1966): 3–20.

81. Lapp, *Blacks in Gold Rush California,* 108.

82. On employment, see Daniels, *Pioneer Urbanites;* Lawrence B. de Graff, "Race, Sex, and Region: Black Women in the American West, 1850–1920," *Pacific Historical Review* 49 (May 1980): 285–313; *The Elevator,* June 19, 1868.

83. Lapp, *Blacks in Gold Rush California;* Holdredge, *Mammy Pleasant,* 47.

84. Charlotte Dennis Downs Interview, April 16, 1950, #26, MEP Coll., SFPL.

85. Quoted in Lapp, *Blacks in Gold Rush California,* 102. Although 1,500 San Franciscans is quite a large increase in the black population, this can be attributed to several factors. The census historically undercounted black and mixed-race citizens, so the 1850 count of 952 California "blacks and mulattoes" probably was low. The Gold Rush did indeed bring hundreds more African Americans to the state, and the institute's figures may have been more accurate. On the question of African Americans and census data, see Leonard P. Curry, *The Free Black in Urban America, 1800–1850: The Shadow of a Dream* (Chicago: University of Chicago Press, 1981).

86. Quoted in Lapp, *Blacks in Gold Rush California,* 102. Similar institutions were created by elite African Americans in other cities. The Banneker Institute in Philadelphia, founded in 1854, also maintained a library and publicized its events in the

local press. However, it did not support a saloon—a telling difference between the two communities. See Emma Jones Lapsansky, "The World the Agitators Made: The Counterculture of Agitation in Urban Philadelphia," in *The Abolitionist Sisterhood: Women's Political Culture in Antebellum America,* ed. Jean Fagan Yellin and John C. Van Horne (Ithaca, N.Y.: Cornell University Press, 1994), 91–99.

87. On the testimony law, see James A. Fisher, "The Struggle for Negro Testimony in California, 1851–1863," *Southern California Quarterly* (January 1969): 313–24.

88. B. Gordon Wheeler, *Black California* (New York: Hippocrene Books, 1993), 105; Joann Levy, *They Saw the Elephant: Women in the California Gold Rush* (San Francisco: Archon Books, 1990), 211.

89. Interview with William Willmore Jr., #26, March 1938, MEP Coll., SFPL.

90. Philip S. Foner and George E. Walker, eds., *Proceedings of the Black State Conventions* (Philadelphia: Temple University Press, 1980), 110–203, for California conventions; Daniels, *Pioneer Urbanites,* 110–11, 117–19. On the city's black press, see William J. Snorgrass, "The Black Press in the San Francisco Bay Area," *California History* 60:4 (1981–82): 306–17.

91. For an insightful discussion on the exclusion of black women from cites of national discourse and their rhetorical strategies, see Carla L. Peterson, *"Doers of the Word": African-American Women Speakers and Writers in the North (1830–1880)* (New York: Oxford University Press, 1995).

92. James Oliver Horton has questioned black Californians' political commitment: "Blacks in California . . . seemed less passionately devoted to the cause of abolition and expressed concern less frequently than blacks in eastern and midwestern cities." Yet evidence from three black newspapers (the *Mirror of the Times,* the *Elevator,* and the *Pacific Appeal*), testimony from the heirs of antebellum black pioneers, and Pleasant's history seem to indicate otherwise. See Horton, *Free People of Color: Inside the African American Community* (Washington, D.C.: Smithsonian Institution Press, 1993), 73.

93. Lapp, *Blacks in Gold Rush California,* 130, 236, 239–40, 255; Eugene Berwanger, *Frontier against Slavery: Western Anti-Negro Prejudice and the Slavery Extension Controversy* (Urbana: University of Illinois Press, 1967), 25; Leon F. Litwack, *North of Slavery,* 66–74. Litwack noted that nearly every northern state considered measures to restrict or prohibit further immigration of African Americans. (66) In the West, anti-immigration bills were considered but not passed in Kansas, New Mexico, and Nebraska. Illinois, Indiana, and Oregon all passed laws that prohibited black immigration.

94. For example, see Lapp, *Blacks in Gold Rush California,* 131–34, 146; Almaguer, *Racial Fault Lines,* 39; Beasley, *Negro Trail Blazers of California,* 72; Delilah L. Beasley, "Slavery in California," *Journal of Negro History* 3 (January 1918): 33–44.

95. Lapp, *Blacks in Gold Rush California,* 147.

96. Charlotte Dennis Downs Interview, #26, April 16, 1950, MEP Coll., SFPL.

97. Lapp, *Blacks in Gold Rush California,* 147.

98. *California Reports* 9 (Sacramento, 1858), 171.

99. According to Beasley, the tugboat rental alone cost $3,050. Beasley, *Negro Trail Blazers of California,* 82–83. See also Rudolph M. Lapp, *Archy Lee: A California Fugitive Slave Case* (San Francisco: Book Club of California, 1969), 22, 45, 61; Rudolph M. Lapp, *Afro-Americans in California* (San Francisco: Boyd and Fraser, 1979), 9–11; Lapp, *Blacks in Gold Rush California,* 152, 256; David W. Ruggles Sr. was one of Pleasant's contemporaries and associates. He is not to be confused with his father, David W. Ruggles, who was a renowned New England abolitionist and died in 1849. His son came to be one of Pleasant's closest associates in San Francisco. His grandson, David W. Ruggles Jr., was one of Holdredge's key interviewees. On the eldest Ruggles, see Dorothy Porter, "David Ruggles, an Apostle of Human Rights," *Journal of Negro History* (January 1943): 23–50.

Ruggles Sr. emigrated to San Francisco during the Gold Rush and, according to his son, took his first job as a cook, just like Pleasant. He became best known for his stove and hardware store on Jackson Street; regular advertisements for Ruggles Stove Shop appeared in the city's black newspapers. Ruggles Sr. stood by Pleasant in the 1880s when she appeared in court.

William Willmore remembered that Ruggles Sr., Pleasant, and John Allen Francis all worked together on fugitive slave cases. Lapp claimed that George Dennis put up the bond money to get Archy Lee out of jail, and David Ruggles gave an address at a meeting about Archy Lee on March 5, 1858.

100. Canada's Imperial Emancipation Act of 1833 outlawed slavery but not, of course, racism. For a discussion of black life in Canada at this time, see Robin Winks, *Blacks in Canada* (New Haven, Conn.: Yale University Press, 1979); Jason H. Silverman, *Unwelcome Guests: Canada West's Response to American Fugitive Slaves, 1800–1865* (Millwood, N.Y.: Associated Faculties Press, 1985).

101. On the exodus to Canada see Lapp, *Blacks in Gold Rush California,* 239–54; Winks, *Blacks in Canada;* C. Peter Ripley, ed., *The Black Abolitionist Papers,* Vol. 2, *Canada, 1830–1865* (Chapel Hill: University of North Carolina Press, 1986); F. W. Howay, "The Negro Immigration into Vancouver Island in 1858," *British Columbia Historical Quarterly* 3 (April 1939): 101–13.

102. Holdredge claimed that the Pleasants left San Francisco on a steamer on April 5, 1858. This seems to contradict other stories claiming that Archy Lee hid at Pleasant's house after the April 14 decision that declared him a free man. Holdredge, *Mammy Pleasant,* 49; Beasley, *Negro Trail Blazers of California,* 83.

103. Rhodes, *Mary Ann Shadd Cary,* 29, 101.

104. Ripley, *Black Abolitionist Papers,* Vol. 2, 425; Benjamin Quarles, *Black Abolitionists* (London: Oxford University Press, 1975), 238.

105. The planning of the raid was a lengthy process for Brown and took place in a variety of locales, but the Chatham convention was critical. For a concise synopsis of the process, see Paul Finkelman, ed., *His Soul Goes Marching On: Responses to John Brown and the Harpers Ferry Raid* (Charlottesville: University Press of Virginia, 1995), 3–9.

106. Winks, *Blacks in Canada*; Ripley, *The Black Abolitionist Papers*, Vol. 2, 3–46; Rhodes, *Mary Ann Shadd Cary*, 100–134.

107. Ripley, *The Black Abolitionist Papers*, Vol. 2, 392–98.

108. Ibid., 393.

109. Davis, "How a Colored Woman Aided John Brown"; Earl Conrad, "She Was a Friend of John Brown," *Negro World Digest* (November 1940): 6–11.

110. On Bell, see Ripley, *The Black Abolitionist Papers*, Vol. 5, 139. Bell's poetry was published often in the San Francisco black newspaper *The Pacific Appeal*.

111. The reference to Pleasant disguised as a male jockey can be found in Du Bois, *The Gifts of Black Folks*, 272; Bettina Aptheker, *Woman's Legacy: Essays on Race, Class, and Sex in American History* (Amherst: Massachusetts University Press, 1981), 38; and Wheeler, *Black Californians*, 88. If the descriptions of Pleasant as a tall, dark woman are accurate, it seems unlikely that she could have traveled through the South in such a disguise.

112. Bennett, "An Historical Detective Story, Parts I and II." On the significance of the raid to the Pleasant legend, see Beasley, *Negro Trail Blazers of California*, 95–96; Thurman, *Pioneers of Negro Origin*, 47.

113. This article was also published in Nantucket in *The Inquirer and Mirror* December 26, 1903.

114. Davis, "How a Colored Woman Aided John Brown."

115. Ibid.

116. Ibid.

117. Recent studies of the "Secret Six" include Edward J. Renehan Jr., *The Secret Six* (New York: Crown, 1995); and Charles E. Heller, *Portrait of an Abolitionist: A Biography of George Luther Stearns, 1809–1867* (Westport, Conn.: Greenwood, 1996).

118. Standard biographies of Brown and recent studies of the "Secret Six" do not mention Pleasant by name. For example, see James Redpath, *The Public Life of Capt. John Brown with an Auto-Biography of His Childhood and Youth* (Boston: Thayer and Eldridge, 1860); Jeffrey Rossbach, *Ambivalent Conspirators: John Brown, the Secret Six, and a Theory of Slave Violence* (Philadelphia: University of Pennsylvania Press, 1982). For an autobiography of a participant, see Osborne P. Anderson, *A Voice from Harpers Ferry, 1859* (Atlanta: World View Publishers, 1861, 1980 reprint).

119. Davis, "How a Colored Woman Aided John Brown."

120. Ibid.

121. Ibid.

122. Ibid.

123. Ibid.

124. Bennett, "An Historical Detective Story, Part II," 80.

125. Holdredge notebook #26, no date, MEP Coll., SFPL.

126. On black Americans and John Brown, see Benjamin Quarles, ed., *Blacks on John Brown* (Urbana: University of Illinois Press, 1972); Philip S. Foner, "Blacks and

John Brown," in *History of Black Americans: From the Compromise of 1850 to the End of the Civil War,* Vol. 3 (Westport, Conn.: Greenwood Press, 1983), 240–65; Daniel C. Littlefield, "Blacks, John Brown, and a Theory of Manhood," in *His Soul Goes Marching On: Responses to John Brown and the Harpers Ferry Raid,* ed. Paul Finkelman (Charlottesville: University Press of Virginia, 1995).

127. Interview with David Ruggles Jr., #24, no date, SFHR.

128. Interview with William Willmore Jr., #26, March 1938, SFHR.

129. Ibid. Holdredge's parenthetical remarks after this interview state, "Willmore was mistaken in thinking that Mammy had, in 1858, tangled with Charles Crocker. This did, indeed, happen but it took place in the 1860s. It was as late as 1887 that Mammy encouraged alien strikers against the railroad."

130. Beasley, *Negro Trail Blazers of California,* 95.

131. More than 100 people attended the dedication program at Tulocay cemetery sponsored by the African American Historical and Cultural Society. *Napa Register,* February 13, 1965.

Chapter 3: Jim Crow San Francisco

1. U.S. Bureau of the Census, *Sixth Census,* 1841.

2. Roger Lotchin, *San Francisco: From Hamlet to City, 1846–1856* (New York: Oxford University Press, 1974), 151.

3. U.S. Bureau of the Census, *Sixth Census,* 1841; Helen Holdredge claims Pleasant was the housekeeper first for Selim Woodworth (for whom she had first worked for beginning in 1856, according to Holdredge) and then his brother Frederick A. Woodworth. Holdredge, *Mammy Pleasant* (New York: G. P. Putnam and Sons, 1953), 60.

4. J. Lloyd Conrich, "The Mammy Pleasant Legend," unpublished manuscript, no date, California Historical Society.

5. Leonard P. Curry, *The Free Black in Urban America, 1800–1850: The Shadow of a Dream* (Chicago: University of Chicago Press, 1981), 15–36.

6. Lawrence B. de Graff, "Race, Sex, and Region: Black Women in the American West, 1850–1920," *Pacific Historical Review* 49 (May 1980): 285–313; Philip M. Montesano, "Some Aspects of the Free Negro Question in San Francisco, 1849–1870," M.A. thesis, University of San Francisco, 1967; Albert S. Broussard, *Black San Francisco: The Struggle for Racial Equality in the West, 1900–1954* (Lawrence: University of Kansas Press, 1993); Douglas Henry Daniels, *Pioneer Urbanites: A Social and Cultural History of Black San Francisco* (Philadelphia: Temple University Press, 1980), 35.

7. Rudolph M. Lapp, "Negro Rights Activities in Gold Rush California," *California Historical Society Quarterly* 45:1 (1966): 3–20.

8. For example, see Rosalyn Terborg-Penn, *African American Women in the Struggle for the Vote, 1850–1920* (Bloomington: Indiana University Press, 1998); Tera W. Hunter, *To 'Joy My Freedom: Southern Black Women's Lives and Labors After the Civil War* (Cambridge, Mass.: Harvard University Press, 1997); Elsa Barkley

Brown, "Negotiating and Transforming the Public Sphere: African American Political Life in the Transition from Slavery to Freedom," in *The Black Public Sphere* (Chicago: University of Chicago Press, 1995); Glenda E. Gilmore, *Gender and Jim Crow: Women and the Politics of White Supremacy in North Carolina, 1896–1920* (Chapel Hill: University of North Carolina Press, 1996); Evelyn Brooks Higginbotham, *Righteous Discontent: The Women's Movement in the Black Baptist Church, 1880–1920* (Cambridge, Mass.: Harvard University Press, 1993); Stephanie J. Shaw, *What a Woman Ought to Be and to Do: Black Professional Women Workers during the Jim Crow Era* (Chicago: University of Chicago Press, 1996).

9. For example, see *Pacific Appeal*, May 24, 1862.

10. List of Negro Business in San Francisco in 1860, in Elena Albert Collection, African American Historical and Cultural Society Library, San Francisco; "Proceedings of the California State Convention of the Colored Citizens, Held in Sacramento on the 25th, 26th, 27th, and 28th of October, 1865," in *Proceedings of the Black State Conventions*, ed. Philip S. Foner and George D. Walker (Philadelphia: Temple University Press, 1980), 180–81.

11. *The Pacific Appeal*, July 25, 1863.

12. *The Pacific Appeal*, November 19, 1870.

13. *The Pacific Appeal*, January 14, 1863; for information on Jeremiah B. Sanderson, see Rudolph M. Lapp, "Jeremiah Sanderson: Early California Negro," *Journal of Negro History* 53:4 (1968): 321–33; Daniels, *Pioneer Urbanites*, 67–68; Lawrence P. Crouchett et al., *Visions toward Tomorrow: The History of the East Bay Afro-American Community, 1852–1977* (Oakland: Northern California Center for Afro-American History and Life, 1989), 5–6.

14. Philip M. Montesano, "San Francisco Black Churches in the Early 1860s: Political Pressure Group," *California Historical Society Quarterly* 52:2 (1973): 145–52. San Francisco City Directories, 1850 to 1870, regularly report on emancipation parades.

15. On the significance of the conventions, see Foner and Walker, *Proceedings of the Black State Conventions*, 110–203, for California conventions; and Daniels, *Pioneer Urbanites*, 110–11, 117–19. On gender and the convention movement, see James O. Horton, "Freedom's Yoke: Gender Conventions among Free Blacks," in Horton, *Free People of Color: Inside the African American Community* (Washington, D.C.: Smithsonian Institution Press, 1993).

16. On Jim Crow and black manhood, see Kevin K. Gaines, *Uplifting the Race: Black Leadership, Politics, and Culture in the Twentieth Century* (Chapel Hill: University of North Carolina Press, 1996).

17. On Philadelphia, see Philip S. Foner, "The Battle to End Discrimination against Negroes on Philadelphia Street Cars: Part I," in *Essays in Afro-American History* (Philadelphia: Temple University Press, 1978), 26; H. E. Cox, "Jim Crow in the City of Brotherly Love: The Segregation of Philadelphia Horse Cars," *Negro History Bulletin* 26:3 (1962): 119–23.

18. *The Pacific Appeal*, May 10, 1862.

19. Gail Bederman, *Manliness and Civilization: A Cultural History of Gender and Race in the United States, 1880–1917* (Chicago: University of Chicago Press, 1995).

20. Edgar M. Kahn, *Cable Car Days in San Francisco* (Stanford, Calif.: Stanford University Press, 1940).

21. James McPherson, *The Negro's Civil War* (New York: Pantheon Books, 1965), 255–56.

22. Evelyn Brooks Higginbotham, "African-American Women's History and the Metalanguage of Race," *Signs* 17 (Winter 1992): 260, 262.

23. Robin D. G. Kelley, *Race Rebels: Culture, Politics, and the Black Working Class* (New York: The Free Press, 1994), 56. Although Kelley's book, especially his third chapter, "Congested Terrain: Resistance on Public Transportation," focuses on twentieth-century resistance, his cogent analysis of its meanings has relevance for the study of Jim Crow protests in the nineteenth century. See also Grace Elizabeth Hale, *Making Whiteness: The Culture of Segregation in the South, 1890–1940* (New York: Pantheon Books, 1998), 125–38.

24. The predecessors of Rosa Parks and the women of the Montgomery Bus Boycott, these nineteenth-century protesters often are overlooked in favor of their twentieth-century counterparts. For a discussion of black women's protests against discrimination in both centuries, see Paula Giddings, *When and Where I Enter: The Impact of Black Women on Race and Sex in America* (New York: William Morrow, 1984); Willi Coleman, "Black Women and Segregated Public Transportation: Ninety Years of Resistance," in *Black Women in United States History*, Vol. 5, ed. Darlene Clark Hine et al. (New York: Carlson, 1990), 295–302. See also Foner, "The Battle to End Discrimination."

25. de Graff, "Race, Sex, and Region," 285–313; Montesano, "Some Aspects of the Free Negro Question"; Broussard, *Black San Francisco*; Daniels, *Pioneer Urbanites*, 35.

26. Mary P. Ryan, *Civic Wars: Democracy and Public Life in the American City during the Nineteenth Century* (Berkeley: University of California Press, 1997), 220–21, 295–96.

27. Ibid., 296.

28. Barbara Y. Welke, "When All the Women Were White, and All the Blacks Were Men: Gender, Class, Race, and the Road to *Plessy*, 1865–1914," *Law and History Review* 13:2 (Fall 1995): 261–316; Higginbotham, "African-American Women's History," 260, 262.

29. *The Pacific Appeal*, March 14, 1863.

30. Reprinted in *The Pacific Appeal*, May 23, 1863.

31. Interview with Charlotte Dennis Downs, #24, MEP Coll., SFPL.

32. *The Pacific Appeal*, July 18, 1863; *Charlotte L. Brown v. Omnibus Railroad Company*, Twelfth District Court, City and County of San Francisco, 1863, manuscript copy, Charlotte L. Brown Papers, California Historical Society. Brown actually sued the Omnibus Railroad Company twice, although it is not clear whether the first case fizzled out. Welke points out that the Omnibus Company defended itself

in the Brown case by claiming that they ejected African American passengers to protect white women and children. Barbara Welke, "Rights of Passage: Gender Rights Consciousness and the Quest for Freedom, San Francisco, California, 1850–1870," in *African American Women Confront the West, 1600–2000*, ed. Quintard Taylor and Shirley Ann Moore (Norman: University of Oklahoma Press, 2003).

33. Ibid. The flurry of activity in the courts came once the ban on African American testimony was lifted.

34. Foner, "The Battle to End Discrimination," 37–38.

35. *The San Francisco Bulletin*, October 3, 1864.

36. *Alta California*, October 17, 1866.

37. Ibid.

38. George W. Tyler was one of the most prominent attorneys in the city.

39. *John J. and Mary E. Pleasants v. NBMRR*, June 20, 1867, California State Archives, Sacramento.

40. Ibid.

41. See W. E. B. Du Bois, *Black Reconstruction in America* (New York: Kraus-Thomson Organization Ltd., 1935); Eric Foner, *Reconstruction: America's Unfinished Revolution* (New York: Harper and Row, 1988).

42. On Reconstruction and black bodies, see Martha Hodes, "The Sexualization of Reconstruction Politics: White Women and Black Men in the South after the Civil War," in *American Sexual Politics: Sex, Gender, and Race since the Civil War*, ed. John C. Fout and Maura Shaw Tantillo (Chicago: University of Chicago Press, 1993), 59–74; Susan Mann, "Slavery, Sharecropping, and Sexual Inequality," *Signs* (Summer 1989): 774–98; Saidiya V. Hartman, *Scenes of Subjection: Terror, Slavery, and Self-Making in Nineteenth-Century America* (New York: Oxford University Press, 1997).

43. The best-known black woman in the crusade against lynching, Ida B. Wells, also fought against Jim Crow transportation in Reconstruction and sued a railway company. On Wells, see Linda O. McMurray, *To Keep the Waters Troubled: The Life of Ida B. Wells* (New York: Oxford University Press, 1998); Giddings, *When and Where I Enter*; and Alfreda M. Duster, ed., *Crusade for Justice: The Autobiography of Ida B. Wells* (Chicago: University of Chicago Press, 1970).

44. Elizabeth B. Clark, "'The Sacred Rights of the Weak': Pain, Sympathy, and the Culture of Individual Rights in Antebellum America," *Journal of American History* 82 (September 1995): 465.

45. "The figure of the slave woman," writes Karen Sanchez-Eppler, "becomes a perfect conduit for the unarticulated and unacknowledged failure of free women to own their own body in marriage." See Karen Sanchez-Eppler, "Bodily Bonds: The Intersecting Rhetorics of Feminism and Abolition," *Representations* 24 (Fall 1988): 28–59.

46. Clark, "Pain, Sympathy," 492.

47. U.S. Bureau of the Census, *Sixth Census*, 1860.

48. *Pleasants v. NBMRR,* June 20, 1867, California State Archives, Sacramento.
49. Ibid.
50. Helen Tunnicliff Catterall, ed., *Judicial Cases Concerning American Slavery and the Negro,* Vol. 5 (Washington, D.C.: Carnegie Institution, 1937).
51. *Pleasants v. NBMRR,* June 20, 1867, California State Archives, Sacramento.
52. On the lives of black domestic workers, see Hunter, *To 'Joy My Freedom.*
53. Ibid.
54. Lynn M. Hudson, "'Strong Animal Passions' in the Gilded Age: Race, Sex, and a Senator on Trial," *Journal of the History of Sexuality* 9:1–2 (January/April 2000): 62–84.
55. For a discussion of the marketing of the mammy, see Cheryl Thurber, "The Development of the Mammy Image and Mythology," in *Southern Women: Histories and Identities,* ed. Virginia Bernhard et al. (Columbia: University of Missouri Press, 1994), 87–108; Patricia A. Turner, *Ceramic Uncles and Celluloid Mammies: Black Images and Their Influence on Culture* (New York: Anchor Books, 1994).
56. *Pleasants v. NBMRR,* California Reports 34, 586 (1868).
57. Ibid.
58. Ibid.
59. *Emma Jane Turner v. NBMRR,* June 20, 1867, California State Archives, Sacramento; Catterall, *Judicial Cases,* 336.
60. Nathaniel S. Colley, "Civil Actions for Damages Arising out of Violations of Civil Rights," *The Hastings Law Journal* 17 (December 1965): 190.
61. Ibid.
62. Harold W. Horowitz, "The 1959 California Equal Rights in Business Establishments Statute: A Problem in Statutory Application," *Southern California Law Review* 33 (1960): 260–305.
63. Ronald P. Klein, "Equal Rights Statutes," *Stanford Law Review* 10 (March 1958): 253–73.
64. Ryan, *Civic Wars;* Mary P. Ryan, *Women in Public: Between Banners and Ballots, 1825–1880* (Baltimore, Md.: Johns Hopkins University Press, 1990), 93, 163.
65. Helen Holdredge claims that in 1868 Pleasant worked as a domestic for George B. Gammons; other sources, including the *City Directory,* indicate that Pleasant was a boardinghouse keeper, not a domestic. Holdredge, *Mammy Pleasant,* 62.
66. For example, see Mary Lee Spence, "They Also Serve Who Wait," *Western Historical Journal* 14 (January 1983); Sandra L. Myres, *Westering Women and the Frontier Experience, 1800–1915* (Albuquerque: University of New Mexico Press), 242–46.
67. Quoted in Gunther Barth, *Instant Cities: Urbanization and the Rise of San Francisco and Denver* (Albuquerque: University of New Mexico Press), 298.
68. Paul Erling Groth, "Forbidden Housing: The Evolution and Exclusion of Hotels, Boarding Houses, Rooming Houses, and Lodging Houses in American Cities, 1880–1938" (Ph.D. diss., University of California at Berkeley, 1983).

69. Philip J. Ethington, *The Public City: The Political Construction of Urban Life in San Francisco, 1850–1900* (Cambridge, England: Cambridge University Press, 1994), 171.

70. Conrich, "Mammy Pleasant Legend," 45.

71. *San Francisco City Directory,* 1869–70.

72. Dupont is now Grant Street, and that corner is in the heart of present-day Chinatown.

73. Ethington, *The Public City,* 59.

74. Polly Welts Kaufman, *Apron Full of Gold: The Letters of Mary Jane Megquier from San Francisco, 1849–1856* (Albuquerque: University of New Mexico Press, 1994), 35.

75. Margaret S. Woyski, "Women and Mining in the Old West," *Journal of the West* 20 (April 1981): 44.

76. Edith Eleanor Sparks, "Capital Instincts: The Economics of Female Proprietorship in San Francisco, 1850–1920" (Ph.D. diss., University of California at Los Angeles, 1999), 82.

77. William Issel and Robert W. Cherny, *San Francisco, 1865–1932: Politics, Power, and Urban Development* (Berkeley: University of California Press, 1986), 58–63.

78. *The Pacific Appeal* carried ads for boardinghouses operated by other African American women; they probably catered to a black clientele. The October 25, 1862 issue noted that Mrs. James Johnson, on the corner of Washington and Stone Streets, could "accommodate a few respectable persons with lodgings, transient or permanent." On the makeup of the Californian elite, see Issel and Cherny, *San Francisco, 1865–1932;* and Lotchin, *San Francisco: From Hamlet to City.*

79. Susan Lee Johnson, "'A Memory Sweet to Soldiers': The Significance of Gender in the History of the American West," *Western Historical Quarterly* 24:4 (November 1993): 495–517; Albert L. Hurtado, "Sex, Gender, Culture, and a Great Event: The California Gold Rush," *Pacific Historical Review* (Summer 1999): 1–19; de Graff, "Race, Sex, and Region"; Susan Armitage and Elizabeth Jameson, eds., *The Women's West* (Norman: Oklahoma University Press, 1987).

80. Conrich, "Mammy Pleasant Legend," 46.

81. Francisco de Talavera Berger and John Parke Custis, *Sumptuous Dining in Gaslight San Francisco, 1875–1915* (Garden City, N.Y.: Doubleday, 1985), 167.

82. William Willmore Interview, #26, March 5, 1938, MEP Coll., SFPL.

83. Kaufman, *Apron Full of Gold,* 99.

84. Ibid., 47.

85. William Willmore Interview, #26, March 5, 1938, MEP Coll., SFPL.

86. Charlotte Dennis Downs Interview, #26, April 1950, MEP Coll., SFPL.

87. Ibid.

88. William Willmore Interview, #26, March 1938, no date specified, MEP Coll., SFPL.

89. William Willmore Interview, #26, March 5, 1938, MEP Coll., SFPL; William Willmore Interview, #24, no date, MEP Coll., SFPL.

90. William Willmore Interview, #24, no date, MEP Coll., SFPL.

91. Elizabeth L. Parker and James Abajian, "A Walking Tour of the Black Presence in San Francisco during the Nineteenth Century" (San Francisco: San Francisco African American Historical and Cultural Society, 1974).

92. The U.S. Census of 1870 lists Newton Booth as a resident of 920 Washington; Lerone Bennett, "An Historical Detective Story," *Ebony* (April 1979): 79.

93. Interview with Edward Bergner, #26, July 1954, no date specified, MEP Coll., SFPL.

94. Ibid.

95. On Whitfield, see Joan R. Sherman, *Invisible Poets: Afro-Americans of the Nineteenth Century* (Urbana: University of Illinois Press, 1974). On Washington Street, see Parker and Abajian, "Walking Tour."

96. Sources are vague on the history of this building. Newspaper reports seem to indicate that the library moved to another location at the end of the 1850s, but it is unclear whether the saloon was still in operation by the time Pleasant moved to the block in the 1860s. See Rudolph M. Lapp, *Blacks in Gold Rush California* (New Haven, Conn.: Yale University Press, 1977), 262.

97. Montesano, "San Francisco Black Churches."

98. See interviews with Willmore, Downs, and Ruggles in MEP Coll., SFPL.

99. This project builds on the work of Mary P. Ryan, Elsa Barkley Brown, and other women's historians who have reconfigured the paradigm of separate spheres; see Mary P. Ryan, *Women in Public*; Elsa Barkley Brown, "Womanist Consciousness: Maggie Lena Walker and the Independent Order of Saint Luke," *Signs* 14:3 (Spring 1989): 610–33; Linda K. Kerber, "Separate Spheres, Female Worlds, Woman's Place: The Rhetoric of Women's History," *The Journal of American History* 75 (June 1988): 9–39.

100. Quoted in Spence, "They Also Serve Who Wait," 12.

101. Charles Caldwell Dobie, *San Francisco: A Pageant* (New York: Appleton-Century, 1933), 316.

102. Boardinghouse keepers were not the only nineteenth-century businesswomen accused of operating bordellos. Wendy Gamber finds female milliners in Boston represented in a similar fashion. See Wendy Gamber, *The Female Economy: The Millinery and Dressmaking Trades, 1860–1930* (Urbana: Illinois University Press, 1997).

103. For example, see Cloyte Murdock, "America's Most Fabulous Black Madam," *Ebony* (April 1954): 46–55; Joseph Horton, "The Happy Black Hooker," *Sepia* 21 (December 1972): 26–28; Eugene Block, *The Immortal San Franciscans: For Whom the Streets Were Named* (San Francisco: Chronicle Books, 1971), 94–96.

104. Mary Murphy, "The Private Lives of Public Women: Prostitution in Butte, Montana, 1878–1917," in *The Women's West*, ed. Susan Armitage et al. (Norman: University of Oklahoma Press, 1987), 193–206; Marion S. Goldman, *Gold Diggers and Silver Miners: Prostitution and the Social Life on the Comstock Lode* (Ann Arbor: University of Michigan, 1981), especially chapter 1. Jacqueline Baker Barn-

hart claims that Pleasant "had in her colorful career in San Francisco been 'kept' by a number of men, had run or owned elegant brothels and assignation houses, and had acted as a marriage broker for some of the women who had worked for her in parlor houses." Barnhart, *The Fair but Frail: Prostitution in San Francisco, 1849–1900* (Reno: University of Nevada Press, 1986), 58; Barnhart cited Helen Holdredge as her source of information on Pleasant. Not all accounts agree that Pleasant's boardinghouses were houses of prostitution. See George Lane interview in MEP Coll., SFPL. When Holdredge asked Lane whether they were houses of prostitution, he stated, "No. They were above anything of the sort. It was considered fashionable to be seen at her 920 Washington boardinghouse."

105. For information on Pleasant's charitable activities, see *The Pacific Appeal,* September 10, 1870, November 19, 1870, January 1, 1871, September 2, 1871, March 2, 1872, August 30, 1873, and May 9, 1874.

106. The history of Maggie Lena Walker indicates that economic self-sufficiency for black women was a significant part of Reconstruction's history; see Brown, "Womanist Consciousness."

107. Bennett, "An Historical Detective Story, Part II," 84.

108. "Servants Tell Tales of Life in Bell Home," *San Francisco Chronicle,* no date.

109. Issel and Cherny, *San Francisco, 1865–1932,* 28–31.

110. Bennett calls Pleasant "that brilliant and knowing manipulator of Western mining stock" and claims she turned Bell into a "financial tiger." Bennett, "An Historical Detective Story, Part II," 84.

111. Dobie, *San Francisco: A Pageant,* 316.

112. *San Francisco Chronicle,* February 12, 1987.

113. Mary Ellen Pleasant file, Bancroft Library, University of California, Berkeley.

114. Interview with Charlotte Downs, #26, no date, MEP Coll., SFPL.

115. For information on Pleasant's holdings in Oakland, see *Oakland Tribune,* September 25, 1889; *Oakland Enquirer,* August 14, 1888, July 5, 1889, and October 10, 1889. The *Enquirer* quote is from the October issue; see also *Cleveland Gazette,* November 29, 1884 and October 23, 1886.

Chapter 4: A Madam on Trial

1. Her case against the North Beach and Mission Railroad had been argued in the District Court of the Twelfth Judicial District and in the California Supreme Court in the 1860s; in 1876 she testified in her husband's suit against A. J. Bowie, which also went before the California Supreme Court.

2. For the purpose of clarity, I will refer to Sarah Althea Hill as Hill or Sarah, although she claimed to be Mrs. Sharon and eventually was Mrs. Terry. Although I acknowledge the problems inherent in naming Sarah Althea Hill "Sarah" and William Sharon "Sharon" I do so intentionally to call attention to the ways they were referred to in the press.

In one month of the 1884 *Sharon v. Sharon* trial the *New York Times,* for example, ran front page stories about it on April 8, 10, and 15. The national significance of the two cases is noted in the journal of former U.S. Supreme Court Justice Stephen J. Field, *Personal Reminiscences of Early Days in California* (New York: Da Capo Press, 1993, originally pub. 1877).

3. Many recent studies analyze late-nineteenth-century courtroom narratives and gendered discourses. For example, see Laura Hanft Korobkin, "The Maintenance of Mutual Confidence: Sentimental Strategies at the Adultery Trial of Henry Ward Beecher," *Yale Journal of Law and the Humanities* 7:1 (1995): 1–48; Richard Wightman Fox, "Intimacy on Trial: Cultural Meanings of the Beecher-Tilton Affair," in *The Power of Culture: Critical Essays in American History,* ed. Richard Wightman Fox and T. J. Jackson Lears (Chicago: University of Chicago Press, 1993); Anne-Louise Shapiro, "Telling Criminal Stories: The *Femme Criminelle* in Late Nineteenth-Century Paris," in *Negotiating at the Margins: The Gendered Discourses of Power and Resistance,* ed. Sue Fisher and Kathy Davis (New Brunswick, N.J.: Rutgers University Press, 1993).

4. There are striking similarities between the enracing of O. J. Simpson in the 1980s and the enracing of Pleasant in the 1880s. And although I do not have the space to discuss them in this book, I am indebted to Ann du Cille for providing an important framework in her study of the Simpson case. Ann du Cille, "The Blacker the Juice: O. J. Simpson and the Squeeze Play of Race," in *Skin Trade* (Cambridge, Mass.: Harvard University Press, 1996).

5. Robert Kroninger, *Sarah and the Senator* (Berkeley, Calif.: Howell-North, 1964), 25–26.

6. See Robert Kroninger and Martin S. Gould, *A Cast of Hawks: A Rowdy Tale of Scandal and Power Politics in Early San Francisco* (La Jolla, Calif.: Copley Books, 1985). This theory received plenty of support in the popular press during the trials and for decades since. For example, see Zoe Battu, "Tin Types," *San Franciscan,* November 29, 1929; Robert O'Brian, "Riptides," *San Francisco Chronicle,* February 18 and 20, 1946.

7. Quoted in John Lawson, ed., *American State Trials* 15 (Saint Louis, Mo.: F. H. Thomas Law Book Co., 1914–36), 505.

8. *San Francisco Examiner,* November 29, 1884.

9. On the economic history of San Francisco's Gilded Age, see William Issel and Robert W. Cherny, *San Francisco, 1865–1932: Politics, Power, and Urban Development* (Berkeley: University of California Press, 1986).

10. William Ralston was the president of Bank of California responsible for the 1875 panic. When he committed suicide, William Sharon inherited his role at the bank and his property, which included the Palace Hotel. See Gray Brechin, *Imperial San Francisco: Urban Power, Earthly Ruin* (Berkeley: University of California Press, 1999); George D. Lyman, *Ralston's Ring: California Plunders the Comstock Lode* (New York: Charles Scribner's Sons, 1937).

11. Although this practice—of living in one state but representing another—was later outlawed, Sharon was well within his rights to do so at the time.

12. Oscar Lewis and Carroll D. Hall, *Bonanza Inn: America's First Luxury Hotel* (New York: Alfred A. Knopf, 1949), 116.

13. William Sharon Manuscripts, Bancroft Library, University of California, Berkeley.

14. Hubert Howe Bancroft and Frances Fuller Victor, *History of Nevada, 1540–1888* (Reno: University of Nevada, 1981), 204.

15. Kroninger, *Sarah and the Senator,* 18.

16. *San Francisco Chronicle,* March 13, 1884.

17. Ibid.

18. Interviews in Tennessee, #4, no date, MEP Coll., SFPL.

19. *San Francisco Chronicle,* March 11, 1884.

20. Ibid.

21. *San Francisco Bulletin,* October 4, 1883.

22. One of the depositions was taken from Freddie Burchard, who claimed to have been engaged to Miss Hill. But Burchard, under cross-examination by Tyler, was forced to admit that he called off the relationship because of his sexual disorders resulting from venereal disease.

23. *San Francisco Chronicle,* March 11, 1884.

24. Transcript of Argument of W. H. L. Barnes, *Sharon v. Sharon* (San Francisco Superior Court, 1883), Bancroft Library, University of California, Berkeley.

25. On the iconography of slavery and the significance of mammy in particular, see Deborah Gray White, *Ar'n't I a Woman: Female Slaves in the Plantation South* (New York: Norton, 1985); Hazel V. Carby, *Reconstructing Womanhood: The Emergence of the Afro-American Woman Novelist* (New York: Oxford University Press, 1987); Cheryl Thurber, "The Development of the Mammy Image and Mythology," in *Southern Women: Histories and Identities,* ed. Virginia Bernhard et al. (Columbia: University of Missouri Press, 1994), 87–108; Patricia A. Turner, *Ceramic Uncles and Celluloid Mammies: Black Images and Their Influence on Culture* (New York: Anchor Books, 1994).

26. I find Korobkin's argument about courtroom storytelling quite compelling: "Lawyers inevitably, and often unconsciously, draw on the story-forms most familiar and powerful within the culture at the time. . . . By suggesting that the facts of a case constitute a story much like others that they know . . . a lawyer can provide jurors with a clear moral framework to use as a guide in making credible determinations and evidentiary assessments." Korobkin, "The Maintenance of Mutual Confidence," 13.

27. Transcript on Appeal, *Sharon v. Sharon* (Supreme Ct. Cal., 1885), California State Archives.

28. Ibid.

29. The original "Bridge of Sighs" connected the Doges Palace with the prison in sixteenth-century Venice; however, the journalists who nicknamed it this probably were taking a swipe at the senator and the traffic—and sighs—his mistresses made on the bridge.

30. Transcript of Argument of William M. Stewart, *Sharon v. Hill* (Ninth District, 1885), Bancroft Library.

31. Ibid.

32. Ibid.

33. For more information on the relationship between Pleasant and the Bells, see Teresa Bell diary, MEP Coll., SFPL; Property Deeds, Pleasant and Bell collections, California Historical Society, San Francisco.

34. On the entertainment value of Victorian courtrooms, see Ginger S. Frost, *Promises Broken: Courtship, Class, and Gender in Victorian England* (Charlottesville: University Press of Virginia, 1995), especially chapter 2, "The Court as Public Theatre."

35. *San Francisco Chronicle*, March 19, 1884.

36. Ibid. Although Barnes and Tyler were the main actors in the courtroom drama, both Sharon and Hill had a team of attorneys.

37. Ibid.

38. *San Francisco Chronicle*, April 15, 1884. On that same day, another woman, Harriet T. Martin, described as "a colored woman well advanced in years," also testified. While working in the Palace Hotel in 1881, Martin said that she saw Sarah Althea hiding behind a door hoping to trap the senator with one of his paramours. Barnes asked the witness, "Did she ever ask you about fortune-tellers?" "Yes; she asked me and offered me $20 for a love powder," stated Martin.

39. *San Francisco Chronicle*, March 19, 1884. This was one of the defense's central arguments: that Sarah had acted like a single woman throughout the period that she claimed to have been married to the senator. See Transcript of Argument of W. H. L. Barnes, *Sharon v. Sharon* (San Francisco Superior Court, 1883), Bancroft Library.

40. On the appeal of spiritualism in the nineteenth century, see Nell Irvin Painter, *Sojourner Truth: A Life, a Symbol* (New York: W. W. Norton, 1996). For information on voodoo in the United States, see Lawrence W. Levine, *Black Culture and Black Consciousness: Afro-American Folk Thought from Slavery to Freedom* (New York: Oxford University Press, 1977); Zora Neale Hurston, *Tell My Horse* (Philadelphia: J. B. Lippincott, 1938), and *Mules and Men* (New York: Negro Universities Press, 1969). For a contemporary account of the significance of voodoo in the United States, see Karen McCarthy Brown, *Mama Lola: A Vodou Priestess in Brooklyn* (Berkeley: University of California Press, 1991). For an insightful analysis of the ways in which voodoo still operates as a code for the primitive in U.S. culture and politics, see Kate Ramsey, "That Old Black Magic: Seeing Haiti through the Wall of Voodoo," *Voice Literary Supplement*, September 27, 1994.

41. On the exoticization of black women and their association with the primitive in the nineteenth century, see Sander Gilman, "Black Bodies, White Bodies: Toward an Iconography of Female Sexuality in Late Nineteenth-Century Art, Medicine, and Literature," in *Race, Writing, and Difference,* ed. Henry Louis Gates, Jr. (Chicago: Chicago University Press, 1986); Nell Irvin Painter, "Representing Truth: Sojourn-

er Truth's Knowing and Becoming Known," *Journal of American History* 81:2 (September 1994): 461–92.

42. Transcript of Argument of W. H. L. Barnes, *Sharon v. Sharon* (San Francisco Superior Court, 1883), Bancroft Library.

43. The witnesses are respectively, Frances Massey, Fred Burchard or "Poor Freddy," and Nellie Brackett.

44. Transcript on Appeal, *Sharon v. Sharon* (Supreme Ct. Cal., 1885); Gould, *A Cast of Hawks,* 217.

45. Transcript of Argument of W. H. L. Barnes, *Sharon v. Sharon* (San Francisco Superior Court, 1883), Bancroft Library.

46. The practice of baby farming—women farming out their often "illegitimate" babies to caretakers—is linked to the unavailability of effective and safe birth control and abortion. It is not coincidental that public attention would be directed to the practice of baby farming in the Victorian era. The Comstock Law, passed in 1873, and the criminalization of birth control continued through the end of the century. See Janet Farrell Brodie, *Contraception and Abortion in Nineteenth-Century America* (Ithaca, N.Y.: Cornell University Press, 1994); Linda Gordon, *Heroes of Their Own Lives: The Politics and History of Family Violence* (New York: Viking, 1988). On the practice of baby farming and its regulation in Great Britain, see Carol Smart, "Disruptive Bodies and Unruly Sex: The Regulation of Reproduction and Sexuality in the Nineteenth Century," in *Regulating Womanhood: Historical Essays on Marriage, Motherhood, and Sexuality,* ed. Carol Smart (New York: Routledge, 1992). Smart notes that several important cases in Britain in the 1870s drew attention to the practice of baby farming.

47. *San Francisco Chronicle,* April 22, 1884.

48. *San Francisco Chronicle,* July 23, 1884; for additional coverage of this episode, see *San Francisco Call,* July 23–26, 1884.

49. *San Francisco Chronicle,* July 23, 1884.

50. *H.M.S. Pinafore,* one of Gilbert and Sullivan's most successful productions, opened in London in 1878. In the second act Little Buttercup sings "A Many Years Ago," which includes the lines "A many years ago, / When I was young and charming, / As some of you may know, / I practiced baby-farming."

51. *San Francisco Chronicle,* July 24, 1884.

52. *San Francisco Chronicle,* August 13, 1884.

53. Ibid.

54. Ibid.

55. Ibid.

56. *San Francisco Chronicle,* March 25, 1884.

57. Transcript of Argument of W. H. L. Barnes, *Sharon v. Sharon* (San Francisco Superior Court, 1883), Bancroft Library.

58. Transcript of Argument of William M. Stewart, *Sharon v. Hill* (Ninth District, 1885), Bancroft Library.

59. Transcript of Argument of W. H. L. Barnes, *Sharon v. Sharon* (San Francisco Superior Court, 1883), Bancroft Library.

60. Ibid.

61. Kroninger, *Sarah and the Senator,* 158.

62. Ibid.

63. Ibid., 168.

64. Ibid., 174.

65. Quoted in Ibid., 185.

66. Ibid.

67. The California Supreme Court ruled that Sharon and Hill were married and then reversed its decision.

68. That David S. Terry and Pleasant would end up on the same side of a court battle was more than a little odd. In 1858, when Terry served as chief justice of the State Supreme Court, he heard California's version of the Dred Scott case, the Archy Lee case. Chief Justice Terry pardoned a slaveholder for keeping Archy Lee as a slave in California, despite the fact that California had outlawed slavery. Terry probably was best known for his 1859 duel against David Broderick; he resigned as chief justice of the State Supreme Court to fight the duel. Terry was a Democrat and vehemently proslavery, whereas Broderick, then U.S. senator, was a leader of the California antislavery Democrats and one of the state's most successful politicians. See Philip J. Ethington, *The Public City: The Political Construction of Urban Life in San Francisco, 1850–1900* (Cambridge, England: Cambridge University Press, 1994). Much has also been written about Terry and the Vigilance Committee; for a less scholarly but lively discussion of the subject, see Gertrude Atherton, *California: An Intimate History* (New York: Blue Ribbon Books, 1936), chapter 14, "The Vigilance Committee and David S. Terry."

69. *San Francisco Chronicle,* February 14, 1892.

70. *San Francisco Chronicle,* March 10, 1892; Sarah Terry lived at the Stockton State Hospital for the Insane for another forty-five years. She died on February 14, 1937.

71. Issel and Cherny, *San Francisco, 1865–1932,* 124; Kroninger, *Sarah and the Senator,* 123.

72. Lloyd J. Conrich, "The Mammy Pleasant Legend" (unpublished manuscript, no date, California Historical Society), 102.

73. Ibid.

74. Michel Foucault, *Power/Knowledge,* ed. Colin Gordon (New York: Random House, 1981).

75. Transcript on Appeal, *Sharon v. Sharon* (California Supreme Court, 1885), California State Archives.

76. Gould, *A Cast of Hawks,* 193.

77. Transcript on Appeal, *Sharon v. Sharon* (California Supreme Court, 1885), California State Archives.

78. Martha Hodes, "The Sexualization of Reconstruction Politics: White Wom-

en and Black Men in the South after the Civil War," *Journal of the History of Sexuality* 3:3 (1993). See also Robyn Wiegman, "The Anatomy of Lynching," *Journal of the History of Sexuality* 3:3 (1993).

79. Mary P. Ryan, *Women in Public: Between Banners and Ballots, 1825–1880* (Baltimore, Md.: Johns Hopkins University Press, 1993).

80. For example, see Ethington, *The Public City.*

81. Lawrence B. de Graff, "Race, Sex, and Region: Black Women in the American West, 1850–1920," *Pacific Historical Review* 49 (May 1980): 285–313.

82. Douglas Henry Daniels, *Pioneer Urbanites: A Social and Cultural History of Black San Francisco* (Philadelphia: Temple University Press, 1980), 54–55.

Chapter 5: The House of Mystery

1. The cases occurred in 1899: *Pleasant v. Solomons, Bell v. Solomons,* Fred Bell's suit against Teresa Bell, and Pleasant's insolvency case.

2. MEP Coll., SFPL, Teresa Bell Diary, #17.

3. *San Francisco Chronicle,* October 17, 1892. Newspaper reports question the eldest son's whereabouts at the time of the fall.

4. Ibid.

5. Lerone Bennett, "An Historical Detective Story: The Mystery of Mary Ellen Pleasant, Part I," *Ebony* (April 1979): 92.

6. Ibid., 95. Probate records from this period were burned in the 1906 fire, hence the reliance on newspapers and secondary sources for information about Bell's will.

7. *San Francisco Examiner,* October 16, 1892.

8. Ibid.

9. *San Francisco Chronicle,* October 17, 1892.

10. Estimates of Thomas Bell's wealth must be determined from newspaper articles and accounts of his will. See MEP Coll., #17, SFPL.

11. *San Francisco Chronicle,* September 9, 1897.

12. The children were ages 17, 16, 14, 14, 12, and 8, respectively, at the time of Bell's death.

13. MEP Coll., #25, no date, SFPL.

14. J. Lloyd Conrich, "The Mammy Pleasant Legend," unpublished manuscript, no date, California Historical Society, 126.

15. The deeds are located at the California Historical Society.

16. Conrich, "The Mammy Pleasant Legend," 126.

17. *San Francisco Chronicle,* October 17, 1892.

18. Ibid.

19. Helen Holdredge, *Mammy Pleasant* (New York: G. P. Putnam's Sons, 1953), 244.

20. For example, see Erin H. Turner, *More Than Petticoats: Remarkable California Women* (Helena, MT: Falcon Publishing, 1999).

21. As quoted in *The San Francisco Call* September 15, 1897.

22. *San Francisco Chronicle,* September 9, 1897. *The San Francisco Call* report-

ed the same scenario slightly differently: "Mammy Pleasant guarded the portals of 'the house of silence'—the home of the Bells—and at her mistress' command allowed no one in to see her."

23. *San Francisco Chronicle*, September 9, 1897.

24. *San Francisco Chronicle*, September 10, 1897.

25. Ibid.

26. *San Francisco Chronicle*, September 16, 1897.

27. Ibid.

28. This is how the *Chronicle* reported the case. September 15, 1897.

29. *San Francisco Call*, September 10, 1897.

30. *San Francisco Call*, September 21, 1897.

31. *San Francisco Chronicle*, September 23, 1897.

32. Ibid.

33. *San Francisco Chronicle*, September 10, 1897.

34. Ibid.

35. "Mammy Pleasant," *The City Argus* (September 1897): 23. For a discussion of maids and their representation, see Trudier Harris, *From Mammies to Militants: Domestics in Black American Literature* (Philadelphia: Temple University Press, 1982); Patricia Morton, *Disfigured Images: The Historical Assault against Black Women* (Westport, Conn.: Greenwood Press, 1991); Minrose C. Gwin, *Black and White Women of the Old South: The Peculiar Sisterhood in American Literature* (Knoxville: University of Tennessee Press, 1985). On the history of black domestics, see Elizabeth Ross Haynes, "Negroes in Domestic Service in the United States," in *Black Women in United States History*, Vol. 2, ed. Darlene Clark Hine et al. (New York: Carlson Publishing, 1990), 507–66; Susan Tucker, "A Complex Bond: Southern Black Domestic Workers and Their White Employers" in *Black Women in United States History*, Vol. 4, ed. Darlene Clark Hine et al. (New York: Carlson Publishing, 1990), 1187–1204; Tera W. Hunter, "Domination and Resistance: The Politics of Wage Household Labor in New South Atlanta," *Labor History* 34 (Spring/Summer 1993): 205–20.

36. For example, see Deborah McDowell and Arnold Rampersad, eds., *Slavery and the Literary Imagination* (Baltimore, Md.: Johns Hopkins University Press, 1989); Elizabeth Fox-Genovese, *Within in the Plantation Household: Black and White Women of the Old South* (Chapel Hill: University of North Carolina Press, 1988).

37. For a discussion of domestic work for wages, see Alice Kessler Harris, *Out to Work: A History of Wage-Earning Women in the United States* (New York: Oxford University Press, 1982; Christine Stansell, *City of Women: Sex and Class in New York, 1789–1860* (Urbana: University of Illinois Press, 1982; 1987 edition), see chapter 8 on servant's work; Jane H. Pease and William H. Pease, *Ladies, Women, and Wenches: Choice and Constraint in Antebellum Charleston and Boston* (Chapel Hill: University of North Carolina Press, 1990), chapter 3. The Peases' study is particularly useful because it compares black and white household workers.

38. List of properties owned by Pleasant and Teresa Bell, MEP Coll., Teresa Bell Diary, #3, SFPL. This folder contains property lists prepared by Holdredge and letters from Teresa Bell to attorneys and applications for bonds. The later documents describe Beltane Ranch and its history.

39. MEP Coll., Teresa Bell Diary, #3, SFPL.

40. MEP Coll., #3, SFPL.

41. Bell Diary, #14, June 25, 1897, MEP Coll., SFPL.

42. Bell Diary, #14, August 3, 1897, MEP Coll., SFPL.

43. Bell Diary, #15, February 3, 1898, MEP Coll., SFPL.

44. Bell Diary #17, March 26 and April 8, 1899, MEP Coll., SFPL.

45. Bell Diary, #17, April 19, 1899, MEP Coll., SFPL. No record of this list exists at the Bancroft Library at University of California, Berkeley.

46. Bell Diary #17, April 19, 1899, MEP Coll., SFPL.

47. Bell Diary #17, April 20, 1899, MEP Coll., SFPL.

48. Bell Diary #17, April 26, 1899, MEP Coll., SFPL. Teresa wrote in her diary that the newspapers reported that Pleasant was kicked out of the house.

49. *San Francisco Call,* May 7, 1899.

50. *San Francisco Call,* May 11, 1899.

51. Ibid.

52. Ibid.

53. Bell Diary #17, May 17, 1899, MEP Coll., SFPL.

54. Bell Diary #17, May 18, 1899, MEP Coll., SFPL.

55. Mary Ellen Pleasant Collection #26, newspaper clipping, September 1899, MEP Coll., SFPL.

56. *San Francisco Chronicle,* September 12, 1899; *Pleasant v. Solomons,* September 1899, California State Archives.

57. *San Francisco Chronicle,* September 21, 1899.

58. Bell Diary #17, September 21, 1899, MEP Coll., SFPL.

59. *San Francisco Chronicle,* September 21, 1899.

60. Bell Diary #17, September 21, 1899, MEP Coll., SFPL.

61. Bell Diary #17, November 3, 1899, MEP Coll., SFPL.

62. Bell Diary #17, May 18, 1899, MEP Coll., SFPL.

63. Bennett, "An Historical Detective Story, Part I," 94.

64. Bell Diary #17, July 7, 1899, MEP Coll., SFPL.

65. Bell Diary, #17, July 9, 1899, MEP Coll., SFPL.

66. *San Francisco Chronicle,* July 9, 1899.

67. Ibid.

68. *San Francisco Call,* November 9, 1899.

69. Ibid.

70. *San Francisco Chronicle,* July 9, 1899.

71. Ibid.

72. *San Francisco Examiner,* January 12, 1904.

73. Mary Ellen Pleasant, "Memoirs and Autobiography," *The Pandex of the Press* 1 (January 1902): 1.

74. Ibid.

75. Conrich, "The Mammy Pleasant Legend," 177.

76. *San Francisco Examiner,* January 12, 1904.

77. *San Francisco Chronicle,* January 12, 1904.

78. Ibid.

79. *San Francisco Examiner,* January 12, 1904.

80. Ibid.

81. *San Francisco Call,* January 16, 1904.

82. *San Francisco Chronicle,* January 16, 1904.

83. *San Francisco Examiner,* January 29, 1904; *San Francisco Call,* January 29, 1904; *San Francisco Chronicle,* January 19, 1904.

84. *San Francisco Call,* January 29, 1904.

85. The claim that Fred Bell cared for Pleasant during her final days seems unlikely given all the lawsuits he had waged.

86. *San Francisco Chronicle,* January 29, 1904.

87. Ibid.

88. *San Francisco Call,* May 17, 1904.

89. Ibid.

90. Mary Ellen Pleasant Collection, #5, #6, #8, #12, MEP Coll., SFPL.

91. *San Francisco Call,* April 16, 1910.

92. Mary Ellen Pleasant Collection, #5, #6, #8, #12, MEP Coll., SFPL.

93. One piece of property that Pleasant and Bell owned was valued at $1,800,000 in 1916. See *Oakland Tribune,* September 3, 1916.

94. Pleasant, "Memoirs," 4. By comparison, the estate of Los Angeles entrepreneur Biddy Mason, also a black woman, was valued at $300,000 in 1896. See Dolores Hayden, "Biddy Mason's Los Angeles, 1856–1891," *California History* 68 (Fall 1989): 69–76; Lawrence B. de Graaf, "Race, Sex, and Region: Black Women in the West, 1850–1920," *Pacific Historical Review* 49 (May 1980): 285–313. For more general information on the wealth of the black elite, see Willard B. Gatewood, *Aristocrats of Color, the Black Elite, 1880–1920* (Bloomington: Indiana University Press, 1990); Leonard P. Curry, *The Free Black in Urban America, 1800–1850: The Shadow of a Dream* (Chicago: University of Chicago Press, 1981), 37–48. Curry's extensive study of census data reveals that antebellum "urban blacks shared the capitalistic zeal for property acquisition" but lagged far behind white capitalists because of limited employment and exclusion from speculative activity (47–48).

95. For example, see the story of the Moss brothers, shopkeepers in Memphis and friends of Ida B. Wells Barnett, in Paula Giddings, *When and Where I Enter: The Impact of Black Women on Race and Sex in America* (New York: William Morrow, 1984), 17–30; see also Elsa Barkley Brown, "Womanist Consciousness: Maggie Lena Walker and the Independent Order of Saint Luke," *Signs* 14:3 (Spring 1989): 610–33; Elsa Barkley Brown, "Negotiating and Transforming the Public Sphere: African

American Political Life in the Transition from Slavery to Freedom," in *The Black Public Sphere,* ed. The Black Public Sphere Collective (Chicago: University of Chicago Press, 1995); Juliet E. K. Walker, *The History of Black Business in America: Capitalism, Race, Entrepreneurship* (New York: Prentice Hall, 1998).

Chapter 6: Making Mammy Work for You

1. The novels include Charles Caldwell Dobie, *Less Than Kin* (New York: John Day & Co., 1926); Evelyn Wells, *The Golden Snare* (serialized in *The San Francisco Call* beginning September 3, 1941); Frank Yerby, *Devilseed* (Garden City, N.Y.: Doubleday, 1984); Jacqueline LaTourrete, *The House on Octavia Street* (New York: Beaufort Books, 1984); Michelle Cliff, *Free Enterprise* (New York: Dutton, 1993); Daniel Alef, *Pale Truth* (Los Angeles: Cahners Publishing Company, 2000); and Karen Joy Fowler, *Sister Noon* (New York: G. P. Putnam's Sons, 2001). The theatrical productions include John Willard, *The Cat and the Canary: A Melodrama in Three Acts* (New York: S. French, 1927); *Dark Cowgirls and Prairie Queens,* Carpet Bag Theatre, Knoxville, Tenn.; and Susheel Bibbs, *On My Journey Now: The Saga of Mary Ellen Pleasant.* Films include *The Cat and the Canary,* Universal Pictures, Los Angeles, 1927; *The Cat Creeps,* Universal Pictures, Los Angeles, 1930; *The Cat and the Canary,* Paramount, Los Angeles, 1939; *The Cat and the Canary,* Gal/Grenadier Productions, Great Britain, 1979. On September 27, 1960, NBC aired a televised version of *The Cat and the Canary* on the *Dow Hour of Great Mysteries.*

These are examples of texts in which Pleasant is portrayed as a central figure. It is by no means a definitive list of the representations of Pleasant in popular culture. She appears briefly or in the periphery in many other novels and productions. For example, see Toni Cade Bambara's *The Salt Eaters* (New York: Random House, 1980), where Pleasant is described as a "boardinghouse keeper from the Coast" who "was prepared to bankroll the original plan for Harpers Ferry." (127)

2. On the representations and marketing of black female historical figures, see Hazel Carby, "The Politics of Fiction, Anthropology, and the Folk," in *History and Memory in African-American Culture,* ed. Geneviève Fabre and Robert O'Meally (New York: Oxford University Press, 1994); Nell Irvin Painter, "Representing Truth: Sojourner Truth's Knowing and Becoming Known," *Journal of American History* 81:2 (September 1994): 461–92.

3. As Jennifer Brody so aptly notes, these fears of miscegenation and hybridity took on new significance in the post-Darwinian era. Jennifer DeVere Brody, *Impossible Purities: Blackness, Femininity, and Victorian Culture* (Durham, N.C.: Duke University Press, 1998).

4. Linda Williams, *Playing the Race Card: Melodramas of Black and White from Uncle Tom to O. J. Simpson* (Princeton, N.J.: Princeton University Press), xiv.

5. Ibid., 6.

6. Eric Lott, *Love and Theft: Blackface Minstrelsy and the American Working Class* (New York: Oxford University Press, 1993), 18.

7. Cheryl Thurber, "The Development of the Mammy Image and Mythology," in

Southern Women: Histories and Identities, ed. Virginia Bernhard et al. (Columbia: University of Missouri Press, 1994), 99. Thurber finds that the actual peak in terms of memoirs and memorials to Mammy was the period between 1906 and 1912, although she finds ample evidence that the fascination continued into the next decade.

8. Grace Elizabeth Hale, *Making Whiteness: The Culture of Segregation in the South, 1890–1940* (New York: Pantheon Books, 1998), especially 85–119.

9. Deborah Gray White, *Ar'n't I a Woman: Female Slaves in the Plantation South* (New York: Norton, 1985), 27–61.

10. On the prevalence of mammies in material and popular culture, see Lisa M. Anderson, *Mammies No More: The Changing Image of Black Women on Stage and Screen* (New York: Bowman and Littlefield, 1997); Patricia A. Turner, *Ceramic Uncles and Celluloid Mammies: Black Images and Their Influence on Culture* (New York: Anchor Books, 1994); Kenneth W. Goings, *Mammy and Uncle Mose: Black Collectibles and American Stereotyping* (Bloomington: Indiana University Press, 1994).

11. Charles Caldwell Dobie, *San Francisco: A Pageant* (New York: D. Appleton-Century, 1933), 316.

12. Ibid.

13. Radio Broadcasts, no date, Charles Caldwell Dobie Papers, Bancroft Library, University of California, Berkeley.

14. *New York Times,* January 9, 1927.

15. Ibid.

16. Hale, *Making Whiteness,* 85–119; Elizabeth Schultz, "Out of the Woods and into the World: A Study of Interracial Friendships between Women in American Novels," in *Conjuring: Black Women, Fiction, and Literary Tradition,* ed. Hortense Spillers and Marjorie Pryse (Bloomington: Indiana University Press, 1985), 67–85.

17. Dobie, *Less than Kin,* 13.

18. Ibid., 291.

19. Mr. Holt to Charles Caldwell Dobie, January 20, 1927, Charles Caldwell Dobie Papers, Bancroft Library.

20. Ibid.

21. Although I do not have publication figures for the 1935 reissue of *Less Than Kin,* even a conservative estimate of 2,000 copies printed would bring the total number of copies printed to 7,000. Atherton herself was a San Francisco legend and a great fan of Dobie. Dobie Papers.

22. Universal Pictures Corporation to Agnes Kerr Crawford, August 3, 1928, Dobie Papers.

23. Helen Holdredge, *Mammy Pleasant* (New York: G. P. Putnam and Sons, 1953), 209.

24. Marvin Lachman and Charles Shibuk, eds., *Encyclopedia of Mystery and Detection* (New York: McGraw-Hill, 1976), 420–21.

25. *New York Tribune,* February 8, 1922; *New York Globe,* February 8, 1922; *New York Mail,* February 8, 1922; *New York Times,* February 8, 1922.

26. As quoted in Anthony Slide, ed., *Selected Theatre Criticism,* Vol. 2, *1920–1930* (Metuchen, N.J.: Scarecrow Press, 1985), 24–25.

27. William Torbert Leonard, *Theatre: From Stage to Screen to Television,* Vol. 1 (Metuchen, N.J.: Scarecrow Press, 1981), 268; J. P. Wearing, *The London Stage 1920–1929: A Calendar of Plays and Players,* Vol. 1, *1920–1924* (Metuchen, N.J.: Scarecrow Press, 1984), 318.

28. *New York Times,* June 15, 1937, p. 26.

29. For example, see Williams, *Playing the Race Card;* Thomas Schatz, "The Family Melodrama," in *Hollywood Genres: Formulas, Filmmaking, and the Studio System* (New York: Random House, 1981); Chuck Kleinhau, "Notes on Melodrama and the Family Under Capitalism," *Film Reader* 3 (February 1978): 40–47; Robert Lang, *American Film Melodrama: Griffith, Vidor, Minnelli* (Princeton, N.J.: Princeton University Press, 1989).

30. John Willard, *The Cat and the Canary* (New York: Samuel French, 1927).

31. Ibid., 5.

32. Ibid., 83.

33. In 1930 the film was remade with sound as *The Cat Creeps;* in 1939, Paramount Pictures remade *The Cat and the Canary,* starring Bob Hope and Paulette Goddard; in 1978 there was a British version.

34. Siegfried Kracauer, *From Caligari to Hitler: A Psychological History of the German Film* (Princeton, N.J.: Princeton University Press, 1946, rpt. 1974), 75, 135.

35. William K. Everson, *American Silent Film* (New York: Oxford University Press, 1978), 13.

36. Daniel Bernardi, "The Voice of Whiteness: D. W. Griffith's Biograph Films (1908–1913)," in *The Birth of Whiteness: Race and the Emergence of U.S. Cinema,* ed. Daniel Bernardi (New Brunswick, N.J.: Rutgers University Press, 1996), 103–28.

37. Lott, *Love and Theft;* Donald Bogle, *Toms, Coons, Mulattoes, Mammies and Bucks: An Interpretive History of Blacks in American Film* (New York: Viking, 1973); Michael Rogin, "Making America Home: Racial Masquerade and Ethnic Assimilation in the Transition to Talking Pictures," *The Journal of American History* 79:3 (December 1972): 1050–77.

38. The campaign to pass the 1924 Racial Integrity Act in Virginia is an excellent example of this heightened concern over racial definitions and categories. See Barbara Bair, "Remapping the Black/White Body: Sexuality, Nationalism, and Biracial Antimiscegenation Activism in 1920s Virginia," in *Sex Love, Race: Crossing Boundaries in North American History,* ed. Martha Hodes (New York: New York University Press, 1999), 399–419.

39. Peggy Pascoe, "Miscegenation Law, Court Cases, and Ideologies of 'Race' in Twentieth-Century America," *The Journal of American History* 83:1 (June 1996): 44–69.

40. For example, see White, *Ar'n't I a Woman;* Catherine Clinton, *The Plantation Mistress: Woman's World in the Old South* (New York: Pantheon Books, 1982);

Angela Y. Davis, *Women, Race, and Class* (New York: Random House, 1981), 87–98.

41. White, *Ar'n't I a Woman;* Walter Johnson, *Soul by Soul: Life Inside the Antebellum Slave Market* (Cambridge, Mass.: Harvard University Press, 1999).

42. Pascoe, "Miscegenation Law"; Robyn Wiegman, *American Anatomies: Theorizing Race and Gender* (Durham, N.C.: Duke University Press, 1995), 21–42; for a discussion of miscegenation in recent fiction, see Barbara Christian, "'Somebody Forgot to Tell Somebody Something': African-American Women's Historical Novels," in *Wild Women in the Whirlwind: Afra-American Culture and the Contemporary Literary Renaissance,* ed. Joanne M. Braxton and Andree Nicola McLaughlin (New Brunswick, N.J.: Rutgers University Press, 1990). On the fear of miscegenation as expressed in film, see Bernardi, *The Birth of Whiteness,* 201–70.

43. Dobie, *Less Than Kin,* 87.

44. Ibid., 172.

45. Ibid., 34.

46. Martin S. Gould, *A Cast of Hawks: A Rowdy Tale of Scandal and Power Politics in Early San Francisco* (La Jolla, Calif.: Copley Books, 1985), 193.

47. Beverley J. Stoeltje, "A Helpmate for Man Indeed: The Image of the Frontier Woman," *Journal of American Folklore* 88 (January–March, 1975): 25–41.

48. According to the *Dictionary of Literary Biography, Foxes of Harrow* sold more than 600,000 copies, and overall Yerby's novels have sold more than 25 million copies; William L. Van DeBurg, *Slavery and Race in American Popular Culture* (Madison: University of Wisconsin Press, 1984), 146.

49. Frank Yerby, "How I Write the Costume Novel," *Harper's Magazine* 219 (October 1959): 145–50.

50. Yerby, *Devilseed,* 99.

51. Ibid., 96.

52. Frank Yerby, *The Dahomeans* (New York: Viking, 1968), xi.

53. Yerby, *Devilseed,* 95.

54. Ibid., 106.

55. Ibid.

56. Ibid., 176.

57. Renee Hausmann Shea, "Interview: Michelle Cliff," *Belle Lettres* 9 (Spring 1994): 32; see also Judith Raiskin, "The Art of History: An Interview with Michelle Cliff," *Kenyon Review* 15:1 (1993): 57–71.

58. Michelle Cliff, "The Resonance of Interruption," *Chrysallis* 8 (Summer 1979).

59. Shea, "Interview," 33.

60. Cliff, *Free Enterprise,* 16–17.

61. Ibid., 100.

62. It was Frederick Douglass's warning about Harpers Ferry, not Harriet Tubman's, that was ignored. Nor did John Brown die in the raid, as Cliff depicts it, but was executed after a well-publicized trial in which he was glorified as a martyr to

the cause of freedom. For example, see Benjamin Quarles, ed., *Blacks on John Brown* (Urbana: University of Illinois Press, 1972).

63. Cliff, *Free Enterprise,* 101.

64. Victoria A. Brownworth, "Capitalism's Costs," *Lambda Book Report* (September–October 1993): 23.

65. Raiskin, "The Art of History," 57.

66. Cliff, *Free Enterprise,* 144.

67. Ibid.

68. Cliff, *Free Enterprise,* 105.

69. Deborah McDowell, "Taking Liberties with History," *Women's Review of Books* 11 (July 1994): 32.

70. Ibid.

71. Stuart Hall, "Subjects in History: Making Diasporic Identities," in *The House That Race Built: Black Americans, U.S. Terrain,* ed. Wahneema Lubiano (New York: Pantheon Books, 1997).

72. Alef, *Pale Truth,* 20.

73. Brad Hooper, review of *Pale Truth* in *Booklist* 97:4 (October 15, 2000): 416; *Publisher's Weekly* 247:38 (September 18, 2000): 86.

74. Fowler, *Sister Noon,* 56.

75. Ibid., 59–62.

76. Ibid., 100.

77. On gender and performativity see Judith Butler, *Gender Trouble: Feminism and the Subversion of Identity* (New York: Routledge, 1990).

Conclusion

1. Alan Trachtenberg, *The Incorporation of America: Culture and Society in the Gilded Age* (New York: Hill and Wang, 1982).

2. Elsa Barkley Brown, "Womanist Consciousness: Maggie Lena Walker and the Independent Order of Saint Luke," *Signs* 14:3 (Spring 1989): 610–33; Paula Giddings, *When and Where I Enter: The Impact of Black Women on Race and Sex in America* (New York: William Morrow, 1988), 104, 187–89.

3. For example, see Sharon R. Ullman, *Sex Seen: The Emergence of Modern Sexuality in America* (Berkeley: University of California Press, 1997); Carroll Smith-Rosenberg, *Disorderly Conduct: Visions of Gender in Victorian America* (New York: Oxford University Press, 1985), 90.

4. Mary P. Ryan, *Women in Public: Between Banners and Ballots, 1825–1880* (Baltimore, Md.: Johns Hopkins University Press, 1990).

5. Kevin K. Gaines, *Uplifting the Race: Black Leadership, Politics, and Culture in the Twentieth Century* (Chapel Hill: University of North Carolina Press, 1996).

6. Elsa Barkley Brown, "Negotiating and Transforming the Public Sphere: African America Political Life in the Transition from Slavery to Freedom," in *The Black Public Sphere: A Public Culture Book,* ed. The Black Public Sphere Collective (Chi-

cago: University of Chicago Press, 1995), 111–50; Evelyn Brooks Higginbotham, *Righteous Discontent: The Women's Movement in the Black Baptist Church, 1880–1920* (Cambridge, Mass.: Harvard University Press, 1993).

7. Mary Ellen Pleasant, "Memoirs and Autobiography," *The Pandex of the Press* 1 (January 1902): 4.

8. Hayden White, "The Value of Narrativity in the Representations of Reality," in *On Narrative*, ed. W. J. T. Mitchell (Chicago: University of Chicago Press, 1981), 23.

9. For an excellent summary and critique of this recent scholarship, see George Lipsitz, "The Possessive Investment in Whiteness: Racialized Social Democracy and the 'White' Problem in American Studies," *American Quarterly* (September 1995): 369–87. See also Alexander Saxton, *The Rise and Fall of the White Republic: Class Politics and Mass Culture in Nineteenth-Century America* (New York: Verso, 1990).

10. Pleasant, "Memoirs and Autobiography," 4.

SELECTED BIBLIOGRAPHY

Primary Sources

Manuscripts

Georgia State Archives, Georgia Department of Archives and History, Atlanta.

Manuscript Census, National Archives of the United States, Washington, D.C.

Massachusetts State Archives and Records Preservation, Boston.

Nantucket Historical Association Research Center & Edouard A. Stackpole Library, Nantucket, Mass.

Mary Ellen Pleasant Collection. San Francisco Public Library (MEP Coll., SFPL)

Mary Ellen Pleasant Collection. San Francisco African American Historical and Cultural Society.

Mary Ellen Pleasant Papers, Sharon Family Papers, William C. Ralston Papers, Papers Related to Quicksilver Mining, James Abajian Collection, and Charles Caldwell Dobie Papers. The Bancroft Library, University of California, Berkeley.

Mary Ellen Pleasant Biography File, Thomas Bell & Family Biography File, and George W. Dennis Biography File. The Society of California Pioneers, San Francisco.

Mary Ellen Pleasant File. Oakland Public Library.

Supreme and Appellate Court Records. California State Archives, Sacramento.

Teresa Bell Collections. California Historical Society, San Francisco.

Government Documents, Reports, and Publications

DeBow, J. D. B., ed. *Statistical View of the United States: . . . Being a Compendium of the Seventh Census to Which Are Added the Results of Every Previous Census, Beginning with 1790. . . .* New York: Gordon and Breach Science Publishers, 1970, originally published 1850.

Hewett, Janet B., ed. *Georgia Confederate Soldiers, 1861–1865, Name Roster.* Vol. 2. Wilmington, N.C.: Broadfoot Publishing Company, 1998.

Jackson, Ronald Vern, et al., eds. *Early America Series: Early Georgia, 1733–1819.* Bountiful, Utah: Accelerated Indexing Systems, n.d.

———. *Georgia 1850 Census Index*. Bountiful, Utah: Accelerated Indexing Systems, n.d.

Register, Alvaretta Kenan, ed. *Index to the 1830 Census of Georgia*. Baltimore, Md.: Genealogical Publishing Company, 1974.

U.S. Bureau of the Census. *Third Census of the United States, 1810*. Washington, D.C., 1812.

———. *Fourth Census of the United States, 1820*. Washington, D.C., 1821.

———. *Fifth Census of the United States, 1830*. Washington, D.C., 1832.

———. *Sixth Census of the United States, 1840*. Washington, D.C., 1841.

———. *Seventh Census of the United States, 1850*. Washington, D.C., 1853.

———. *Eighth Census of the United States, 1860*. Washington, D.C., 1864.

———. *Ninth Census of the United States, 1870*. Washington, D.C., 1872.

———. *Tenth Census of the United States, 1880*. Washington, D.C., 1883.

———. *Negro Population, 1790–1915*. Washington, D.C.: GPO, 1918.

Secondary Sources

Alef, Daniel. *Pale Truth*. Los Angeles: Cahners Publishing Company, 2000.

Almaguer, Tomás. *Racial Fault Lines: The Historical Origins of White Supremacy in California*. Berkeley: University of California Press, 1994.

Anderson, Lisa M. *Mammies No More: The Changing Image of Black Women on Stage and Screen*. New York: Bowman and Littlefield, 1997.

Anderson, Osborne P. *A Voice from Harpers Ferry, 1859*. Atlanta: World View Publishers, 1861; 1980 reprint.

Aptheker, Bettina. *Women's Legacy: Essays on Race, Sex, and Class in American History*. Amherst: University of Massachusetts Press, 1982.

Armitage, Susan, and Elizabeth Jameson, eds. *The Women's West*. Norman: University of Oklahoma Press, 1987.

Asbury, Herbert. *The Barbary Coast*. New York: Alfred A. Knopf, 1933; Pocket Books edition, 1947.

Atherton, Gertrude. *California: An Intimate History*. New York: Blue Ribbon Books, 1914; 1936 edition.

Bair, Barbara. "Remapping the Black/White Body: Sexuality, Nationalism, and Biracial Antimiscegenation Activism in 1920s Virginia." In *Sex Love, Race: Crossing Boundaries in North American History*. Ed. Martha Hodes. 399–419. New York: New York University Press, 1999.

Baker, Paula. "The Domestication of Politics: Women and American Political Society, 1780–1920." *American Historical Review* 89 (1984): 620–47.

Bambara, Toni Cade. *The Salt Eaters*. New York: Random House, 1980.

Bancroft, Hubert Howe. *History of California*. 7 vols. San Francisco: History Co. Publishers, 1884–90.

———, and Frances Fuller Victor. *History of Nevada, 1540–1888*. Reno: University of Nevada Press, 1981.

Bargo, Michael "Women's Occupations in the West in 1870." *Journal of the West* 32:1 (January 1993): 30–45.

Barnhart, Jacqueline. *The Fair but Frail: Prostitution in San Francisco, 1849–1900*. Reno: University of Nevada Press, 1986.

Barry, Kathleen. "The New Historical Syntheses: Women's Biography." *Journal of Women's History* 1:3 (Winter): 75–105.

Barth, Gunther. *Instant Cities: Urbanization and the Rise of San Francisco and Denver*. Albuquerque: University of New Mexico Press, 1988.

Battu, Zoe. "Tin Types." *San Franciscan* (November 29, 1929): 17–30.

Bean, Walton, and James J. Rawls. *California: An Interpretative History*. 4th ed. New York: McGraw-Hill, 1988.

Beasley, Delilah L. *The Negro Trail Blazers of California*. Los Angeles: Times Mirror Printing and Binding House, 1919.

———. "Slavery in California." *Journal of Negro History* 3 (January 1918): 33–44.

Bederman, Gail. *Manliness and Civilization: A Cultural History of Gender and Race in the United States, 1880–1917*. Chicago: University of Chicago Press, 1995.

Beegel, Susan F. "The Brotherhood of Thieves Riot of 1842." *Historic Nantucket* 40:3 (Fall 1992): 45–48.

Bennett, Lerone. "An Historical Detective Story: The Mystery of Mary Ellen Pleasant." *Ebony* (April and May 1979): 90–96, 71–86.

Berger, Francisco de Talavera, and John Parke Custis. *Sumptuous Dining in Gaslight San Francisco, 1875–1915*. Garden City, N.Y.: Doubleday, 1985.

Berry, Mary Frances. "Judging Morality: Sexual Behavior and Legal Consequences in the Late Nineteenth-Century South." *Journal of American History* 78:3 (December 1991): 835–56.

———. *The Pig Farmer's Daughter and Other Tales of American Justice: Episodes of Racism and Sexism in the Courts from 1865 to the Present*. New York: Alfred A. Knopf, 1999.

Bernardi, Daniel. "The Voice of Whiteness: D. W. Griffith's Biograph Films, 1908–1913." In *The Birth of Whiteness: Race and the Emergence of U.S. Cinema*. Ed. Daniel Bernardi. 103–28. New Brunswick, N.J.: Rutgers University Press, 1996.

Berwanger, Eugene. "The 'Black Law' Question in Antebellum California." *Journal of the West* 6:2 (1967): 205–20.

———. *Frontier against Slavery: Western Anti-Negro Prejudice and the Slavery Extension Controversy*. Urbana: University of Illinois Press, 1967.

———. *The West and Reconstruction*. Urbana: University of Illinois Press, 1981.

Bibbs, Susheel. *A Heritage of Power: Marie LaVeau, Mary Ellen Pleasant*. San Francisco: MEP Publications, 1998.

———. "Mary Ellen Pleasant: Mother of Civil Rights in California." *Historic Nantucket* 44:1 (1995): 9–13.

———. *Mary Ellen Pleasant, 1817–1904: Mother of Human Rights in California*. San Francisco: MEP Publications, 1996.

Birmingham, Stephan. *California Rich*. New York: Simon and Schuster, 1986.

Blackett, R. J. M. *Beating against the Barriers: The Lives of Six Nineteenth-Century Afro-Americans*. Baton Rouge: Louisiana State University Press, 1986.

———. *Building an Antislavery Wall: Black Americans in the Atlantic Abolitionist Movement, 1830–1860*. Ithaca, N.Y.: Cornell University Press, 1983.

Blight, David W. "'For Something Beyond the Battlefield': Frederick Douglass and the Memory of the Civil War." *The Journal of American History* 75:4 (March 1989): 1156–78.

———. *Frederick Douglass' Civil War: Keeping Faith in Jubilee*. Baton Rouge: Louisiana State University Press, 1989.

Block, Eugene. *The Immortal San Franciscans: For Whom the Streets Were Named*. San Francisco: Chronicle Books, 1971.

Blockson, Charles L. *The Underground Railroad*. New York: Prentice Hall, 1987.

Bogle, Donald. *Toms, Coons, Mulattoes, Mammies, and Bucks: An Interpretive History of Blacks in American Film*. New York: Viking, 1973.

Bolster, Jeffrey W. *Black Jacks: African American Seamen in the Age of Sail*. Cambridge, Mass.: Harvard University Press, 1997.

———. "'To Feel Like a Man': Black Seamen in the Northern States, 1800–1860." *Journal of American History* 76 (March 1990): 1173–99.

Brechin, Gray. *Imperial San Francisco: Urban Power, Earthly Ruin*. Berkeley: University of California Press, 1999.

Brodie, Janet Farrell. *Contraception and Abortion in Nineteenth-Century America*. Ithaca, N.Y.: Cornell University Press, 1994.

Brody, Jennifer DeVere. *Impossible Purities: Blackness, Femininity, and Victorian Culture*. Durham, N.C.: Duke University Press, 1998.

Bronson, Samuel. *Dueling in America*. San Diego: Joseph Tabler Books, 1884; 1992 edition.

Broussard, Albert S. *Black San Francisco: The Struggle for Racial Equality in the West, 1900–1954*. Lawrence: University Press of Kansas, 1993.

———. "Slavery in California Revisited: The Fate of a Kentucky Slave in Gold Rush California." *Pacific Historian* 29:1 (Spring 1985): 17–21.

Brown, Elsa Barkley. "Negotiating and Transforming the Public Sphere: African American Political Life in the Transition from Slavery to Freedom." In *The Black Public Sphere*. Ed. The Black Public Sphere Collective. 111–50. Chicago: University of Chicago Press, 1995.

———. "Womanist Consciousness: Maggie Lena Walker and the Independent Order of Saint Luke." *Signs* 14:3 (Spring 1989): 610–33.

Brown, Karen McCarthy. *Mama Lola: A Vodou Priestess in Brooklyn*. Berkeley: University of California Press, 1991.

———. "Women's Leadership in Haitian Vodou." In *Weaving the Visions: New Patterns in Feminist Spirituality*. Ed. Judith Plaskow and Carol Christ. 226–234. San Francisco: Harper and Row, 1989.

Brown, William Wells. *Clotel; or, The President's Daughter: A Narrative of Slave Life in the United States*. New York: Collier, 1853; 1972 edition.

Brownworth, Victoria A. "Capitalism's Costs." *Lambda Book Report* (September–October 1993): 23.

Buckbee, Edna Bryan. "The Boys Called Her 'Mammy' Pleasant." *The Pony Express* (October 1953): 1–14.

Bundles, A'Lelia Perry. *On Her Own Ground: The Life and Times of Madam C. J. Walker*. New York: Scribner, 2001.

Butler, Judith. *Gender Trouble: Feminism and the Subversion of Identity*. New York: Routledge, 1990.

Byers, Edward. *The Nation of Nantucket: Society and Politics in an Early American Commercial Center, 1660–1820*. Boston: Northeastern University Press, 1987.

Campbell, Lindsay. "Gambling in San Francisco in the Days of Gold as Seen by a Slave." *San Francisco Sunday Call*, July 16, 1911.

Carby, Hazel V. "On the Threshold of Woman's Era: Lynching, Empire, and Sexuality in Black Feminist Theory." *Critical Inquiry* 12 (Autumn 1985): 262–77.

————. "The Politics of Fiction, Anthropology, and the Folk: Zora Neale Hurston." In *History and Memory in African-American Culture*. Ed. Geneviève Fabre and Robert O'Meally. 28–44. New York: Oxford University Press, 1994.

————. *Reconstructing Womanhood: The Emergence of the Afro-American Woman Novelist*. New York: Oxford University Press, 1987.

Cary, Lorin Lee, and Francine C. Cary. "Absalom F. Boston, His Family, and Nantucket's Black Community." *Historic Nantucket* 25:1 (Summer 1977): 15–23.

Castañeda, Antonia. "Women of Color and the Rewriting of Western History: The Discourse, Politics, and Decolonization of History." *Pacific Historical Review* (1992): 501–33.

Catterall, Helen Tunnicliff, ed. *Judicial Cases Concerning American Slavery and the Negro*. Vol. 5. Washington, D.C.: Carnegie Institution, 1937.

Chan, Sucheng. "A People of Exceptional Character: Ethnic Diversity, Nativism, and Racism in the California Gold Rush." *California History* 79:2 (Summer 2000): 44–85.

Chandler, Robert J. "Integrity amid Tumult: Wells Fargo and Co.'s Gold Rush Banking." *California History* 70:3 (Fall 1991): 258–77.

Christian, Barbara. "'Somebody Forgot to Tell Somebody Something': African-American Women's Historical Novels." In *Wild Women in the Whirlwind: Afra-American Culture and the Contemporary Literary Renaissance*. Ed. Joanne M. Braxton and Andree Nicola McLaughlin. 326–41. New Brunswick, N.J.: Rutgers University Press, 1990.

————. *Black Women Novelists: The Development of a Tradition, 1892–1976*. Westport, Conn.: Greenwood Press, 1980.

Clark, Elizabeth B. "'The Sacred Rights of the Weak': Pain, Sympathy, and the

Culture of Individual Rights in Antebellum America." *Journal of American History* 82 (September 1995): 463–93.

Clark-Lewis, Elizabeth. *Living In, Living Out: African American Domestics in Washington, D.C., 1910–1940*. Washington, D.C.: Smithsonian Institution Press, 1994.

Cliff, Michelle. *Free Enterprise*. New York: Dutton, 1993.

———. "The Resonance of Interruption." *Chrysallis* 8 (Summer 1979): 29–37.

Clinton, Catherine. *The Plantation Mistress: Woman's World in the Old South*. New York: Pantheon Books, 1982.

Coleman, Willi. "African American Women and Community Development in California, 1848–1900." In *Seeking El Dorado: African Americans in California*. Ed. Lawrence B. de Graaf, Kevin Mulroy, and Quintard Taylor. 98–125. Los Angeles: Autry Museum of Western Heritage, 2001.

———. "Black Women and Segregated Public Transportation: Ninety Years of Resistance." In *Black Women in United States History*. Vol. 5. Ed. Darlene Clark Hine et al. 295–302. New York: Carlson, 1990.

Colley, Nathaniel S. "Civil Actions for Damages Arising out of Violations of Civil Rights." *The Hastings Law Journal* 17 (December 1965): 189–215.

Conrad, Earl. "She Was a Friend of John Brown." *Negro World Digest* (November 1940): 6–11.

Conrich, J. Lloyd. "The Mammy Pleasant Legend." Ms., California Historical Society, n.d.

Cott, Nancy F. *The Bonds of Womanhood*. New Haven, Conn.: Yale University Press, 1977.

Cox, H. E. "Jim Crow in the City of Brotherly Love: The Segregation of Philadelphia Horse Cars." *Negro History Bulletin* 26:3 (1962): 119–23.

Crevecoeur, J. Hector St. John de. *Letters from an American Farmer and Sketches of Eighteenth-Century America*. Ed. Albert Stone. New York: Viking Penguin, 1981.

Cromwell, Otelia. *Lucretia Mott*. Cambridge, Mass.: Harvard University Press, 1958.

Crouchett, Lawrence P., et al. *Visions toward Tomorrow: The History of the East Bay Afro-American Community, 1852–1977*. Oakland: Northern California Center for Afro-American History and Life, 1989.

Curry, Leonard P. *The Free Black in Urban America, 1800–1850: The Shadow of a Dream*. Chicago: University of Chicago Press, 1981.

Cushman, Sean Dennis. *America in the Gilded Age: From the Death of Lincoln to the Rise of Theodore Roosevelt*. 3d ed. New York: New York University Press, 1993.

Davis, Angela Y. *Women, Race, and Class*. New York: Random House, 1981.

Davis, Sam. "How a Colored Woman Aided John Brown." *The Inquirer and Mirror*, December 26, 1901.

Daniels, Douglas Henry. *Pioneer Urbanites: A Social and Cultural History of Black San Francisco*. Philadelphia: Temple University Press, 1980.

de Graaf, Lawrence B. "The City of Black Angels: Emergence of the Los Angeles Ghetto, 1890–1930." *Pacific Historical Review* 39:3 (August 1970): 323–52.

———. "Race, Sex, and Region: Black Women in the American West, 1850–1920." *Pacific Historical Review* 49 (May 1980): 285–313.

———, Kevin Mulroy, and Quintard Taylor, eds. *Seeking El Dorado: African Americans in California*. Los Angeles: Autry Museum of Western Heritage, 2001.

Decker, Peter R. *Fortune and Failure: White-Collar Mobility in Nineteenth-Century San Francisco*. Cambridge, Mass.: Harvard University Press, 1978.

Delgado, James P. *To California by Sea: A Maritime History of the California Gold Rush*. Columbia: University of South Carolina Press, 1990.

D'Emilio, John, and Estelle D. Freedmen. *Intimate Matters: A History of Sexuality in America*. New York: Harper and Row, 1988.

Deutsch, Sarah. "Landscape of Enclaves: Race Relations in the West, 1865–1990." In *Under an Open Sky: Rethinking America's Western Past*. Ed. William Cronan et al. 110–31. New York: W. W. Norton, 1992.

Dobie, Charles Caldwell. *Less Than Kin*. New York: John Day and Co., 1926.

———. *San Francisco: A Pageant*. New York: Appleton-Century, 1933.

Dobkowski, Michael N. *The Tarnished Dream: The Basis of American Anti-Semitism*. Westport, Conn.: Greenwood Press, 1979.

Douglass, Frederick. *My Bondage, My Freedom*. Salem, N.H.: Ayer Co., 1984 ed.; originally pub. 1855.

———. *Narrative of the Life of Frederick Douglass*. Cambridge, Mass.: Harvard University Press, 1988; originally pub. 1845.

Du Bois, W. E. B. *Black Reconstruction in America*. New York: Kraus-Thomson Organization, 1935.

———. *The Gift of Black Folk: The Negroes in the Making of America*. Boston: Stratford Co., 1924.

———. *John Brown*. New York: Kraus-Thomson Organization, 1973.

———. *The Philadelphia Negro: A Social Study*. New York: Schoken Books, 1967.

Du Cille, Ann. "The Blacker the Juice: O.J. Simpson and the Squeeze Play of Race." In *Skin Trade*. Ed. Ann Du Cille. 136–69. Cambridge, Mass.: Harvard University Press, 1996.

Duster, Alfreda M., ed. *Crusade for Justice: The Autobiography of Ida B. Wells*. Chicago: University of Chicago Press, 1970.

Ethington, Philip J. *The Public City: The Political Construction of Urban Life in San Francisco, 1850–1900*. Cambridge, England: Cambridge University Press, 1994.

Everson, William K. *American Silent Film*. New York: Oxford University Press, 1978.

Farnham, Eliza W. *California: In-Doors and Out*. New York: Dix, Edwards and Co., 1856.

Field, Stephen J. *Personal Reminiscences of Early Days in California*. New York: Da Capo Press, 1993; originally pub. 1877.

Fields, Barbara J. "Ideology and Race in American History." In *Region, Race, and Reconstruction: Essays in Honor of C. Vann Woodward*. Ed. J. Morgan Kousser and James M. McPherson. 142–47. New York: Oxford University Press, 1982.

Finkelman, Paul, ed. *His Soul Goes Marching On: Responses to John Brown and the Harpers Ferry Raid.* Charlottesville: University Press of Virginia, 1995.

Fisher, James A. "The Political Development of the Black Community in California, 1850–1950." *California Historical Society Quarterly* 1 (1971): 256–66.

———. "The Struggle for Negro Testimony in California, 1851–1863." *Southern California Quarterly* 51 (January 1969): 313–24.

Foner, Eric. *Reconstruction: America's Unfinished Revolution.* New York: Harper and Row, 1988.

Foner, Philip S. "The Battle to End Discrimination against Negroes on Philadelphia Street Cars, Part 1." In *Essays in Afro-American History.* 19–50. Philadelphia: Temple University Press, 1978.

———. "Blacks and John Brown." In *History of Black Americans: From the Compromise of 1850 to the End of the Civil War.* Vol. 3. 240–65. Westport, Conn.: Greenwood Press, 1983.

———, and George E. Walker, eds., *Proceedings of the Black State Conventions.* Philadelphia: Temple University Press, 1980.

Foucault, Michel. *Power/Knowledge.* Ed. Colin Gordon. New York: Random House, 1981.

Fowler, Karen Joy. *Sister Noon.* New York: G. P. Putnam's Sons, 2001.

Fox, Richard Wightman. "Intimacy on Trial." In *The Power of Culture: Critical Essays in American History.* Ed. Richard Wightman Fox and T. J. Jackson Lears. 103–32. Chicago: University of Chicago Press, 1993.

Fox-Genovese, Elizabeth. *Within the Plantation Household: Black and White Women of the Old South.* Chapel Hill: University of North Carolina Press, 1988.

Fraser, Isabel. "Mammy Pleasant: The Woman." *San Francisco Call* (July 9, 1901): 2.

Fraser, Nancy. "Rethinking the Public Sphere: A Contribution to the Critique of Actually Existing Democracy." *Social Text* 25/26 (1990): 56–80.

Fredrickson, George M. *The Black Image in the White Mind: The Debate on Afro-American Character and Destiny, 1817–1914.* New York: Harper and Row, 1971.

Frost, Ginger S. *Promises Broken: Courtship, Class, and Gender in Victorian England.* Charlottesville: University Press of Virginia, 1995.

Frye, Hardy. "Negroes in California, 1841–1870." Ms., San Francisco Afro-American Historical and Cultural Society, 1976.

Gaines, Kevin K. *Uplifting the Race: Black Leadership, Politics, and Culture in the Twentieth Century.* Chapel Hill: University of North Carolina Press, 1996.

Gamber, Wendy. *The Female Economy: The Millinery and Dressmaking Trades, 1860–1930.* Urbana: University of Illinois Press, 1997.

———. "A Precarious Independence: Milliners and Dressmakers in Boston, 1860–1890." *Journal of Women's History* 4 (Spring 1992): 60–88.

Garcia, Mikel. "Black Women as Community Builders, Los Angeles, 1886–1920." *NWSA Perspectives* 5:3 (Spring–Summer 1987): 1–8.

Gardner, Anna. "The Antislavery Phase of Our Island's History." *The Inquirer and Mirror,* July 11, 1895.

Gatewood, Willard B. *Aristocrats of Color: The Black Elite, 1880–1920*. Bloomington: Indiana University Press, 1990.

Giddings, Paula. *When and Where I Enter: The Impact of Black Women on Race and Sex in America*. New York: William Morrow, 1984.

Gilman, Sander. "Black Bodies, White Bodies: Toward an Iconography of Female Sexuality in Late Nineteenth-Century Art, Medicine, and Literature." In *Race, Writing, and Difference*. Ed. Henry Louis Gates Jr. 223–61. Chicago: Chicago University Press, 1986.

Gilmore, Glenda E. *Gender and Jim Crow: Women and the Politics of White Supremacy in North Carolina, 1896–1920*. Chapel Hill: University of North Carolina Press, 1996.

Gilroy, Paul. *The Black Atlantic: Modernity and Double Consciousness*. Cambridge, Mass.: Harvard University Press, 1993.

Glenn, Evelyn Nakano. "From Servitude to Service Work: Historical Continuities in the Racial Division of Paid Reproductive Labor." *Signs* 18:1 (1992): 1–43.

Goings, Kenneth W. *Mammy and Uncle Mose: Black Collectibles and American Stereotyping*. Bloomington: Indiana University Press, 1994.

Goldman, Marion S. *Gold Diggers and Silver Miners: Prostitution and the Social Life on the Comstock Lode*. Ann Arbor: University of Michigan, 1981.

González, Deena J. "La Tules of Image and Reality: Euro-American Attitudes and Legend Formation on a Spanish-Mexican Frontier." In *Unequal Sisters: A Multicultural Reader in U.S. Women's History*. 2d ed. Ed. Vicki L. Ruiz and Ellen Carol DuBois. 57–69. New York: Routledge, 1994.

Goode, Gloria Davis. "African-American Women in Nineteenth-Century Nantucket: Wives, Mothers, Modistes, and Visionaries." *Historic Nantucket* 40:3 (Fall 1992): 76–78.

Goode, Kenneth G. *California's Black Pioneers: A Brief Historical Survey*. Santa Barbara, Calif.: McNally and Loftin Publishers, 1974.

Gordon, Linda. *Heroes of Their Own Lives: The Politics and History of Family Violence*. New York: Viking, 1988.

Gould, Milton S. *A Cast of Hawks: A Rowdy Tale of Scandal and Power Politics in Early San Francisco*. La Jolla, Calif.: Copley Books, 1985.

Greene, Lorenzo. *The Negro in Colonial New England*. Washington, N.Y.: Kennicat Press, 1966.

Grossberg, Michael. *Governing the Hearth: Law and the Family in Nineteenth-Century America*. Chapel Hill: University of North Carolina Press, 1985.

———. *A Judgment for Solomon: The D'Hauteville Case and Legal Experience in Antebellum America*. New York: Cambridge University Press, 1996.

Groth, Paul Erling. "Forbidden Housing: The Evolution and Exclusion of Hotels, Boarding Houses, Rooming Houses, and Lodging Houses in American Cities, 1880–1938." Ph.D. diss., University of California, Berkeley, 1983.

Gutman, Herbert G. *The Black Family in Slavery and Freedom, 1750–1925*. New York: Random House, 1976.

Guy-Sheftall, Beverly. *Daughters of Sorrow: Attitudes toward Black Women, 1880–1920*. New York: Carlson Publishing, 1990.

Gwin, Minrose C. *Black and White Women of the Old South: The Peculiar Sisterhood in American Literature*. Knoxville: University of Tennessee Press, 1985.

Haas, Lisbeth. *Conquests and Historical Identities in California, 1769–1936*. Berkeley: University of California Press, 1995.

Habermas, Jürgen. *The Structural Transformation of the Public Sphere: An Inquiry into a Category of Bourgeois Society*. Trans. Thomas Burger. Cambridge: MIT Press, 1989.

Hale, Grace Elizabeth. *Making Whiteness: The Culture of Segregation in the South, 1890–1940*. New York: Pantheon Books, 1998.

Hall, Jacquelyn Dowd. "Disorderly Conduct: Gender and Labor Militancy in the Appalachian South." *Journal of American History* 73 (1986): 354–82.

———. "Partial Truths." *Signs* 14:4 (1989): 902–11.

Hall, Stuart. "Subjects in History: Making Diasporic Identities." In *The House That Race Built: Black Americans, U.S. Terrain*. Ed. Wahneema Lubiano. 289–99. New York: Pantheon Books, 1997.

———. "What Is This 'Black' in Black Popular Culture?" In *Black Popular Culture*. Ed. Gina Dent. 21–33. Seattle: Bay Press, 1992.

Hanaford, Phebe Ann. *Daughters of America or Women of the Century*. Augusta, Maine: True and Co., 1883.

Harding, Vincent. *There Is a River: The Black Struggle for Freedom in America*. New York: Random House, 1981.

Harlan, Louis R. *Booker T. Washington: The Making of a Black Leader, 1856–1901*. New York: Oxford University Press, 1972.

Harley, Sharon. "For the Good of Family and Race: Gender, Work, and Domestic Roles in the Black Community," In *Black Women in America: Social Science Perspectives*. Ed. Micheline R. Malson et al. 159–72. Chicago: University of Chicago Press, 1990.

Harris, Alice Kessler. *Out to Work: A History of Wage-Earning Women in the United States*. New York: Oxford University Press, 1982.

Harris, Trudier. *From Mammies to Militants: Domestics in Black American Literature*. Philadelphia: Temple University Press, 1982.

Hart, James D. *A Companion Guide to California*. New York: Oxford University Press, 1978.

Hartman, Saidiya V. *Scenes of Subjection: Terror, Slavery, and Self-Making in Nineteenth-Century America*. New York: Oxford University Press, 1997.

Hayden, Dolores. "Biddy Mason's Los Angeles, 1856–1891." *California History* 68 (Fall 1989): 69–76.

———. *The Power of Place: Urban Landscapes as Public History*. Cambridge, Mass.: MIT Press, 1995.

Haynes, Elizabeth Ross. "Negroes in Domestic Service in the United States." In *Black*

Women in United States History. Vol. 2. Ed. Darlene Clark Hine et al. 507–66. New York: Carlson Publishing, 1990.

Heilbrun, Carolyn G. *Writing a Woman's Life.* New York: Ballantine Books, 1988.

Heizer, Robert F., and Alan J. Almquist. *The Other Californians: Prejudice and Discrimination under Spain, Mexico, and the United States to 1920.* Berkeley: University of California Press, 1971.

Heller, Charles E. *Portrait of an Abolitionist: A Biography of George Luther Stearns, 1809–1867.* Westport, Conn.: Greenwood Press, 1996.

Higginbotham, Evelyn Brooks. "African-American Women's History and the Meta-language of Race." *Signs* 17 (Winter 1992): 251–74.

———. "Beyond the Sound of Silence: Afro-American Women in History." *Gender and History* 1 (Spring 1989): 50–67.

———. *Righteous Discontent: The Women's Movement in the Black Baptist Church, 1880–1920.* Cambridge, Mass.: Harvard University Press, 1993.

Higham, John. "Anti-Semitism in the Gilded Age: A Reinterpretation." *Mississippi Valley Historical Review* 43 (March 1957): 559–78.

Hine, Darlene Clark. "Lifting the Veil, Shattering the Silence: Black Women's History in Slavery and Freedom." In *The State of Afro-American History: Past, Present and Future.* Ed. Darlene Clark Hine. 224–49. Baton Rouge: Louisiana State University Press, 1986.

———. "Rape and the Inner Lives of Black Women in the Middle West: Preliminary Thoughts on the Culture of Dissemblance." *Signs* 14 (Summer 1989): 912–20.

Hodes, Martha. "The Sexualization of Reconstruction Politics: White Women and Black Men in the South after the Civil War." *Journal of the History of Sexuality* 3:3 (1993).

Holdredge, Helen. *Firebelle Lillie.* New York: Meredith Press, 1967.

———. *The House of the Strange Woman.* San Carlos, Calif.: Nourse Publishing, 1961.

———. *Mammy Pleasant.* New York: G. P. Putnam's Sons, 1953.

———. *Mammy Pleasant's Cookbook.* San Francisco: 101 Productions, 1970.

———. *Mammy Pleasant's Partner.* New York: G. P. Putnam's Sons, 1954.

———. *The Woman in Black: The Life of Lola Montez.* New York: G. P. Putnam's Sons, 1955.

Holloway, Karla F. C. *Moorings and Metaphors: Figures of Culture and Gender in Black Women's Literature.* New Brunswick, N.J.: Rutgers University Press, 1992.

Hooper, Brad. "Review of *Pale Truth.*" *Booklist* 97:4 (October 15, 2000): 416.

Horowitz, Harold W. "The 1959 California Equal Rights in Business Establishments Statute: A Problem in Statutory Application." *Southern California Law Review* 33 (1960): 260–305.

Horton, James Oliver. *Free People of Color: Inside the African American Community.* Washington, D.C.: Smithsonian Institution Press, 1993.

————, and Lois E. Horton. *In Hope of Liberty: Culture, Community, and Protest among Northern Free Blacks, 1700–1860*. New York: Oxford University Press, 1997.

Horton, Joseph. "The Happy Black Hooker." *Sepia* 21 (December 1972): 26–28.

Howard, Brett. "The Boarding House Reach." *Mankind* 7 (1982): 25–26, 50.

Howay, F. W. "The Negro Immigration into Vancouver Island in 1858." *British Columbia Historical Quarterly* 3 (April 1939): 101–13.

Hudson, Lynn M. "'Strong Animal Passions' in the Gilded Age: Race, Sex, and a Senator on Trial." *Journal of the History of Sexuality* 9:1–2 (January/April 2000): 62–84.

Hunter, Tera W. "Domination and Resistance: The Politics of Wage Household Labor in New South Atlanta." *Labor History* 34 (Spring/Summer 1993): 205–20.

————. *To 'Joy My Freedom: Southern Black Women's Lives and Labors after the Civil War*. Cambridge, Mass.: Harvard University Press, 1997.

Hurston, Zora Neale. *Mules and Men*. New York: Negro Universities Press, 1969.

————. *Tell My Horse*. Philadelphia: J. B. Lippincott, 1938.

Hurtado, Albert L. *Intimate Frontiers: Sex, Gender, and Culture in Old California*. Albuquerque: University of New Mexico Press, 1999.

————. "Sex, Gender, Culture, and a Great Event: The California Gold Rush." *Pacific Historical Review* 68 (Summer 1999): 1–19.

Issel, William, and Robert W. Cherny. *San Francisco, 1865–1932: Politics, Power, and Urban Development*. Berkeley: University of California Press, 1986.

Jameson, Elizabeth, and Susan Armitage. *Writing the Range: Race, Class, and Culture in the Women's West*. Norman: University of Oklahoma Press, 1997.

Jensen, Joan M., and Gloria Ricci Lothrop. *California Women: A History*. San Francisco: Boyd and Fraser, 1987.

————, and Darlis Miller. "Gentle Tamers Revisited: New Approaches to the History of Women in the American West." *Pacific Historical Review* 49 (May 1980): 173–212.

Johnsen, Leigh Dana. "Equal Rights and the 'Heathen Chinee': Black Activism in San Francisco, 1865–1875." *Western Historical Quarterly* 11:1 (1980): 57–68.

Johnson, Susan Lee. "'A Memory Sweet to Soldiers': The Significance of Gender in the History of the American West." *Western Historical Quarterly* 24 (November 1993): 495–517.

————. *Roaring Camp: The Social World of the California Gold Rush*. New York: W. W. Norton, 2000.

Johnson, Walter. *Soul by Soul: Life Inside the Antebellum Slave Market*. Cambridge, Mass.: Harvard University Press, 1999.

Jones, Jacqueline. *Labor of Love, Labor of Sorrow: Black Women, Work, and the Family from Slavery to the Present*. New York: Basic Books, 1985.

Jordan, Winthrop D. *Tumult and Silence at Second Creek: An Inquiry into a Civil War Slave Conspiracy*. Baton Rouge: Louisiana State University Press, 1993.

————. *White over Black: American Attitudes toward the Negro, 1550–1812*. New York: W. W. Norton, 1977.

Josephy, Alvin. *The Civil War in the American West*. New York: Vintage Books/ Random House, 1991.

Kahn, Edgar M. *Cable Car Days in San Francisco*. Stanford, Calif.: Stanford University Press, 1940.

Kaldenbach-Montemayor, Isabel. "Black on Grey: Negroes on Nantucket in the Nineteenth Century." B.A. thesis, Princeton University, 1983.

————. "Blacks on the High Seas: The Arrival of Negroes in Nantucket." Ms., Nantucket Historical Association, 1982.

Katz, William Loren. *Black People Who Made the Old West*. Trenton, N.J.: Africa World Press, 1992.

————. *The Black West*. Seattle: Open Hand Publishing, 1987.

Kaufman, Polly Welts, ed. *Apron Full of Gold: The Letters of Mary Jane Megquier from San Francisco, 1849–1856*. Albuquerque: University of New Mexico Press, 1994.

Kelley, Mary. *Private Woman, Public Stage: Literary Domesticity in Nineteenth-Century America*. New York: Oxford University Press, 1984.

Kelley, Robin D. G. *Race Rebels: Culture, Politics, and the Black Working Class*. New York: Free Press, 1994.

Kerber, Linda K. "Separate Spheres, Female Worlds, Woman's Place: The Rhetoric of Women's History." *Journal of American History* 75 (June 1988): 9–39.

Kimball, Charles P. *San Francisco City Directory: 1821–1894* (San Mateo, Calif.: D. I. Lamphier, 1997.

Klein, Ronald P. "Equal Rights Statutes." *Stanford Law Review* 10 (March 1958): 253–73.

Kleinhau, Chuck. "Notes on Melodrama and the Family Under Capitalism." *Film Reader* 3 (February 1978): 40–47.

Korobkin, Laura Hanft. "The Maintenance of Mutual Confidence: Sentimental Strategies at the Adultery Trial of Henry Ward Beecher." *Yale Journal of Law and the Humanities* 7:1 (1995): 1–48.

Kracauer, Siegfried. *From Caligari to Hitler: A Psychological History of the German Film*. Princeton, N.J.: Princeton University Press, 1946; rpt. 1974.

Kraemer, Kristi. "Background and Resolution of the Eunice Ross Controversy." *Historic Nantucket* 29:1 (July 1981): 11–18.

Kroninger, Robert H. *Sarah and the Senator*. Berkeley, Calif.: Howell-North, 1964.

————, and Martin S. Gould. *A Cast of Hawks: A Rowdy Tale of Scandal and Power Politics in Early San Francisco*. La Jolla, Calif.: Copley Books, 1985.

Kusmer, Kenneth L. "The Black Urban Experience in American History." In *The State of Afro-American History: Past, Present, and Future*. Ed. Darlene Clark Hine. 91–129. Baton Rouge: Louisiana State University Press, 1986.

Kwolek-Folland, Angel. *Engendering Business: Men and Women in the Corporate Office, 1870–1930.* Baltimore, Md.: Johns Hopkins University Press, 1994.

Lachman, Marvin, and Charles Shibuk, eds. *Encyclopedia of Mystery and Detection.* New York: McGraw-Hill, 1976.

Lang, Robert. *American Film Melodrama: Griffith, Vidor, Minnelli.* Princeton, N.J.: Princeton University Press, 1989.

Lapp, Rudolph M. *Afro-Americans in California.* San Francisco: Boyd and Fraser Publishing Co., 1979.

———. *Archy Lee: A California Fugitive Slave Case.* San Francisco: Book Club of California, 1969.

———. *Blacks in Gold Rush California.* New Haven, Conn.: Yale University Press, 1977.

———. "Jeremiah Sanderson: Early California Negro." *Journal of Negro History* 53:4 (1968): 321–33.

———. "Negro Rights Activities in Gold Rush California." *California Historical Society Quarterly* 45 (March 1966): 3–20.

Lapsansky, Emma Jones. "The World the Agitators Made: The Counterculture of Agitation in Urban Philadelphia." In *The Abolitionist Sisterhood: Women's Political Culture in Antebellum America.* Ed. Jean Fagan Yellin and John C. Van Horne. 91–99. Ithaca, N.Y.: Cornell University Press, 1994.

Larson, Jane E. "'Women Understand So Little, They Call My Good Nature Deceit': A Feminist Rethinking of Seduction." *Columbia Law Review* 374 (1993): 375–459.

LaTourrete, Jacqueline. *The House on Octavia Street.* New York: Beaufort Books, 1984.

Lawson, John, ed. *American State Trials.* Vol. 15. 465–592. St. Louis: F. H. Thomas Law Book Co., 1914–36.

Lebsock, Suzanne. *The Free Women of Petersburg: Status and Culture in a Southern Town, 1784–1860.* New York: W. W. Norton, 1984.

Leonard, William Torbert. *Theatre: From Stage to Screen to Television.* Metuchen, N.J.: Scarecrow Press, 1981.

Leslie, Kent Anderson. *Woman of Color, Daughter of Privilege: Amanda America Dickson, 1849–1893.* Athens: University of Georgia Press, 1995.

Levine, Lawrence W. *Black Culture and Black Consciousness: Afro-American Folk Thought from Slavery to Freedom.* New York: Oxford University Press, 1977.

———. *Highbrow Lowbrow: The Emergence of Cultural Hierarchy in America.* Cambridge, Mass.: Harvard University Press, 1988.

Levy, Joann. *They Saw the Elephant: Women in the California Gold Rush.* San Francisco: Anchor Books, 1990.

Lewis, Oscar. *Silver Kings.* Reno: University of Nevada Press, 1986.

———, and Carroll D. Hall. *Bonanza Inn: America's First Luxury Hotel.* New York: Alfred A. Knopf, 1949.

Linebaugh, Barbara. *The African School and the Integration of Nantucket Public*

Schools, 1825–1847. Boston: African-American Studies Center, Boston University, 1978.

Lipsitz, George. "The Possessive Investment in Whiteness: Racialized Social Democracy and the 'White' Problem in American Studies." *American Quarterly* 52 (September 1995): 369–87.

Littlefield, Daniel C. "Blacks, John Brown, and a Theory of Manhood." In *His Soul Goes Marching On: Responses to John Brown and the Harpers Ferry Raid.* Ed. Paul Finkelman. 67–97. Charlottesville: University Press of Virginia, 1995.

Litwack, Leon F. *Been in the Storm So Long: The Aftermath of Slavery.* New York: Random House, 1979.

———. *North of Slavery: The Negro in the Free States, 1790–1860.* Chicago: University of Chicago Press, 1961.

Loewenberg, Bert, and Ruth Bogin. *Black Women in Nineteenth-Century American Life: Their Words, Their Thoughts, Their Feelings.* University Park: Pennsylvania State University Press, 1976.

Lortie, Francis N., Jr. "San Francisco's Black Community, 1870–1890: Dilemmas in the Struggle for Equality." M.A. thesis, San Francisco State University, 1970.

Lotchin, Roger. *San Francisco: From Hamlet to City, 1846–1856.* New York: Oxford University Press, 1974.

Lott, Eric. *Love and Theft: Blackface Minstrelsy and the American Working Class.* New York: Oxford University Press, 1993.

Love, Spencie. *One Blood: The Legend of Charles Drew.* New York: W. W. Norton, 1996.

Lyman, George D. *Ralston's Ring: California Plunders the Comstock Lode.* New York: Charles Scribner's Sons, 1937.

Mabee, Carleton. *Sojourner Truth.* New York: New York University Press, 1993.

Mann, Susan. "Slavery, Sharecropping, and Sexual Inequality." *Signs* 14 (Summer 1989): 774–98.

McDowell, Deborah. "Taking Liberties with History." *Women's Review of Books* 11 (July 1994): 32–34.

———, and Arnold Rampersad, eds. *Slavery and the Literary Imagination.* Baltimore, Md.: Johns Hopkins University Press, 1989.

McFeely, William S. *Frederick Douglass.* New York: W. W. Norton, 1991.

McGlone, Robert E. "Rescripting a Troubled Past: John Brown's Family and the Harpers Ferry Conspiracy." *Journal of American History* 75:4 (March 1989): 1179–1200.

McMurray, Linda O. *To Keep the Waters Troubled: The Life of Ida B. Wells.* New York: Oxford University Press, 1998.

McPherson, James M. *The Abolitionist Legacy: From Reconstruction to the NAACP.* Princeton, N.J.: Princeton University Press, 1975.

———. *Battle Cry of Freedom: The Civil War Era.* New York: Oxford University Press, 1988.

———. *The Negro's Civil War.* New York: Pantheon Books, 1965.

Meehan, Johanna. *Feminists Read Habermas*. New York: Routledge, 1995.

Mercer, Kobena. *Welcome to the Jungle: New Positions in Black Cultural Studies*. New York: Routledge, 1994.

Miller, Ronald Dean. *Shady Ladies of the West*. Los Angeles: Westernlore Press, 1964.

Montesano, Philip M. "San Francisco Black Churches in the Early 1860s: Political Pressure Group." *California Historical Society Quarterly* 52:2 (1973): 145–52.

———. "Some Aspects of the Free Negro Question in San Francisco, 1849–1870." M.A. thesis, University of San Francisco, 1967.

Moore, Shirley Ann Wilson. *To Place Our Deeds: The African American Community in Richmond, California, 1910–1963*. Berkeley: University of California Press, 2000.

———. "'Your Life Is Really Not Just Your Own': African American Women in Twentieth Century California." In *Seeking El Dorado: African Americans in California*. Ed. Lawrence B. de Graaf, Kevin Mulroy, and Quintard Taylor. 210–46. Los Angeles: Autry Museum of Western Heritage, 2000.

Morrison, Toni. *Playing in the Dark: Whiteness and the Literary Imagination* Cambridge, Mass.: Harvard University Press, 1992.

Morton, Patricia. *Disfigured Images: The Historical Assault against Black Women*. Westport, Conn.: Greenwood Press, 1991.

Murdock, Cloyte. "America's Most Fabulous Black Madam." *Ebony* (April 1954): 46–55.

Murphy, Mary. "The Private Lives of Public Women: Prostitution in Butte, Montana, 1878–1917." In *The Women's West*. Ed. Susan Armitage et al. 193–206. Norman: University of Oklahoma Press, 1987.

Myres, Sandra L. *Westering Women and the Frontier Experience, 1800–1915*. Albuquerque: University of New Mexico Press.

Nash, Gary B. *Forging Freedom: The Formation of Philadelphia's Black Community, 1720–1840*. Cambridge, Mass.: Harvard University Press.

Nieman, Donald G. ed. *The Politics of Freedom: African Americans and the Political Process during Reconstruction*. New York: Garland, 1994.

Norling, Lisa. *Captain Ahab Had a Wife: New England Women and the Whalefishery, 1720–1870*. Chapel Hill: University of North Carolina Press, 2000.

O'Brian, Robert. "Riptides." *San Francisco Chronicle*, February 18 and 20, 1946.

Older, Cora. *San Francisco: Magic City*. New York: Longmans, Green and Co., 1961.

Olsen, Tillie. *Silences*. New York: Dell Publishing, 1979.

Ong, Paul. "An Ethnic Trade: The Chinese Laundries in Early California." *Journal of Ethnic Studies* 8:4 (Winter 1981):95–113.

Paine, Swift. *Eilley Orrum: Queen of the Comstock*. Indianapolis: Bobbs-Merrill, 1929.

Painter, Nell Irvin. *Exodusters: Black Migration to Kansas after Reconstruction*. New York: W. W. Norton, 1976.

———. "Of Lily, Linda Brent, and Freud: A Non-Exceptionalist Approach to Race, Class, and Gender in the Slave South." *Georgia Historical Quarterly* 76 (Summer 1992): 241–59.

————. "Representing Truth: Sojourner Truth's Knowing and Becoming Known." *Journal of American History* 81:2 (September 1994): 461–92.

————. *Sojourner Truth: A Life, a Symbol.* New York: W. W. Norton, 1996.

————. "Sojourner Truth in Life and Memory: Writing the Biography of an American Exotic." *Gender and History* 2 (Spring 1990): 3–16.

Parent, Anthony S., Jr., and Susan Brown Wallace. "Childhood and Sexual Identity under Slavery." In *American Sexual Politics: Sex, Gender, and Race since the Civil War.* Ed. John C. Fout and Maura Shaw Tantillo. 19–57. Chicago: University of Chicago Press, 1993.

Parker, Elizabeth L., and James Abajian. *A Walking Tour of the Black Presence in San Francisco during the Nineteenth Century.* San Francisco: San Francisco African American Historical and Cultural Society, 1974.

Pascoe, Peggy. "Miscegenation Law, Court Cases, and Ideologies of 'Race' in Twentieth-Century America." *Journal of American History* 83:1 (June 1996): 44–69.

Paul, Rodman Wilson. *Mining Frontiers in the Far West, 1848–1880.* New York: Holt, Rinehart, and Winston, 1963.

Pease, Jane H., and William H. Pease. *Ladies, Women, and Wenches: Choice and Constraint in Antebellum Charleston and Boston.* Chapel Hill: University of North Carolina Press, 1990.

Peterson, Carla L. *"Doers of the Word": African-American Women Speakers and Writers in the North, 1830–1880.* New York: Oxford University Press, 1995.

Peterson, Richard H. *The Bonanza Kings: The Social Origins and Business Behavior of Western Mining Entrepreneurs, 1870–1900.* Norman: University of Oklahoma Press, 1971; 1991 edition.

Philbrick, Nathaniel. *"Away Off Shore": Nantucket Island and Its People, 1602–1890.* Nantucket, Mass.: Mill Hill Press, 1994.

————. "'Every Wave Is a Fortune': Nantucket Island and the Making of an American Icon." *New England Quarterly* 66 (September 1993): 434–47.

————. "'I Will Take to the Water': Frederick Douglass, the Sea, and the Nantucket Whale Fishery." *Historical Nantucket* 40:3 (Fall 1992): 49–51.

————. "The Nantucket Sequence in Crevecoeur's *Letters from an American Farmer.*" *New England Quarterly* 64 (September 1991): 414–32.

Pierce, J. Kingston. *San Francisco, You're History!* Seattle: Sasquatch Books, 1995.

Pleasant, Mary Ellen. "Memoirs and Autobiography." *The Pandex of the Press* 1 (January 1902): 1–6.

Porter, Dorothy B. "David Ruggles, an Apostle of Human Rights." *Journal of Negro History* (January–October 1943): 23–50.

Quarles, Benjamin. *Black Abolitionists.* London: Oxford University Press, 1969.

————, ed. *Blacks on John Brown.* Urbana: University of Illinois Press, 1972.

Raboteau, Albert J. *Slave Religion: The "Invisible" Institution in the Antebellum South.* New York: Oxford University Press, 1978.

Raiskin, Judith. "The Art of History: An Interview with Michelle Cliff." *Kenyon Review* 15(1) (1993): 57–71.

Ramsey, Kate. "That Old Black Magic: Seeing Haiti through the Wall of Voodoo." *Voice Literary Supplement,* September 27, 1994.

Rasmussen, Louis J. *San Francisco Ship Passenger Lists: Names of Passengers Arriving by Vessels into the Port of San Francisco, 1850–1875.* Colma, Calif.: San Francisco Historic Records, 1966.

Redpath, James. *The Public Life of Capt. John Brown with an Auto-Biography of His Childhood and Youth.* Boston: Thayer and Eldridge, 1860.

Renehan, Edward J., Jr. *The Secret Six.* New York: Crown, 1995.

Rhodes, Jane. *Mary Ann Shadd Cary: The Black Press and Protest in the Nineteenth Century.* Bloomington: Indiana University Press, 1998.

———. "The Politics of (In)visibility in the Life of Mary Ann Shadd Cary." Paper presented at the annual meeting of the Organization of American Historians, Washington, D.C., April 1, 1995.

Riggs, Marlon, dir./prod. *Ethnic Notions.* California Newsreel, 1989.

Riley, Glenda. "American Daughters: Black Women in the West." *Montana: The Magazine of Western History* 38 (Spring 1988): 14–27.

———. *The Female Frontier: A Comparative View of Women on the Prairie and the Plains.* Lawrence: University Press of Kansas, 1988.

———. *A Place to Grow: Women in the American West.* Arlington Heights, Ill.: Harlan Davidson, 1992.

Ripley, Peter, ed. *The Black Abolitionist Papers.* Vol. 2. Chapel Hill: University of North Carolina Press, 1986.

Roberts, Brian. *The California Gold Rush and Middle-Class Culture.* Chapel Hill: University of North Carolina Press, 2000.

Roediger, David R. *The Wages of Whiteness: Race and the Making of the American Working Class.* New York: Verso, 1991.

Rogers, J. A. *Sex and Race.* Vol. 3. New York: Author, 1944.

Rogin, Michael. "Making America Home: Racial Masquerade and Ethnic Assimilation in the Transition to Talking Pictures." *Journal of American History* 79:3 (December 1972): 1050–77.

Rohrbough, Malcolm J. *Days of Gold: The California Gold Rush and the American Nation.* Berkeley: University of California Press, 1997.

Rosen, Ruth. *The Lost Sisterhood: Prostitution in America, 1900–1918.* Baltimore, Md.: Johns Hopkins University Press, 1982.

Rossbach, Jeffrey. *Ambivalent Conspirators: John Brown, the Secret Six, and a Theory of Slave Violence.* Philadelphia: University of Pennsylvania Press, 1982.

Ryan, Mary P. *Civic Wars: Democracy and Public Life in the American City during the Nineteenth Century.* Berkeley: University of California Press, 1997.

———. *Women in Public: Between Banners and Ballots, 1825–1880.* Baltimore, Md.: Johns Hopkins University Press, 1990.

Salvatore, Nick. *We All Got History: The Memory Books of Amos Weber.* New York: Random House, 1996.

Sanchez-Eppler, Karen. "Bodily Bonds: The Intersecting Rhetorics of Feminism and Abolition." *Representations* 24 (Fall 1988): 28–59.

Savage, William Sherman. *Blacks in the West.* Westport, Conn.: Greenwood Press, 1976.

———. "Mary Ellen Pleasant." In *Notable American Women.* Ed. Edward T. James. Cambridge, Mass.: Belknap Press, 1971.

———, and Rayford W. Logan. "Mary Ellen Pleasant." In *Dictionary of Negro Biography.* Ed. Rayford W. Logan and Michael R. Winston. New York: W. W. Norton, 1982.

Saxton, Alexander. *The Indispensable Enemy: Labor and the Anti-Chinese Movement in California.* Berkeley: University of California Press, 1971.

———. *The Rise and Fall of the White Republic: Class Politics and Mass Culture in Nineteenth-Century America.* New York: Verso, 1990.

Schatz, Thomas. "The Family Melodrama." In *Hollywood Genres: Formulas, Filmmaking, and the Studio System.* 221–60. New York: Random House, 1981.

Schultz, Elizabeth. "Out of the Woods and into the World: A Study of Interracial Friendships between Women in American Novels." In *Conjuring: Black Women, Fiction, and Literary Tradition.* Ed. Hortense Spillers and Marjorie Pryse. 67–85. Bloomington: Indiana University Press, 1985.

Schweninger, Loren. *Black Property Owners in the South, 1790–1915.* Urbana: University of Illinois Press, 1990.

———. "Property-Owning Free African-American Women in the South, 1800–1870." *Journal of Women's History* 1:3 (Winter 1990): 13–44.

Secrest, William B., Sr. "The Strange Book of Helen Holdredge." *The Californians* 12:5 (1995): 42–49.

Seiter, Ellen. "The Promise of Melodrama: Recent Women's Film and Soap Operas." Ph.D. diss., Northwestern University, 1981.

Shapiro, Anne-Louise. "Telling Criminal Stories: The *Femme Criminelle* in Late Nineteenth-Century Paris." In *Negotiating at the Margins: The Gendered Discourses of Power and Resistance.* Ed. Sue Fisher and Kathy Davis. 145–71. New Brunswick, N.J.: Rutgers University Press, 1993.

Shaw, Stephanie J. *What a Woman Ought to Be and to Do: Black Professional Women Workers during the Jim Crow Era.* Chicago: University of Chicago Press, 1996.

Shea, Renee Hausmann. "Interview: Michelle Cliff." *Belle Lettres* 9 (Spring 1994): 32–33.

Sherman, Joan R. *Invisible Poets: Afro-Americans of the Nineteenth Century.* Urbana: University of Illinois Press, 1974.

Silber, Nina. *The Romance of Reunion: Northerners and the South, 1865–1900.* Chapel Hill: University of North Carolina Press, 1993.

Silverman, Jason H., *Unwelcome Guests: Canada West's Response to American Fugitive Slaves, 1800–1865.* Millwood, N.Y.: Associated Faculties Press, 1985.

Slide, Anthony, ed. *Selected Theatre Criticism*. Vol. 2: *1920–1930*. Metuchen, N.J.: Scarecrow Press, 1985.

Smart, Carol. "Disruptive Bodies and Unruly Sex: The Regulation of Reproduction and Sexuality in the Nineteenth Century." In *Regulating Womanhood: Historical Essays on Marriage, Motherhood, and Sexuality*. Ed. Carol Smart. 7–32. New York: Routledge, 1992.

Smith-Rosenberg, Carroll. *Disorderly Conduct: Visions of Gender in Victorian America*. New York: Oxford University Press, 1985.

Snorgrass, William J. "The Black Press in the San Francisco Bay Area." *California History* 60:4 (1981–82): 306–17.

Soderlund, Jean R. *Quakers and Slavery: A Divided Spirit*. Princeton, N.J.: Princeton University Press, 1985.

Sokolow, Michael. "'New Guinea at One End, and a View of the Alm's House at the Other': The Decline of Black Salem, 1850–1920." *New England Quarterly* 71 (June 1998): 204–28.

Sparks, Edith Eleanor. "Capital Instincts: The Economics of Female Proprietorship in San Francisco, 1850–1920." Ph.D. diss., University of California at Los Angeles, 1999.

Spence, Mary Lee. "They Also Serve Who Wait." *Western Historical Journal* 14 (January 1983): 5–28.

Spillers, Hortense J. "Mama's Baby, Papa's Maybe: An American Grammar Book." *Diacritics* 17 (Summer 1987): 65–81.

St. Clair, David J. "New Almaden and California Quicksilver in the Pacific Rim Economy." *California History* 73 (Winter 1994–95): 279–95.

Stackpole, Edouard A. "A Plan Has Been Advanced for the Restoration of the Old African Baptist Church on Nantucket." *Historic Nantucket* 36:2 (1988): 7–10.

Stansell, Christine. *City of Women: Sex and Class in New York, 1789–1860*. Urbana: University of Illinois Press, 1982; 1987 edition.

Starbuck, Mary Eliza. *My House and I: A Chronicle of Nantucket*. Boston: Houghton Mifflin, 1929.

Sterling, Dorothy, ed. *We Are Your Sisters: Black Women in the Nineteenth Century*. New York: W. W. Norton, 1984.

Still, William. *The Underground Railroad*. Philadelphia: William Still Publishers, 1883.

Stoeltje, Beverly J. "'A Helpmate for Man Indeed': The Image of the Frontier Woman." *Journal of American Folklore* 88 (January–March 1975): 25–41.

Taylor, Quintard. *In Search of the Racial Frontier: African Americans in the American West, 1528–1990*. New York: W. W. Norton, 1998.

Teish, Luisah. *Jambalaya*. New York: HarperCollins, 1987.

Terborg-Penn, Rosalyn. *African American Women in the Struggle for the Vote, 1850–1920*. Bloomington: Indiana University Press, 1998.

Thurber, Cheryl. "The Development of the Mammy Image and Mythology." In

Southern Women: Histories and Identities. Ed. Virginia Bernhard et al. 87–108. Columbia: University of Missouri Press, 1994.

Thurman, Sue Bailey. *Pioneers of Negro Origin in California.* San Francisco: Acme Publishing Co., 1971.

Trachtenberg, Alan. *The Incorporation of America: Culture and Society in the Gilded Age.* New York: Hill and Wang, 1982.

Trouillot, Michel-Rolph. *Silencing the Past: Power and the Production of History.* Boston: Beacon Press, 1995.

Tucker, Susan. "A Complex Bond: Southern Black Domestic Workers and Their White Employers." In *Black Women in United States History.* Vol. 4. Ed. Darlene Clark Hine et al. 1187–1204. New York: Carlson Publishing, 1990.

Turner, Erin H. *More Than Petticoats: Remarkable California Women.* Helena, Mont.: Falcon Publishing, 1999.

Turner, Patricia A. *Ceramic Uncles and Celluloid Mammies: Black Images and Their Influence on Culture.* New York: Anchor Books, 1994.

———. *I Heard It through the Grapevine: Rumor in African-American Culture.* Berkeley: University of California Press, 1993.

Ullman, Sharon R. *Sex Seen: The Emergence of Modern Sexuality in America.* Berkeley: University of California Press, 1997.

Van DeBurg, William L. *Slavery and Race in American Popular Culture.* Madison: University of Wisconsin Press, 1984.

Vickers, Daniel. "Nantucket Whalemen in the Deep-Sea Fishery: The Changing Anatomy of an Early American Workforce." *Journal of American History* 72 (September 1985): 277–96.

Walker, Clarence E. *Deromanticizing Black History: Critical Essays and Reappraisals.* Knoxville: University of Tennessee Press, 1991.

Walker, Juliet E. K. "Black Entrepreneurship: An Historical Inquiry." *Business and Economic History* (2d ser.) 12 (1983): 37–55.

———. *Free Frank: A Black Pioneer on the Antebellum Frontier.* Lexington: University Press of Kentucky, 1983.

———. *The History of Black Business in America: Capitalism, Race, Entrepreneurship.* New York: Prentice Hall, 1998.

———. "Racism, Slavery, and Free Enterprise: Black Entrepreneurship in the United States." *Business History Review* 60 (Autumn 1986): 343–82.

Walkowitz, Judith R. *Prostitution and Victorian Society: Women, Class, and the State.* New York: Cambridge University Press, 1980.

Wearing, J. P., ed. *The London Stage, 1920–1929: A Calendar of Plays and Players.* Vol. 1: *1920–1924.* Metuchen, N.J.: Scarecrow Press, 1984.

Welke, Barbara Y. "Rights of Passage: Gender Rights Consciousness and the Quest for Freedom, San Francisco, California, 1850–1870." In *African American Women Confront the West, 1600–2000.* Ed. Quintard Taylor and Shirley Ann Moore. Norman: University of Oklahoma Press, 2003.

———. "When All the Women Were White, and All the Blacks Were Men: Gender, Class, Race, and the Road to *Plessy,* 1865–1914." *Law and History Review* 13:2 (Fall 1995): 261–316.

Wells, Evelyn. *Champagne Days of San Francisco.* New York: D. Appleton-Century, 1939.

———. *The Golden Snare.* Serialized in *The San Francisco Call* beginning September 3, 1941.

Wheeler, B. Gordon. *Black California.* New York: Hippocrene Books, 1993.

Whipple, A. B. C. *Vintage Nantucket.* New York: Dodd, Mead and Company, 1978.

White, Barbara. "The Integration of Nantucket Public Schools." *Historic Nantucket* 40:3 (Fall 1992): 59–62.

White, Deborah Gray. *Ar'n't I a Woman: Female Slaves in the Plantation South.* New York: W. W. Norton, 1985.

———. "Mining the Forgotten: Manuscript Sources for Black Women's History." *Journal of American History* 74 (June 1987): 237–42.

White, Hayden. "The Value of Narrativity in the Representations of Reality." In *On Narrative.* Ed. W. J. T. Mitchell. 1–23. Chicago: University of Chicago Press, 1981.

Whitfield, Stephen J. *The Culture of the Cold War.* Baltimore, Md.: Johns Hopkins University Press, 1991.

Wiegman, Robyn. *American Anatomies: Theorizing Race and Gender.* Durham, N.C.: Duke University Press, 1995.

———. "The Anatomy of Lynching." *Journal of the History of Sexuality* 3:3 (1993).

Wiggins, Rosalind Cobb. *Captain Paul Cuffe's Logs and Letters, 1808–1817: A Black Quaker's "Voice from within the Veil."* Washington, D.C.: Howard University Press, 1996.

Wiley, Catherine. "Free Enterprise." *The Bloomsbury Review* 14 (May/June 1994): 9.

Willard, John. *The Cat and the Canary: A Melodrama in Three Acts.* New York: Samuel French, 1927.

Williams, Brad. *Legendary Women of the West.* New York: David McKay, 1978.

Williams, Linda. *Playing the Race Card: Melodramas of Black and White from Uncle Tom to O. J. Simpson.* Princeton, N.J.: Princeton University Press, 2001.

Winch, Julie. *Philadelphia's Black Elite: Activism, Accommodation, and the Struggle for Autonomy, 1787–1848.* Philadelphia: Temple University Press, 1988.

Winks, Robin. *Blacks in Canada.* New Haven, Conn.: Yale University Press, 1979.

Wollenberg, Charles, ed. *Ethnic Conflict in California.* Los Angeles: Tinnon-Brown Publishers, 1970.

Woodson, Carter G., "The Negroes of Cincinnati prior to the Civil War." *Journal of Negro History* 1 (January 1916): 1–22.

Work Projects Administration. *American Guide Series: San Francisco—The Bay and Its Cities.* New York: Hastings House, 1947.

Woyski, Margaret S. "Women and Mining in the Old West." *Journal of the West* 20 (April 1981): 38–46.

Yee, Shirley J. *Black Women Abolitionists: A Study in Activism, 1828–1860.* Knoxville: University of Tennessee Press, 1992.

Yellin, Jean Fagan. *Women and Sisters: The Antislavery Feminists in American Culture.* New Haven, Conn.: Yale University Press, 1989.

———, and John C. Van Horne, eds. *Abolitionist Sisterhood: Women's Political Culture in Antebellum America.* Ithaca, N.Y.: Cornell University Press, 1994.

Yerby, Frank. *The Dahomeans.* New York: Viking, 1968.

———. *Devilseed.* Garden City, N.Y.: Doubleday, 1984.

———. "How I Write the Costume Novel." *Harper's Magazine* 219 (October 1959): 145–50.

INDEX

LYNN M. HUDSON is an associate professor in the Department of History at Macalester College, St. Paul, Minnesota, where she also teaches in the department of American Studies and Women, Gender, and Sexuality Studies.

The University of Illinois Press
is a founding member of the
Association of American University Presses.

Composed in 10/13 Sabon
with Sabon display
by Jim Proefrock
at the University of Illinois Press
Designed by Dennis Roberts

University of Illinois Press
1325 South Oak Street
Champaign, IL 61820-6903
www.press.uillinois.edu